A
View
from
Above

○ ○ ○

A View from Above

o o o

WILT CHAMBERLAIN

VILLARD BOOKS   NEW YORK   1991

Riverside Community College
Library
4800 Magnolia Avenue
Riverside, California 92506

JAN '93

Copyright © 1991 by Wilt Chamberlain

All rights reserved under International and Pan-American Copyright
Conventions. Published in the United States by Villard Books, a
division of Random House, Inc., New York, and simultaneously in
Canada by Random House of Canada Limited, Toronto.

Villard Books is a registered trademark of Random House, Inc.

Library of Congress Cataloging-in-Publication Data

Chamberlain, Wilt
A view from above/Wilt Chamberlain.
p. cm.
ISBN 0-679-40455-4
1. Chamberlain, Wilt. 2. Basketball players—United
States—Biography. I. Title.
GV884.C5A3 1991
796.323′092—dc20
[B]   91-50057
9 8 7 6 5 4 3 2
First Edition

IN MEMORY

To my mother and father, who were the two greatest teachers in my life

Contents

CONTENTS

Introduction

Although I am a big man, and have been a big man for a long time, I am certainly not *the* Big Man, if you know what I mean. So, for those of you who picked up this book somehow thinking that you were getting The Word from The Big Man Himself, I want to assure you that this is not the case.

However, I must confess that as a young kid growing up I was, for a brief period, confused about my actual identity because when so many people first saw me they would say things like:

"Oh, GOD! How tall are you?"

"My GOD!!! Are you tall!"

"My LORD! When are you going to stop growing?"

"Good GOD!! How did you get so tall?"

"JESUS! Are those stilts you have on?"

These kinds of utterances started when I was thirteen years old, and to this day they have never stopped—although I no longer get confused about my humble humanity. (Of course, this is helped by the people who simply say, "HOLY SHIT!")

But being tall is just one part of being Wilt Chamberlain—a very large part, sure, but only one part. My close friends know that there are other sides to me: a lighter side, an angry side, a funny side, a contemplative as well as a sensual side. These friends also know that on certain subjects I feel very strongly. For years they have urged me to write about myself—the inner me. So now I have.

I wrote a book eighteen years ago; it was called *Wilt.* I thought it was pretty good, but there are many reasons for writing another one. For one thing, I have changed and the world has changed around me. I'm freer to say certain things (and, I hope, people are more receptive and more open to the things I have to say). For another thing, I really feel I am one of the most misunderstood celebrities of the century. The misunderstandings come about because of my size, my demeanor, my race, the media. For some inexplicable reason, people assume they *know* me and know what I think and feel. My guess is, if you're reading this book, you have certain preconceptions about me. My guess is, too, that you're wrong.

Humor me for a moment. Let me pick a few subjects: Bill Russell . . . race relations . . . the NBA . . . sex . . . women . . . Kareem Abdul-Jabbar . . . money . . .

You think you know what I have to say about these things, don't you? Well, I say, "The hell you do!" Very few people know my inner thoughts because I haven't gone public too many times over the years. If you want to learn the truth, you'll have to keep reading. Personally, I think it's worth it.

I said in the final paragraph of *Wilt* that the book didn't really have an ending—a denouement, as they say in the movies. By the same token, this book has no real beginning. Nor is it a continuation, a sequel. This book is a collection of thoughts, my honest feelings about life and my living of life.

Some say I have lived a charmed life. True, I have been blessed, but like most people, there are some things that, if given a chance, I would indeed do differently.

If I could do it all over I would continue my bass violin studies; I was a good string bassist in junior high school, but my music teacher told me I had to choose between furthering my studies in music and my athletic pursuits. I have always wondered whether I made the right choice.

My dream of becoming a world-class decathlete ended when I realized that I had to choose between becoming a pro or staying an amateur, and I chose the way to financial gain.

Given the chance, I would spend as much time as possible studying as many languages as I could. The one thing I have no excuse for and should be more adroit at is foreign languages. I have traveled so much it is a shame I didn't get a stronger foundation and didn't take more time to learn to speak more languages fluently. (When we are young, we don't consider the learning of languages very important, and I was no different. When we grow up and realize how important it really is, it is too late.)

And (this one is hard for me to believe, even as I write it) I would have a serious relationship with just one lady.

All in all, though, I have few regrets. But I do have a

plethora of ideas and observations about life and people. The Harlem Globetrotters, for whom I played, have an honor they bestow on a select few: "Thirty Years on the Road." I explain this fully later on, but it basically means that you've been out there a long time, long enough to know what's happenin' in the world and how to deal with most of it. A lot of my musings come from my personal Thirty Years on the Road.

My observations have been gleaned from a lifetime of (usually) being the tallest man in the room, which enables me to see things, I feel, from a different but truer perspective than those average-size people who are caught up in the average-size maze of life. That's why I call these observations *A View from Above.*

I have sprinkled these observations with what I call Wiltisms. Wiltisms are sayings, witticisms, musings, poems, philosophies, and some of my deepest gut feelings. A Wiltism is not to be confused with a Confucianism. But then again, who knows; maybe a thousand years from now . . .

Another reason for writing this book is, perhaps, the toughest one for me to admit: I'm getting older.

I know, I know, it happens to the best of us. But I'm used to doing things not everyone is used to doing. I'm used to being great at what I do, whether it's basketball, volleyball, sex, whatever. Age is a hell of an equalizer, however, and it tends to make one a bit reflective.

A quick story to illustrate my point . . .

Recently, I started playing tennis. Again, you have to understand that when I played basketball, I was, in my opinion, one of the best players in the game. Hell, I might as well say it—one of the best players who ever lived. When I took up volleyball, I think I was one of the best at that, too. There were a lot of world-class volleyball players who weren't too damn thrilled to see a fiercely competitive seven-foot-tall competitor leaping up to spike a ball straight down at their head. I mean, when I walked out on a court—*any* court—I could intimidate. But now, walking onto a tennis court is a different story. I'm *good*—I'm not being overly humble here—but I'm not great. I'm not the best. And at my age, which is fifty-five, I'll *never* be the best. I've been volleying with Jennifer Capriati and I can hold my own, but I know that by the time I really learn to serve and volley the way one is meant to, I'll be too old to ever beat Ivan Lendl or Pete Sampras or Boris Becker.

It makes you stop and think. At least, it makes *me* stop and think.

Some athletes can't handle it. Jim Brown, for instance. Jim is so competitive, he scares people. If he loses a tennis game—a friendly weekend tennis game—it's not a pretty sight. That's rage that comes pouring out of him. That's fear of getting old.

I don't think I'm full of rage or even full of fear. Some people say I'm full of something else—but I don't believe that either.

I do think I'm full of curiosity, which has made my life interesting.

So here we go. I sincerely hope you enjoy my view.

Bel Air, California

A
View
from
Above

○ ○ ○

On Height: A View from Above

Recently I was out with a young lady. A fine young lady, according to my standards. My standards, I might add, are fairly high. Even though beauty is only skin deep, I am still very impressed with great-looking bodies. Young ladies don't have to get a "boob job" for me, though. I am a leg and, as the Hawaiians say, an '*ōkole* man. (A Hawaiian is very capable of spotting a young lady and saying, "She's got an awfully nice '*ōkole*.") Strong, healthy-looking ladies are a joy to me. Dark hair has always been my choice. There *is* one change I have gone through over the last couple of decades. I used to prefer women who were five feet, four inches to five feet, five inches; now I like them a few inches taller. Yet height is the least of my concerns. Once there's a physical attraction—which there must be—then a warm and caring personality is what's most important. A woman can be smart, book-wise, or not so smart, as long as she's *open* to learning. More than anything, that openness and flexibility are what turns me on.

Anyway, over dinner, during our conversation, this particular young lady said, "I would love to see you play and I'm really looking forward to your next home game." I was quite surprised (and, I admit, a little flattered).

Later that evening, a man interrupted me on the dance floor with a surprised look on his face. He blurted out, "Wilt! I thought you died years ago!" I didn't know whether he meant literally or figuratively, but fearing both of us would be embarrassed I carried the conversation no further.

Needless to say, both my date and the gentleman were terribly confused. I haven't played a game of professional basketball in over seventeen years, since 1974; however, life certainly did not end for me with the playing of that last game.

Most of the past seventeen years have been exciting and fulfilling for me. I have had time to reflect; time to mellow out; time to put things in their proper perspective.

Proper perspective for *me,* that is. To the average person my perspective may seem a little aberrant at first, but remember: a perspective is a representation of a subject as it appears to an observer when viewed from a given position. My perspective, good or bad, is a view from this seven-foot-plus frame. This perspective started to take shape when I was a gangling kid on the streets of Philadelphia and has continued developing in my present perch, as a fairly successful businessman who lives high above the busy freeways of southern California.

So yes, my perspective is different. But even that has changed some over the years. I said in my first book that I'm just like "any other seven-foot black millionaire who lives next door." Twenty years ago, that line was very appropriate in getting my point across about how different I was. But these days, with the unbelievable salaries available in sports, there are plenty of seven-foot black millionaires out there, and they must be living next to somebody.

Now, I am set apart by being a member of some other minorities. After all, do you know any other person of color (a phrase I prefer to black) who is seven feet tall, over fifty, has never been married, owns a car he helped design and build with over $1 million of his own money, is in the top 1 percent of all Americans financially, is a Republican (but not a Reagan or Bush fan), and—last but not least—is tall, dark, and handsome?

Well, maybe handsome is presumptuous of me. But two out of three ain't bad, especially in sports.

Still, out of those many minorities, the one people notice most is my tallness. Since being tall often determines how I react to people—and how people react to me—I begin my musings with thoughts about height.

I should also begin by admitting these thoughts are quite personal. I don't know if other people at my altitude feel the same way I do about most of you down there. I'm sure I'll find out after they read this book. And if, after reading this book, you down there doubt my perspective, or still wonder what it's like up here, I have a suggestion.

It is said that you should not pass judgment on someone

until you have walked a mile in his shoes. In this case, forget about my shoes.

I suggest you buy a pair of stilts, and see the world—and the likes of all of you—from my point of view.

P.S. I'm thinking of opening a stilt company. Called, of course:

"Wilt the Stilts"

☛ WILTISM 🐟

If you only appreciate the old-fashioned things and ways, the only time you will appreciate anything from today will be tomorrow.

There has always been something majestic about height. I've come to the conclusion that humans have always been fascinated by and in awe of things that are taller than everything else: the tallest building, particularly the Empire State Building (even though other buildings have more cubic space), the tallest mountain, the giant sequoia.

We always refer to good things as being up and we refer to bad or evil as being down. Believers consider their God to be on a higher plane; heaven is always portrayed as being up high.

Kings and other leaders always elevate themselves on a throne so they will be above their subjects, knowing that no matter how powerful they are, if they are looked down on physically they will not have the same mystique for the masses.

In our society, things that are down are held in low esteem, and are often spat upon—literally and figuratively. Things that are up are respected.

Yet, despite this reverence for height, when it comes to

people, I often wonder if the average person doesn't actually resent people who are a lot taller than they are. I mean, short people have hang-ups, like a Napoleonic complex, and are often overachievers because of this. At the same time, many tall people never reach their potential because of the superior status society automatically gives them.

People think being tall is always better than being small, but we who stand head and shoulders above the masses have our hang-ups and problems, too. Because we tall people are such a minority we often take the ostrich approach, but instead of sticking our heads in a hole in the ground we stick our heads in the clouds and pretend that what goes on down there has little or no effect on us.

Since most things in our society were not built with us in mind we pretend the problems they cause us don't exist. You never see us lobbying for bigger telephone booths, higher toilet seats in public places, or johns on airplanes that we can fit into. We don't fuss no matter how ridiculous it gets when we almost have to get on our knees to duck through those security screening machines they have at airports. We don't demand that seats in movie houses and trains and planes have enough room for our legs. Everywhere you turn there are special areas for the physically handicapped, but even though it is obvious that our height can be a handicap there are no special accommodations for us.

And we often get insult added to our injury. When we board a plane and go to the front seat, which usually has the most leg room, we find it occupied by children or older couples whose legs don't even reach the floor. Don't you think the airline industry should reserve these seats for people who are six feet or taller? I sure as hell do.

And what about if you are on the broad side? Or just

plain fat? You know what the airlines give you then? An extra-long seat belt, even though you might not fit in the seat. I suppose we should be grateful that at least they're *somewhat* concerned about your being oversized.

The government does help us tall folks on one occasion: They won't draft a person over six foot, six inches. They reason that GI (government issue) items won't fit, and it would be too expensive to custom fit us.

Back when there was a draft, you were sent a letter to report for a physical examination and then, when measured, you were told you were too tall for the service.

I never even got a letter to report. I guess it was obvious they didn't need to measure me.

Here's one of my favorite tall stories:

I got on an elevator in a hotel, going up to the ninth floor, and there was this little boy and his mother on the elevator. The little boy said to his mother as I entered, "Gee, Mom, he must be a hundred years old!" His mother immediately turned to me, and, in a very embarrassed state, she explained, "I . . . um . . . I've been telling my son that the older you get, the taller you get."

As I stepped off the elevator I said, "It sounds good to me, ma'am, but my friend Bill Shoemaker might tell you to stop lying to your kid."

☞ **WILTISM** 🐘

Does wisdom come with age or does age come from the lack of wisdom? Example: If you are not smart enough to take care of your body you can get old fast.

When I was in Hartford, Connecticut, for my induction into the basketball Hall of Fame in 1978, I had an odd encounter, one that made me understand a little better what it's like *not* being tall.

I had traveled all the way from Australia to get there for the ceremony and was very tired. Whenever I'm tired I like to do something physical, so I went for a run. When I returned I was totally exhausted, and my head was down when I entered the elevator. I just pushed the button to my floor without looking at who else was in it. Then I straightened up a bit and looked around. To my amazement there were three guys in there, each taller than me.

And if that wasn't amazing enough, when I looked into their faces I realized that if you added the ages of all three together, the total was probably equal to my age. I couldn't believe my eyes: three guys, so young, and each taller than I was.

I thought that maybe I was stooped low and they just appeared taller, so I straightened up even more and stood as straight as I could. They were all *still* taller. I was so astonished, I forgot to get off at my floor.

I learned later that they were three high school All-Americans, in town to be honored at the same time I was inducted into the Hall of Fame. One of the boys was Ralph Sampson, who is seven foot four. The second was Sam Bowie, seven-two. I don't know who the third was, but he was somewhere in between Sampson's and Bowie's height, about seven-three.

It sure was a different experience for me. But I kept my cool. I never asked them, "Hey, what do you guys eat to get that tall?"

A similar thing occurred in 1976. I went to Montreal to watch the Russian basketball team. They had a player who was seven-five, and when I walked past him I realized how impressive his size was.

When they played the national anthem before the game I stood up, and to my amazement there was someone staring me right in the eye. And that someone was a lady! She was Iuliyana Semenova, a member of the Russian women's team. Not only was she as tall as I was, she was a lot broader. I mean, she was truly a broad!

But once again I kept my cool. I didn't ask her, "Is it hard to find a boyfriend? Or do you prefer SSS—strong, short Soviets?"

Which brings me to the subject of questions.

If you see a fat guy walking down the street, would you go up to him and blurt out, "Is your mother fat? Are your sisters fat? How fat is your father?" Would you walk up to a one-legged man and ask him if his father had only one leg? Or his mother?

Of course not. And yet, I get these questions about my height all the time from well-meaning and in a lot of cases sensitive and intelligent people. Recently I was at a bakery and a saleslady (an incredibly fat saleslady, actually) said with disdain in her voice, "Hey, how tall are you anyway?" (Don't worry, I didn't ask her how fat she was. I was tempted, but I like to think I'm more mature than that.)

Even though curiosity has no bounds (or, in this last case, pounds), I find it hard to understand why some people would not be a little more sensitive in asking personal questions about people's anatomy. How dare she ask me that question—and in a manner that implied "You are ridiculously tall"—when she looked to be well over three hundred pounds? (By the way, for her height that would make her three times the weight she should have been. So if I was three times the average guy's height—or eighteen feet tall—her question would have been more warranted.) I *was* curious about her weight, but no amount of curiosity could have made me ask her that kind of personal question.

WILTISM

No one seems to equate
Inquiries regarding size and weight.
The questions on weight are not so polite
But asking how tall you are seems quite all right.

All my life I've been asked questions about my size. Total strangers will walk up to me and ask personal questions like, "What size shoe do you wear?" Would the same people walk up to a lady with large breasts and ask, "What size bra do you wear?" Or to a fat man and blurt out, "What size is your belt?" Of course not, but for some strange reason people feel they can ask a tall person anything.

As a kid, being a foot taller than most of my friends never seemed to have much effect on me. Can you imagine, though, that at the age of fourteen I had almost reached my present-day height? That's right, at fourteen I was seven feet tall. I can remember one boy who lived down the street from me and was about the same age I was, telling me that his mother did not want him to play with me because I was too tall. I was about twelve years old. Can you believe that? I wasn't too mean, I wasn't the wrong color or a bad influence, I was just too tall?

In those early days, around my friends and family I felt I was normal in height. It was only when I used to take the El (which was a subway above ground—a trolley car in Philadelphia) to other parts of the city and I had to bend way over when standing in the compartment that I began to feel uncomfortable. If there were no empty seats, it seemed to me that *everyone* was staring at me. My parents had taught us to stand and give our seats to a lady on a crowded bus or train, but when I was sitting on a crowded El and a woman boarded, I wouldn't get up to give her my seat—I didn't want to be embarrassed.

Other than being charged adult prices to go to movies when I was three or six years too young, I adjusted surprisingly easily to all that extra height.

Except, now that my memory is taking me back to those early days, for one thing: When I first started playing basketball in junior high, I had a real fear of putting on my uniform shorts and showing my long, skinny legs. I had to totally concentrate on my game or I would have been unable to continue playing. Eventually, as the game progressed, I could relax and feel the audience was focusing on my play, not my legs. But, man, that wasn't just nervousness on my part—it was a real phobia. As I got a little older, of course, I got over it.

People *I have* never seen before have walked up to me and said, "Man, I sure would hate to feed you." Do they think my legs are hollow? Every time I sit down to eat do I have to fill my legs with food?

I often ask myself why people feel they can ask idiotic, personal questions of tall people, but not of *other* people who are physically different from the norm. Do they think we're not sensitive, or we don't get tired of these meaningless, thoughtless jabs?

"Where do you sleep?" is one of the questions I'm asked the most. Often I'll tell one of my harmless little lies. I say, "I sleep like a horse does. I learned the technique from the horses I've owned. Just find me an ol' corner and I'll just stand up and sleep." And the people who ask the question usually buy my answer. For the record, because I like to sleep with my feet over the end of the bed, a mere king-size bed is sufficient for me. I became accustomed to sleeping this way in days gone by when my beds were not large enough. My home in Bel Air has a truly Goliath-size bed. Would you believe it's eight feet wide and nine feet long? I use about one fifth of it—what a waste.

I *guess I've made* my point that I find it rude when people, even little old ladies just five feet tall, put their hand inside of mine and exclaim, "Whoo! What a big hand!" I sometimes reply, "Do you *really* expect my hand to be the same size as yours?! For my size, my hands and feet are normal to small. My fourteen-and-a-half shoe is small for a seven-footer." If they still don't believe me, I remind them that Bob Lanier, who is a few inches shorter than I am, wears size twenty-two. As the beer commercial said, he was responsible for "the biggest feets in basketball."

I went to a dentist when I was on the road once and when he looked into my mouth he seemed stunned. "Your teeth are normal size," he said. I wanted to bite his normal-size hand off.

Just because your legs are a little longer than the average, most people think *everything* has to be longer. A great many people believe I'm hung like a horse.

(As to that: for the record, I say I'm not, and thank God. Why? Because I've owned a lot of horses, and all horses are *not* hung alike.)

. . . .

Tall people and basketball have been given a bum rap because they have become synonymous. I've been stopped on the street a million times and told, "You must play basketball," only because I'm tall. I think that statement, and the assumption that all you need to play the game of basketball is height, does a disservice to the game of basketball and to tall people.

🖙 WILTISM 🖙

They say that good things come in small packages, but, all things being equal, wouldn't you rather have a ten-carat diamond than a one-carat diamond?

In a similar vein, I have noticed that these days, people's eyes seem to register dollar signs when they see someone as tall as I am. When I was a kid, being tall just brought amazement. Now, people think of all the money a tall kid is going to automatically make from basketball. There's a whole new aura surrounding tall kids. It's a green aura and I guess it takes away some of the stigma that comes with being so much bigger than the norm.

I realize that all this may sound like I'm complaining about being tall. Not so. All the little negative things associated with being tall are nothing compared to the advantages of being above the masses. Like:

In an elevator your nose is well above everyone else's armpits.

If you live in a cold region you always stay warmer,

because heat goes up. If it gets too warm, you merely sit down to get cooler.

When viewing any event, such as a parade or a sporting event, you have a decided edge.

Almost anyone can touch the floor, but reaching that top shelf can be a bitch for some people.

You are never confused for your average rapist or bank robber or other wanted man.

People have to look up to you whether they want to or not.

And best of all, you are farther away from most assholes, literally and figuratively.

People make a big deal out of me ducking under doorways. It's a strange phenomenon, I have to admit. If you are average in size and you travel with me for a period of time, you will find yourself ducking with me as we walk through doorways. Sometimes the doorways are high enough so I don't have to duck, but because it is a reflex action with me, I duck anyway. And the shorter people with me also stoop down. Usually we look at each other and laugh afterward.

I've seen supposedly mature CEOs in their gray pin-striped suits tap their friends and say, "Watch this," like something amazing and amusing is about to happen, then they stop and watch as I duck under a doorway. The same people will stop and watch this amazing event time after time after time.

I wonder: Are these the same people who used to go to the local barbershop and watch the barber cut hair on Saturday nights as their big thrill?

Or are they just waiting for the time when I don't duck?

☞ WILTISM ☜

Enthusiasm can't be taught but can be caught.

Sometimes when people see me for the first time they burst out laughing.

One time I asked this lady, "Excuse me, ma'am. What the *hell* are you laughing at?"

She immediately apologized and said, "What a handsome man you are."

And I said, "Do you normally laugh at people that you find good-looking?"

"Oh, no!" she said.

"Then why are you laughing now?"

"I just think it's funny," she said.

Now, *you* figure that one out.

In *the summer* of 1984, I was on my way to Finland to attend the track and field championships in Helsinki. I had a five-hour stopover at Heathrow Airport in London. As I was walking around the terminal killing time I ran into a very attractive lady who had been on my flight from the States. I was to find out later she was on her way to Frankfurt, Germany, and also had a five-hour layover. I asked if she spoke English and it turned out she did; at least she spoke a little. She said, "Boy, you are tall. You must be the tallest man in the world." Trying to look modest, I said, "Yes, I am." And she believed me.

She asked me where I was going, and I could tell she assumed I was a participant in the track and field championships that I was going to. Now who am I to shatter a pretty girl's fantasy? She wanted to know if my height

16

helped me in my event. "Yes, it does," I told her. I was laying it on thick about how great it was to be the tallest man in the world and how unique I was. She was gullible and was hanging on to my every word, when someone walked up behind me and said rather casually, *"What's going on?"*

I turned around and gasped.

It was Kareem Abdul-Jabbar. (He was on his way to Paris.)

The lady did a double take like you wouldn't believe. So, without breaking stride in our conversation, I nonchalantly said to her, "Would you believe, I'm the *second* tallest guy in the world?"

 WILTISM

AMERICAN EXPRESS: "Don't leave home without it."
WILT: "If you don't leave home you won't need it."

You've heard the statement that a good big man can always beat a good little man. To me, that is flat-out ridiculous.

I have never seen a tall man win a marathon. Has there ever been a world-class gymnast over six feet? No. In fact, the best gymnasts are usually smaller than the norm. All of this leads me to a favorite WILTISM:

 WILTISM

Size has never been a barometer for measuring the worth of a man. Unless you are talking about the size of his heart.

I mentioned in the introduction that I left amateur sports because of financial opportunities. Those financial opportunities—obviously basketball-related—came about because of my size. One of the reasons I have regrets about that decision is because I excelled in amateur sports *despite* my size. As usual, I went against the grain.

I feel there are certain sports that I was just a plain natural for. (Is that conceited? Am I full of myself? I'll leave that up to you.) The decathlon was one of these. The decathlon, for you non–track-and-field enthusiasts, is a ten-event competition that is performed in two days, five events each day. The events are the shot put, javelin toss, high jump, long jump, pole vault, discus throw, 100 meters, 400 meters, 1500 meters, and the 110-meter high hurdles, and, in the Olympics, the winner in this competition is considered the greatest athlete in the world. The three talents needed most for the decathlon are speed, strength, and endurance. As I said before, I was a natural for this competition. Being blessed with speed, I was able to race and defeat the fastest men in the NBA from one end of the court to the other. I took great pride in beating Hal Greer, the sensational guard who was considered the fastest man in the NBA, in a race. In the forty-yard dash, I blew away with ease the likes of Jim Brown, who was pretty powerful and fast himself. When I was in college I defeated guys like Ernie Shelby, a long jumper who also ran a 9.3 hundred-yard dash.

Once, Hank Stram, the coach of the Kansas City Chiefs (he's now a sportscaster), wanted me to play for them. He took me to a football field and started throwing passes to me. Stram couldn't believe how well I was able to catch the football. Next, he asked me if he could time me in the forty-yard sprint. At the time I didn't have any cleats on, just sneakers, so I took my shoes off and ran barefoot in the grass. They timed me at 4.4 and then 4.5 seconds in the forty. That, as you may know, is world-class speed—especially in bare feet.

Strength I was blessed with and I enhanced it with weight training way before that was fashionable. I was an undefeated shot-putter in high school and during my freshman year at the University of Kansas, when I won the national championship in this event. I could tell you hundreds of stories about the unbelievable amounts of weight I have lifted, but the two stories I am relating should be indicative enough of my strength. When I was in college the world record holder in the shot put, the one event that requires more brute strength than anything else, was a guy named Bill Nieder. Well, every time Nieder had a few beers, he used to challenge me to an arm-wrestling contest. Bill was six feet, five inches tall, weighed between 260 and 270 pounds, and his body was as hard as granite. I was this skinny 210-pound freshman basketball player—but I would whip his ass *every* time. I've had a chance to wrestle guys with unbelievable strength, and I'm still undefeated in arm wrestling.

If you still doubt my strength, ask one of the strongest men I've ever met, Arnold Schwarzenegger. As a general rule, bodybuilders are not very strong, but Schwarzenegger was a power-lifter before he became a bodybuilder. I had the pleasure of working out with Arnold for half a year. During this period he could not believe some of the things I did. He would not even *attempt* some of them. The one that really astonished him was when I'd put five fifty-pound plates on my chest, while lying on an incline board, and do up to thirty sit-ups.

The one time I actually astonished *myself* with my own

strength came on the basketball court. We were playing the Celtics and I remember K.C. Jones was driving by me on the baseline. K.C. was six-two and weighed 205 or 210; he was built like a football player. Well, he was going full speed when he passed me—and I just stuck out my left hand, grabbed him, stopped him cold, stone dead in his tracks and picked him up as if he were a rag doll. K.C. absolutely couldn't believe it. Up to that moment, I'd always taken my strength for granted, but even I was startled.

Okay, now we've established strength along with speed, wouldn't you say?

When I was with the Harlem Globetrotters, my vertical leap was measured at around fifty inches. Spud Webb, who at five-eight dunks a basketball, has a vertical jump of just over forty inches. So imagine a seven-footer with a fifty-inch vertical. It may be half a foot higher than that of Michael Jordan. (Check out some of the pictures in this book of me jumping.)

A little bit more about my vertical leap: When I jumped I felt like a bird. I felt like I was flying. It's tough to call it a superhuman feeling, but *damn*, it was exhilarating. When I jumped, I really felt there were no limitations on how high I could go. It was as if I was above the limits of mere mortals. Here's a secret: I loved to demonstrate my jumping ability so much, loved to test it so much, that sometimes I wouldn't try to block a shot I knew I could easily block. I used to like to time my leaps so I could simply grab the ball out of my opponent's hand when he was in midair. Try it sometime; you'll like it.

When I was with the Globies, playing in Europe, I used to walk around whatever country we were in, exploring, usually with my teammates "Showboat" Hall and Tom "Tarzan" Spencer. We'd be walking and we'd see a tree limb, let's say eleven feet off the ground. In Europe, it was attention-getting enough just being three giant black men—but we'd play a game and draw even more attention to ourselves. I'd point at the limb, then point at Showboat. Boat would then jump and easily touch the limb. We'd do that until we came to something so high that Boat couldn't reach it—then we'd move on to Spencer, who was five inches taller, around six-eight. When we'd come to something so high it looked to be *impossible* to touch, they'd both point at me. By this time, we'd have a crowd of people watching. The crowd, thinking I could never reach the object, would go, "Noooooo." I'd play along with them, pretending it was out of my reach—then I'd leap up and touch it. Nothing was ever too high for me. It was the closest thing I've ever felt to being the fastest gun in town.

You must give me some credit for being agile (which is one of the things that kept me from ever fouling out of a basketball game) as well. Put these things together—along with my strong love for track and field and my passion for competition—and you have the makings of what may have been the world's greatest decathlete.

I wish now I'd stuck with the decathlon—if only to show people that a seven-footer can do the things normally associated with much shorter men.

Y*ou may find* this hard to believe, but I've had an encounter or two—"encounter" is what I like to call a sexual experience—with girls under five feet tall. I've had many, many encounters with women who were hovering around the five-foot mark. Even though we may have seemed comical to the average observer, there was nothing we didn't do—with the exception of slow dancing.

For the curious, it's amazing how a girl who is two feet shorter than I am when the two of us are standing is only a few inches shorter than I am when we're sitting—and if we're lucky enough to lie down together, we almost seem to become the same size. So it works out—or works in—just fine, thank you. The strange thing is that small ladies never seem to complain about my being too big for them. When I get that complaint, it always comes from one of the taller types (I have dated girls up to six foot two). I get the feeling that many smaller women are fascinated by my size; they're consumed with the belief that no matter how tall I may be, they want to prove to me and themselves that they can deal with it. I am personally glad to oblige. I think of these small women as Spinners, my pet name for little doll-like ladies I can just sit on my lap and spin around like tops. Size *does* have more than just ups and downs.

He*re's an old* cliché I've heard since I was thirteen years old, but with a different twist.

I was in the lobby of a hotel in Florida waiting for the elevator. The doors opened, and a lady stepped off the elevator. Without hesitation she blurted out, "How's the weather up there?"

I gave her one of my meanest looks and her husband saw me. This prompted him to say to her, "What did you ask him?" When she told him, he replied, "You *know* how it is up there. We just came down from the second floor."

I get that stupid question so often from people that I'm

thinking of coming up with a consistent answer. How do you like this:

"My head is warm since heat goes up, but my ass is cold. Since you're so full of hot air, blow some of it there."

Or maybe I'll go back to the old standby from my younger days. When I used to get too fed up with the "How's the weather up there?" question, I'd spit on the sucker and say, "It's raining up here. Are you getting wet down there?"

Because of my size most people think that there is not a car in the world large enough for me to drive, and that any car I drive has to be specially made. This is not true. You may remember that some years ago I won a Cleo for the television commercial I did with Volkswagen. I drove one of the VW Bugs in the commercial, but people who saw it refused to believe it was an ordinary VW. The commercial got so much response that even I got caught up in the hype. I drove my VW everywhere and delighted in watching the expressions of the people as I parked and got out.

During that same time I bought a Lamborghini Countach, which is as small as the VW and a lot lower. Whenever I got out of the Countach, eyes bulged and jaws dropped. Some people, after seeing me get out, would ask, "Man, how do you drive that car?"

I'd reply, "Where there's a Wilt, there's a way."

On Myself: Where There's a Wilt, There's a Way

Coming from a large family—not in physical size but in numbers—on both sides, it's hard to believe that my father, God rest his soul, was the tallest at five foot eight. Now, that may seem short to you, but since there was nothing he couldn't do, he always appeared taller—above all the rest—to me. The things he passed down to me and the deeds he did formed my backbone, my mettle, and are the true reflections of what my life is all about. Among many other things, I get my love of games from him, though he never touched a basketball in his life. He was a champion card player. In games like pinochle, whist, and bridge he was a true master. I never learned to beat him in a game of checkers (not even *once*). I became his equal in many card games, but that was where the equality stopped. If you needed a plumber, an electrician, a carpenter, a mason, or anything else, you just called on William (Bill, his friends called him; I always called him Dad). My father was an avid sports lover and from the time I was two he found time to take me to boxing matches and baseball games. He never implored me to indulge in any of these sports—just allowed me the opportunity to enjoy them. The only thing my parents pushed me to do was to share. They also instilled in me a strong work ethic.

There seemed to be no subject that Dad wasn't well versed in, yet only by directly questioning him could you tell he knew anything at all, and then he always left you wondering how he got to know so much, having only a sixth-grade education.

If my father was considered the strong, silent type, my mother's strength was more pronounced. With six sisters, and two brothers, and a constant horde of cousins and friends at our house, it was obvious to all that Olivia Ruth Chamberlain ran a tight ship. But it was a ship with open doors; anyone could come in and partake of a meal or have a bed. She would always find room. How the two of them raised all of us without a day of hunger and with a permanent supply of clean clothes is beyond my comprehension.

Being the fourth from the youngest (number six), of the Chamberlain brood, I was born in the University of Pennsylvania Hospital in 1936. There was absolutely nothing special about me. I was a little over twenty-two inches long and weighed eight pounds ten ounces.

Growing up with all those sisters—who were considered to be the neighborhood beauties and who had a multitude of suitors—I learned firsthand about the power of women. They were very fashionable in their dress (even today they influence my choice in women and my taste in what they should wear). I was from a tough neighborhood but I never feared gangs or other boys messing with me. Not because of my size but because of my sisters. They were very protective and everyone knew it. You just didn't mess with the Chamberlains. A couple of my sisters could have been great athletes (world class) of the Wilma Rudolph type, but in those days women didn't have many opportunities, especially women of color. This is why I have always had a special place in my heart for women in sports, and why I've sponsored girls' volleyball teams. I have also coached some national volleyball champions and sponsored women's track and field teams. Here I was really fortunate to have athletes like Florence Griffith Joyner, Jackie Joyner-Kersee, and other world-class track stars on my teams.

Since boxing was my dad's favorite sport, it's easy to understand why, when I was young, all my heroes were boxing greats. The number one was, of course, the greatest heavyweight of all time, Joe Louis. Then came Sugar Ray.

From the time I was around four years of age and making pennies by helping the milkman carry empty bottles to his truck, I have known the value of a buck. I have never been afraid to work for that buck, either.

I am not impressed with people who are impressed with me because they think I am rich. Likewise, I am not impressed with people who are rich. I am impressed with people who use their money wisely. I have never aspired to be among the world's richest people; I never cared to be a Jack Kent Cooke or a Donald Trump. I only wanted enough to make myself happy.

Of course, it didn't take me long to realize that money played a major part in making me happy. But it also didn't take long to realize that it's not the amount of money you have, it's what you do with it that brings pleasure and contentment.

I owe this way of thinking to my mom and dad, who were two very giving people. Even though they had all us kids, and often there wasn't a lot to go around, they always had enough to share with neighbors or unexpected visitors. That has stayed with me, the feeling of wanting to share.

I *like the* Ted Turners of the world. By that I mean people who use their money to get involved in enterprises that help provide jobs for many. I'm impressed when they do things like sponsor such events as the Goodwill Games; but I am *more* impressed when they take chances and get involved in activities that create equal opportunity for all.

All too often, many of us only make money to put ourselves in a more powerful position in society. Many never caring about making society stronger. I must admit, I don't feel kindly toward all those homeless people out there in the streets. Many of them take advantage of our welfare system. This is where I feel our government totally sucks. A country with so much going for it should be able to afford a job for *anyone* who wants to work. There is not a city that doesn't have a traffic problem. Why don't we use homeless people and people on welfare to build better highway systems? We all could profit from that. *Think* of all the productive jobs that could be provided!

What about the millions we spend on people in prison, people who do nothing in return but cost us money? They should all be forced to do more in the way of supporting themselves, thus defraying the cost to the taxpayers. I am definitely for the death penalty—and once enacted, execution should be immediate.

I *feel guilty* sometimes about the big house I have and the cars I have owned, knowing that money could have been put to better use. I do focus on this whenever I am in the position to make money. Since I'm fortunate enough to be blessed with the ability to make money—in commercials, business endeavors and such—I remember to always give a part of this money to the less fortunate. I always have that in mind first and foremost when I make a business deal. In fact, I sometimes feel guilty when I turn down an opportunity to make money, knowing that some of that money could have gone to help others. But let me tell you, I have also taken moneymaking opportunities that I would otherwise have turned down, so that I could give some of that money to the less fortunate.

People call me lucky because I'm rich. They are right, but not because of the dollars I have. I'm rich because of the wisdom I have to use those dollars as I see fit. And I thank my parents for that.

☞ WILTISM ☜

I have often heard it said, the apple doesn't fall far from the tree. So thanks, Mom and Dad, for all the good things you instilled in me. With all the things I have done and the places I have gotten to see I have come to realize it was possible because you two were my tree.

Here's a surprising confession: I love to curl up in bed alone with a good book. This is hardly the image I portray to people, including many of my own friends. They always assume that if I'm in bed with something, it has to be a female—and a good-looking one at that. But you see, that's how they imagine themselves if *they* were Wilt Chamberlain. If you are a bachelor and successful and famous and not altogether a nerd and you live in a great house and drive nice cars, well, you *must* have a different lady every night. That's what they believe. It's hard to convince people that some seemingly mundane things can also be my cup of tea.

So I don't fight the image. When they ask, often with a leer, "Hey, Wilt, what did you do last night?" instead of telling them I read the latest issue of *Smithsonian* or *National Geographic,* I give them what they want to hear. Like, "Would you believe this incredible lady came over to cook for me? And boy, could she 'cook.'"

I *mentioned earlier* that one of the reasons for writing this book was to reveal different—and surprising—sides of my personality. Many of my friends do, of course, realize that I can be very funny and introspective. Yet, even among my closest friends, very few, I believe, recognize the sensuality I have in this seven-foot frame. It's as if I'm too big, much too much larger than life to have the softer, sensual side that smaller, less hulking, less intimidating people are allowed to have. Whenever we talk about gladiators—of which I'm apparently one—we use adjectives and phrases like strength, power, courage, obliviousness to pain. In some ways it's nice to be described with all those superhuman characteristics, but why is it gladiators are never allowed to have *real* human traits? When is the last time you've seen one of those huge guys in a love scene in a movie? Never! I have read a zillion words about me and *never* has anyone talked of my sensuality or sensitivity. Granted, I don't expect to find my picture in the dictionary next to the word "sensual." But my point is, people give you labels, they pigeonhole you—especially big guys like me. Maybe that kind of awareness has to come one on one. Certainly, the only time I am ever graced with this type of awareness from others is after lovemaking. Maybe women are shocked to learn that I have real feelings, that size does not preclude what they may take for granted in a lesser-size person.

There is one side of me that is still mystifying even to me. I guess you can call it my angry side. When you are my size you have to be extra careful about expressing anger. Just raising my voice to a level that would go unnoticed coming from a normal mortal creates a response of extraordinary fear. It's a strange restriction, one that most people wouldn't think of—but I really am not allowed the freedom of blowing off steam. Little dogs can yelp and bark any time, but if a big dog barks, people run for the damn hills. Size creates a fear factor, which is stupid because usually the larger the animal the more docile he is. Nothing pisses me off more than those narrow-minded people who lump certain people together because of their physicality, their color, religion, or whatever. The only thing that I see as a reason for putting people together in a group is that they're all of the same mind.

I can't tell you how many times I've practically thrown up because some person I hardly knew decided he had the perfect girl for me. Without asking, I immediately know that "perfect" means six feet or taller, of color, and, in the matchmaker's view, beautiful. I know many tall ladies, many ladies of every race, religion, color, and creed, many damn fine-looking ladies. And guess what? I don't want to sleep with all of them. Do you think every fat guy wants a fat girl—or a skinny one, for that matter? No! They want what they feel like at a particular time. But as long as I can remember, people have been trying to unite me with some "perfect" physical match. When are they going to start to look at where my mind is and not how my body is?

Another reason I'm suspicious of matchmaking acquaintances: If the girl they're trying to fix me up with is so damn great, why doesn't the matchmaker grab her for himself?! I don't see too many people giving away a million dollars these days!

People only see what they want to see. For instance, people think I only like blondes. In fact, many of the white girls I date are brunettes—but people know that by saying, "I saw Wilt with a blonde," they're making a stronger impression that I date white women. I think it's pretty goddamn strange. When I lived in Hawaii and had a strong fascination for Oriental girls, no one said, "He only dates Chinese or Japanese or Koreans," which I did almost exclusively for ten years. I never heard anyone commenting on my dating Indian girls. But people—white *and* of color—still have strong feelings about my dating white girls. So be it. My head doesn't know color, creed, or religion, only what turns me on.

One of the questions I am most often asked is, "When are you going to get married?" And I usually reply, "Well, if it happens, it happens."

Invariably the next question is, "Don't you want to have

little 'Wilties'?" What they really want to know is, "Wouldn't I like to see my athletic prowess embodied in offspring?"

I truly believe that the biggest problem facing the world today is overpopulation. I would like to see the world's birth rate decrease. I believe in adoption and doing as much as we can for the kids who are already here. At this point in time I am still too much of a vagabond to adopt. My life-style is not conducive to my raising a family. But I do see a time when I settle down. And the woman I settle down with will understand my position on this issue, because we will discuss it beforehand, believe me. I will not settle down with anyone who won't adopt.

WILTISM

Any idiot can father a child, and too many of them do.

Wendell Willkie said it best for me. Practically any citizen of our great country can, if he is able and willing to work for it, attain the highest levels of education. That is why the only man I look down on is the one who is not willing to work.

One thing that has been hard for me to find is people who will tell me what I need to hear rather than what they think I *want* to hear. It may be a common occurrence to all people, or it may be because of my station in life. But I hate to be placated, especially by so-called friends. That is why I don't like traveling in an entourage. I don't need to be surrounded by yes-men.

Many star athletes, boxers in particular, always seem to be surrounded by these yes-men. My theory is that they, the athletes, equate the number of people in their entourage with their own success. It's like going out and eating alone. Many people can't or won't; they feel it's like saying you have no friends. Also, when there are multitudes of hangers-on to always agree with you, you can always blame them when things go wrong.

It may seem to you all that I spend all of my time in fun and frolic. Not true. I spend a great deal of time doing something that is *not* fun—but *is* very rewarding. This is my involvement in drug abuse prevention. It has a very high priority in my life, which I mention not for self-acclaim but to let you know that I am trying to make a difference.

I do and always will travel around the country to raise money, counsel kids, and try to bring attention to this problem, which, believe me, is destroying the country. I have little sympathy for the affluent and sports stars who fall prey to drugs. I realize they are vulnerable and need help like anyone else, but my sympathies lie elsewhere. When I see so many people in Harlem and East L.A. and other underprivileged areas of our country with nothing to look forward to except the same squalor they are looking at today, it is a hell of a lot easier for me to understand their involvement with drugs—using and selling—than that of the affluent and the sports star.

What do you say to a guy who can make a thousand dollars a day for selling drugs when he can't get a decent job otherwise? I'm often confronted with that dilemma.

They say to me, "Yeah, Wilt, you live in a big house and drive expensive cars, so it's easy for you to say don't do drugs, but what would you be doing if you were me?"

My answer is not profound or new. I tell them there are many ways to make a buck, and if you want to spend the rest of your life looking over your shoulder, then drug selling is one of them. But if you're willing to work and look for a little luck, you can do an honest day's work and feel good about yourself. I tell them that I do believe luck plays a major part in any game, including the game of life. But the key is working hard to put yourself in a position to take advantage of the luck when it comes your way. I can remember losing a lot of tough games in the last second by opponents' lucky shots, but if the other team had not worked damn hard to put themselves in a position to allow that shot to be the winner, there would have been no point in even taking it. So I say to people I talk to: Put yourself in a position to take advantage of that lucky shot when it comes your way.

I am fearful that our leaders like Bush and Quayle don't view the ghettos as a real part of American society. That's why they do so little to help and instill the American spirit in ghetto kids. These kids aren't given any educational advantages. They are just pushed aside. It's taken for granted that life in the Bush-lane will work without them. As a result, they grow up with a certain hopelessness. They feel they can have no real impact on the American way of life. That's the big reason they take drugs. And it's only because of those drugs—and their danger to all society—that attention has been focused on this segment of our society. Not until we make the ghettos a real part of our America will this drug problem subside.

It is said that good things come to those who wait. I believe that good things come to those who work.

When I was playing for the 76ers—from 1965 to 1968—I commuted between Philadelphia and New York City. I would get home at about two in the morning and then around three I would walk my dogs, two black Great Dane puppies. I was giving them obedience training, teaching them to wait at the corner until I gave them the command to cross the street on the green light. On one of these occasions I noticed that a stretch limousine was following me. After a block or two the limo pulls alongside of me and the window rolls down. This very distinguished lady sticks her head out and says, "Excuse me, sir. I've been watching you train your dogs and you are really wonderful. How much do you charge to train them?"

At that time the Philadelphia 76ers were having a terrible season, so I replied without missing a beat, "I'm very expensive, ma'am, but right now I have no time, because I have a whole *team* of dogs I'm working with."

She said, "I'm so sorry." And she drove off.

I *find that* the busier I am the more projects I am able to take on and complete. I also find that when I'm in one of those lazy moods and doing nothing, I can't find time to do anything.

The moral here is to stay busy. Leonardo da Vinci, one of my idols, is the best example of this. He did in one lifetime what it would have taken a normal person four or five lifetimes to accomplish.

If you want something done, give it to a busy person, not to that guy in the rocking chair.

I *'ve probably signed* a million autographs, but I feel like I have yet to sign one to the person who's asking for it. It's always: "Would you please give me an autograph? It's for my son, my daughter, my wife's brother, my uncle's other nephew, my husband's mistress's stepson, my grand-mother's lover's illegitimate granduncle," and on and on.

In the old days you would buy a program to see someone perform, perhaps someone like the great opera singer Enrico Caruso, and after the performance you would say, "Please, Mr. Caruso, will you sign my program? I enjoyed your performance very much, you were wonderful."

But that's all changed. Now it's: "Hey, Wilt, gimme your autograph!" And believe me, autograph hounds will stop you *anywhere*. I've been stopped in the middle of meals and in the middle of taking a leak. I would not be surprised, one of these days, to look up while I was making love—and find somebody standing there, holding out a pen, saying, "Hey, Wilt, gimme an autograph!" Many of the people asking don't even know who I am. But they see others asking—it's monkey see, monkey do. I really believe that most of the people they say they're getting it for really don't know who I am. Autograph seekers should just ask for the autograph and skip the explanations. The people who are signing the autograph don't care who it's for; not really.

It also disturbs me when moms and pops push their kids to get autographs from their parents' heroes. Most of these kids don't know who the hell Wilt Chamberlain is—or Bob Cousy or Bill Russell, either. We're from a different era.

Parents, allow your kids to make a choice about getting an autograph or not. Don't force Frank Sinatra on your kids, and they won't force Run-D.M.C. on you.

I often hear, "My son is a great basketball fan. Will you sign for him?" If the kid really is a fan, the odds are he doesn't like every player. Maybe I'm one of the players he doesn't like at all. If the kid had once said, "Hey, Dad, if you ever meet Wilt Chamberlain will you get his autograph for me?" that would be fine. No problem. But to say the kid is a basketball fan so sign here is an imposition on the player and does nothing for the kid.

And to those of you who might want an autograph from me in the future, I personally was raised to appreciate "please" and "thank you," especially when asking for something.

Some *athletes are* chosen from the outset of their careers to be the good guys (the winners, the ones you want your sons and daughters to emulate) and some are chosen to be controversial—like me. I believe this is a premeditated decision by members of the media. And most members of the media are like sheep. If one influential reporter tags an athlete as a good guy, most of the other reporters follow along docilely without a moment's thought.

We're *all* involved with controversy at some point. Some, like the Jerry Wests and the Julius Ervings, manage to slide through it unscathed. Others, like Darryl Dawkins and World B. Free—and Wilt Chamberlain—have controversy used against them. I discussed this with a writer for the *Los Angeles Times* once, and he as much as admitted it. He told me, "Wilt, people don't want to read anything negative about Jerry West. They do with you."

All satisfying stories have a bad guy, a villain, to make the good guy look even better. Many times, though, the bad guy *becomes* a good guy as the plot unfolds. During my playing days, I was the classic bad guy. Controversy followed me wherever I went. When I was traded to the Los Angeles Lakers, writers immediately wanted to know if there were going to be enough balls to go around for Jerry West, Elgin Baylor, and me. They fostered the belief that I was a ball hog—even though I had just led the league in assists the year before! Neither Jerry nor Elgin ever led the league in assists, so who was the better team player?

The coach, Butch van Breda Kolff, was asked how he was going to deal with me. He instantly set another controversy into motion by saying, "He'll play it my way or not play at all." All that brilliant statement did was make people—who were already aware of my "stormy personality"—ready for the unavoidable clash.

My first pro coach, Neil Johnston, was responsible for my first controversy. He was the center whose job I took. He was never a big fan of mine to begin with, since I used to kick his butt playing in the summer leagues back in Philadelphia while I was still in high school and he was the leading NBA scorer and rebounder. This was his first coaching assignment and it was only given to him out of kindness and the gratitude of our owner, Eddie Gottlieb, who felt he owed him something. Later, Gottlieb admitted he was wrong to have hired a neophyte like Johnston because he had no ability to deal with all of the unique things I brought to the team and the league. Whenever we lost, Johnston would bring up how much money I was making, exactly how I should be playing, and why I should be doing even more than I was.

Well, why don't you check my first-year stats? No player

in pro sports *ever* dominated their sport as I did. To tell you the truth, I believe it embarrassed people—players and coaches. It made them feel inadequate. There was a lot of jealousy over the attention and money I was earning. The white basketball society couldn't accept all that. Thank God for my second pro coach, Frank McGuire, who respected my ability, but most of all treated me as an equal. He understood my volatile position in both basketball and society.

I was *chosen* to be a man of controversy. It was surprising to me when it happened—and I'm sure it happened just because I believed in speaking my mind. Is it the speaking of my mind that makes me controversial, or is it that people don't like what I'm saying?

In the long run, controversy has been good for me. Writing and reading about the good guys can get very boring. On the other hand, controversy sells papers and gets viewers. My career in commercials, movies, and TV commentating has had longevity, I believe, because of the controversial role I was cast in (justly or unjustly). My contemporaries who were chosen as the good guys have long since slipped into obscurity.

Have *you heard* the expression "I am a camera"? You know how some people will act out of character when they know a camera is on them? Well, for some odd reason, I also bring that same response out of some people. When they see me they act in ways that they wouldn't normally act. I believe that's why so many people can ask me incredibly stupid questions, make crass remarks, give me unbelievable looks—all things that wouldn't be a normal part of their character.

. . .

I *believe that* we need to go back to some of our old values. Most important among these values is the time when we had a strong belief in others. We have become a very distrusting people, and that is disturbing to me. We need to bring back trust, the kind of trust the old neighborhood grocer had for your mother or father.

Remember when we were able to go into the corner store and say, "I need some groceries, but I won't be able to pay you until Friday"? The grocer would let people have the four or five dollars' worth of food just by signing their name to a tattered old book. In most cases not even your signature was needed. A lot of these trusting grocers were from the old ethnic backgrounds (in my neighborhood they were either Jewish or Italian). The grocer trusted his customers and he very seldom if ever got burned. The amount that food costs today is far greater than when I was a kid. But it's not the cost of the food that's making the difference—it's the lack of respect and trust.

This mind-set is no longer with us. I don't know whether it's because these stores seem to be owned by other minority groups who no longer deem it the proper thing to do, or whether it's just a product of our times, but we seem to have very few people we fully trust. Now, if you don't have money you better have your credit card with you. Or else you are dead meat, and if it's food you need you won't get to eat.

E*verything is subject* to change, and another thing I wish would hurry and change back to the old ways is the sense of home. It seems hard to find that homey feeling anymore.

For instance, I miss home cooking. The sociability and grace that goes with having people over for home-cooked meals has given way to attending the plentiful restaurants that now grace our cities. These restaurants are quite pleasant, with great chefs and delicious food, but they don't mash potatoes or make gravy, fry a chicken or a pork chop, bake an apple cobbler or a lemon meringue pie, the food you can only find in a good home-cooked meal.

I could go on and on, but you get the idea. Some things need that homey touch.

WILTISM

When it comes to food I am not hard to please. I only like one kind: the best.

This same personal touch is gone from the performances of our great singers and musicians. At one time you could go see them in some intimate room or nightclub. Now, the only time you can see the great ones is with tens of thousands of fans in an arena big enough to house a football game. Granted, they may give good performances here, but these concerts provoke an entirely different feeling in the audience.

I remember, years ago, watching the great Sam Cookc, Nat King Cole, Miles Davis, and Frank Sinatra in those small, quiet, comfortable rooms. I can only hope those days are not gone forever. For those of you who have never had the chance to hear music in an intimate room, it has its own special flavor—just like home cooking. Even the performers of that day—Sarah Vaughan, Dinah Washington, Billie Holiday—had the gift of making you feel you were at home.

Money has caused musicians and singers to opt to play only in huge, impersonal places. It's had the same effect on jocks. Now, everything a jock does or does not do is predicated on how it may affect his or her salary. I hate it. It's ruined music and it's ruining sports.

As *long as* I'm on the subject of change . . .

I know we can all get to our destinations faster by airplane, and that this allows us to stay longer and see more, but oh! there was something so charming and relaxing when I used to travel by train.

Remember those convenient little shopping malls that were built to save us from the hazards of shopping downtown? They have now all gone berserk! Every city is trying to build the biggest, grandest mall of them all, mega-malls with parking lots so large you need a bus to get from your car to the entrance—if you know which entrance you want, because there are so many stores and floors, you don't have a clue. Malls are sure no longer convenient for me.

Have you tried to watch a basketball game in one of those huge arenas? Come on! How much fun can it be?! You need to carry a radio to hear what's happening, 'cause you sure can't see it.

☞ **WILTISM** 🐟

Some change is for the better. But sometimes it's better if we change things back.

Every time someone asks me, "Wilt, wouldn't you like to be playing today and making all of that money that the players are making now?" I always reply, "Not really. I enjoyed the time I was playing and I made plenty of money, relatively speaking."

Well, I'm here to tell you all that's a bunch of bull. I don't know why I say it. Come on. Wouldn't anyone want to be twenty or thirty years younger and playing today, especially compared to the conditions I had to play and get paid under?

Today, the bylaws won't allow an NBA team to travel and play on the same day. When I played for the Philadelphia Warriors, we once had a night game in Los Angeles. We flew out of Philly on a TWA Super Constellation; the flight was scheduled to take ten to eleven hours, and we were to land in L.A. around three or four in the afternoon. We had strong headwinds and landed at *nine.* Nine thousand fans waited patiently at the Sports Arena for us to arrive. We hurried from the airport to the arena. On the bus to the game, we rushed to get taped and dressed. It reminded me of my old days with the Globetrotters, when we played three games a day and dressing on the bus was common. Well, to make a long story shorter, the game started at 10:00 P.M.—which was 1:00 A.M. in Philadelphia. The game lasted three hours—4:00 A.M. Philadelphia time. And no one even made a statement about it; no one seemed at all upset. It was commonplace and natural in the NBA in those days. By the way, we kicked their butts. One last difference: On that trip there was no first-class section. All basketball players traveled coach and sat three across in cramped seats.

Centers now are making $2 million a year, averaging six points and four rebounds a game. If you prorated my salary for what I did and compared it with what they are doing now, I'd be making $20 million a season.

So how obvious is the answer to that question now?

. . .

On the other hand, some people think I am still playing, like my date I mentioned in the first chapter. To this day many people ask me what team I play for. Considering my age, that could be a compliment. Of course, most of the people who ask questions like that know nothing at all about basketball. (I truly believe these people don't know much about *anything*. These same people would probably ask President Reagan, while he was in his second term of office, "Are you filming today, Ronnie?")

When I travel the world I often find myself at the great monuments built by man, like the pyramids of Egypt. I often wonder how many people, when they view the pyramids, pay homage to the thousands of lives that were lost in the building of what is essentially just a tomb.

Most of the so-called great manmade monuments were built by enslaved people who were forced to endure great hardships to complete them. How many died in the building of the Great Wall of China? I believe we should view these great monuments with more compassion for who built them, and at what cost they were built.

☞ **WILTISM** 🐾

Of all our faculties the most important one is our ability to imagine. Can you imagine how it would be not to be able to imagine?

What was the single biggest thrill in my life? Winning the NBA championship? Scoring a hundred points in one game? No. Witnessing the first night flight of the space shuttle.

I was flown by NASA into Washington, D.C., and then on to Cape Kennedy, with dignitaries of various backgrounds. We had the closest view possible for watching this overwhelming event.

I was invited because of my color. NASA was trying to do more in the way of public relations. The connection was that one of the crew members was the first astronaut of color. (I wondered for a moment whether they had the launching at night so no one could see him—*only kidding.*)

It was a very special experience for me. Not only was he a man of color, but he was also from my alma mater, Overbrook High School back in Philly.

(They said he was the first of his race in space, but I'm not so sure. There was another guy who graduated from Overbrook a little before his time and everyone who knew him believed that he had already been "up there" for a long time—in a beautifully strange way, in some spiritual way. His name was Wali Jones, alias Wali Wonder. He went on to become a professional basketball player, and I had the pleasure of playing with him on the Philadelphia 76ers.)

Without being at the launch I could have never in a million years imagined the impact the takeoff would have on me. It was an awesome display of power and of man's incredible ingenuity. At blast-off, the dark night sky was lit for over twenty square miles with such brightness that you had to shield your eyes, as if you were staring directly into a thousand-watt bulb that had just been turned on in a small, dark room. It was hard for me to believe as I watched the rocket ascend that there could be anyone or anything alive inside. Only when it disappeared into the blackness of the night, and my heart started to beat again, did I fully grasp what I had just seen.

It was a view that I was definitely not above, but oh, how high it made me feel.

I *like games:* chess, dominoes, cards, backgammon, and most any game that challenges your mind. We were all raised on games and I believe that games mirror life. Sure, they're fun and can be taken lightly. But if you take them seriously you can tell a lot about a person you're playing against.

I'm suspicious of people who won't play games. I wonder if they're afraid you'll get to know the real them.

Most people don't see the way they play their weekend sports as a barometer for measuring their values (and value) in life. Basketball is just another game to them when they shoot around in their driveway or in a schoolyard. Yet people seem to measure an athlete's worth *completely* on what they see in the athlete's performance on the court. This is sad. Hey, some people are lousy card players but very worthwhile citizens. There are basketball players who are brilliant on the floor but have no real merit in other facets of life. People often judge good players as good people and, of course, this is not necessarily the case.

I take games very seriously; that way I get the most out of them. Yet the more seriously I take them the more fun they are. (Though I am careful not to take them so seriously that they stress me out.)

When I play a game of dominoes, I don't just sit down to fill in some time that I have on my hands. For me, it's dominoes time and that's prime time. I have time for work, I have time for love, I have time for dominoes. It isn't just to fill in some loose hours or moments—it's as much a part of my life as going to see a play or a sporting event or reading a book.

I like to relate life to games because I think life *is* a game. The game of life, if we play it correctly, can be a lot of fun. Like most games there are winners and losers. But the real deal is to have fun while you're playing—especially because any game may end a lot sooner than you think. If you play it wrong you could be disqualified, and—tilt!—the game's over. When the game is dominoes, you can always play again. But when it's the game of life . . . On the other hand, a game can last a long time if you play—or live—it right.

Some say that the last true winner is death. But does anybody know for sure? Could we just move on to play another game on another plane?

When I play games I am so competitive that I very seldom lose. I will take full advantage of any slip on my opponent's part, even to the point where many of my opponents kiddingly accuse me of cheating. (How else are you going to accuse a seven-foot, three-hundred-pound guy of cheating but kiddingly?) I will take a peek if my adversary is not playing his cards close enough to his chest. I will bend a rule in my favor if they are not quite sure what the rule is. But my real advantage here is giving the *illusion* that I'm cheating. My opponent spends so much time trying to figure out *how* I'm cheating that he's distracted from giving his full attention to what he should be doing if he hopes to win the game.

This I call gamesmanship. You, like my opponents, may call it gamesman-*shit*.

. . .

Back in 1984, while I was filming *Conan the Destroyer* with Arnold Schwarzenegger, I got the opportunity to begin to realize a dream that is now almost fulfilled.

I've always loved automobiles, and on the movie set in Mexico City I became associated with a gentleman who did some designing of cars and boats. We became friends and decided to build a car together. ("Together" meant my money and his brains.) Actually I did a lot of the designing and had a lot of input into how I wanted it and what I was looking for. Since I have owned many exotic cars in the past, I tried to build a car that included the good things some of my cars had but avoided the bad things that these cars had. I thought the project would take a year.

I am now into the sixth year of building that car. But by the time this book is published the car should be completed. It was a great undertaking. During this period I've had to change designers and builders and build several different engines, all the while dealing with the things that go along with creating a prototype of anything. As much as I love cars, and the challenge was one that I relished, I doubt sincerely that I would ever want to tackle that kind of a job again. You have too many things going against you.

Still, I feel I've been lucky. I think I'll wind up with a great car that is, in my opinion, also a work of art. You can see from the picture in the photo section that the car is quite a looker. I guarantee it's also going to be quite a mover.

I was always at a loss as to what I would call this vehicle. When you put a great deal of your own money and six years of your time into it, why not give it your own name? Ford gave his car his name and so did almost everyone else who built one. So I'm not trying to be vain; I'm just being practical when I call it The Chamberlain.

Or would you rather I call it The Jordan?

Speaking of vanity, I never thought of myself as being vain, yet the older I get the more I worry about my appearance. I am trying to change this about myself. I'm not saying you should stop worrying about things like controlling your weight, just don't let a few extra pounds or inches control you. It's more than just growing old gracefully. It's realizing that trying to act younger and appear younger only makes you look older and feel older.

I'm also trying to change my attitudes toward today's music. I am far too critical and I should know better, because when I was younger and in college at the University of Kansas, I was a DJ with a call-in music program. My older listeners would call in and complain about how bad they thought the music of the day was—especially Elvis Presley—and I remember thinking, "These old fogies! They only like a song if it's thirty years old!" Now here I am, thirty years later, feeling the same way about contemporary music. Shame on me!

So I am going to stop worrying about those extra pounds, and learn to appreciate today's sounds. I hope my contemporaries will join me in this change of attitude— and not in the rocking chair with the old fogies.

There are a couple of things I like about myself that I feel have played a major part in the shaping of my life.

One of these is this: I have forever believed the choosing of friends is the single most important thing one can do to enhance one's well-being and help in leading oneself toward an honest, worthwhile, and productive life. When I do any antidrug lectures and speak to the youth of our great country, I tell them that choosing their friends should be thought of in the same way as choosing a good basketball team.

You want to pick a guard with good ball-handling ability; in the same manner you should pick a friend with good morals. A center that rebounds and blocks shots is like a friend who helps to block you from liars and dealers and all the other bad elements out there. Picking a forward who can make that clutch basket for your team when needed is like picking a friend you can count on in the clutch, which we all need from time to time.

I hope I'm not jinxing myself, but I've avoided some of the pitfalls that have trapped many of my contemporaries simply by surrounding myself with good people who have become good friends. We keep each other straight.

We learn to act through our associations—observing, absorbing, then simulating the actions that appeal to us—and therefore our friends play a great role in determining what we become.

WILTISM

Many people say we are what we eat. But I believe we are shaped by who we meet.

Toward the end of my basketball career, the last two or three years of it anyway, my favorite thoughts used to occur while I was on the foul line getting ready to attempt the one part of my game I dreaded the most. These thoughts never helped me to actually make a foul shot, but they were refreshing and cool. That's because they were on how nice it would be to be in some wonderful place—like skiing on the slopes of the Swiss Alps—instead of in a hot, sweaty, demanding arena getting ready to be booed for missing yet another free throw.

Since I've been retired from basketball I have tried skiing a couple of times, but like my foul shooting—and maybe because my skiing desire was born at the foul line—I am the world's worst skier. And boy, was it cold there!

If there is a moral to this story it is that the grass is often the same color on both sides of the fence.

All right, I suppose this is the time and place to finally tell the truth about why I was such a lousy foul shooter.

Believe it or not, in high school, I was an 80-percent shooter from the free throw line. Look it up. Then, my freshman year at Kansas, I hurt my knee.

When I shot free throws, I used to have this deep, deep knee bend. But after the knee injury, I had to change my style of shooting. When I started to miss from the line— using this new style—I changed to a third style. The more I kept missing, the more I kept messing around with different methods and techniques. People started giving me advice. I started listening—to anybody and everybody. But the whole thing became a major psychological hang-up. I knew I'd been good—but now I knew I was awful. Once your brain is giving you that message, forget it. So what started out as just a slump turned into a careerlong slide.

The weird thing was, in practice I was as sharp from the line as I'd been in high school. With the Lakers, fooling around between games, I could shoot free throws as well as Gail Goodrich. Fooling around, I used to beat Calvin Murphy—the all-time best foul shooter—from the line. I could routinely sink forty or forty-five out of fifty. But in a game, my head was too messed up.

Ike Richman, the owner of the 76ers, sent me to a shrink to see if that would help me solve the problem.

It didn't.

Ike was paying $100 an hour for me to tell that psychiatrist my problems, which I did for four months. All that happened is that the shrink became a really good foul shooter and I became a good analyst.

I'm *still* a good free throw shooter. At UCLA or Pepperdine, if I go over to fool around with some kids, I never miss. Oh well.

I will tell you one thing, though, and this proves how sports are so psychologically oriented. The one time I was good in real games was in clutch situations. With the game on the line, I was an excellent foul shooter. I won a lot of games in the closing minutes because opposing teams would always decide I was the person they should foul. But I sure as hell never *wanted* to go to that foul line. I didn't like it. That's one of the reasons I admire Larry Bird. If his team's down by a point with little or no time on the clock, he *loves* to step up to that foul line. His brain is telling him there's no way he can miss. Unfortunately, my brain used to give me just the opposite message.

Number *13 was* my uniform number. I know of no one who wore it before me, and that may have been the reason I chose it. Most people who are superstitious consider thirteen to be an unlucky number. I also felt it was bad luck—it was bad luck for those people I was going to play against.

I remember playing in the Boston Garden and hearing the announcer say, "And here is number thirteen . . . Wilt Chamberlain." I mumbled to myself, "Yeah, number thirteen on the scoreboard, but number one in your hearts." And then I ran on the floor with a little laugh because I knew I was truly number one in their hearts—if only as their number-one villain.

Who could be a better villain than I? Like Goliath, I was (and am) much bigger than anyone else, dark and mysterious. I was impossible to relate to. Even my beard often gave me a devillike image. I didn't wear a black hat but I did wear that 13, which had the same effect.

There have been times when I have not been invited to some affairs because I would overshadow the event itself or create an adverse effect. Usually, I don't care. But I'll tell you one instance that stung. A few years ago, the NBA picked the best players and teams of the first thirty-five years of the league. They chose Russell as the best player and my teams, the 1967 76ers and the '72 Lakers, as the best teams. Russell was invited to the ceremony but I never was. Can you believe it? They never even *invited* me. I'm sure the NBA would deny this, but I believe they knew that many people would make a big deal out of my not being picked as the best player of all time—and they wanted to stay away from that controversy. From that point of view, they were probably right. Why do you think I have never formally been asked to play in the Old-Timers' Game on the celebrated All-Star Game weekend? Well, whatever the reason, I'm not ready to be an old-timer anyway.

. . .

One of the biggest lies of my life was one that I tried to live for a long while. A year or so after I retired, I bought a residence in Hawaii. It wasn't my only residence but it was the one I spent the most time at for quite a few years. I considered it my home away from the real world and I thought Hawaii would be my last haven on earth—the place where I would finish out the rest of my life. I became enamored with the life-style—playing games in the sun all day and chasing *wahines* all night.

I saw this life-style as an extended vacation, one that I had earned and that I deserved. I no longer cared about making money or being goal-oriented in any way, except maybe to become a better racquetball player on the courts at Fort De Russy. I had closed my eyes to the fact that vacations are most enjoyed by people who use them as a brief interlude that punctuates meaningful work.

I am sure that most of us from time to time have wished we had nothing to do but lie on some idyllic island. But most of what I have in life and most of what I feel about life was passed on to me by two perpetually hard-working people, my mother and father. So I learned very early that work was and is quite wholesome and rewarding. There are few things more satisfying than achieving a good day's work or seeing a job well done. So why did I ever think that I could fool myself into believing that doing nothing could ever have any redeeming value?

I lived this lie for a lot longer time than I care to remember.

What brought me out of it? As many of us do, come New Year's I reflect on the year gone by. I started my reflections on 1989 late in December of that year and I began to realize that it was very much like '87 and '88. I did a little thinking and I realized the entire decade of the 1980s was reminiscent of '89—full of far too much nothingness. So then and there I started to plan to be a more productive individual in the 1990s. So far, I'm not doing a bad job. I have written this little thing you are reading all by myself—in longhand at that. I'm writing two more books, one fiction, the other nonfiction. I have written two screenplays, and started a chain of Wilt Chamberlain restaurants. The first one is in Boca Raton, Florida, and in its first month of operation, it was in the top 1 percent of the highest grossing restaurants in America. It's a sports restaurant, with the emphases on family, fun, and good food. With all these new endeavors I have still found time to get more involved in my favorite charities, Best Buddies and the Special Olympics. Best Buddies is an organization where college students take mentally handicapped children one on one and do the same kinds of things Big Brothers do. I also work with a charitable organization called Operation Smile. In this organization, doctors correct facial defects in children in the Third World. The work they do is amazing. I am also heavily involved working with drug abuse programs for our youth.

With all my new work, volleyball and women have been cut way down—not out, but down.

I hope I haven't taken too much for granted, now that I think about it. Writing a book is strange because I have to assume people already know a lot about me—or why would they bother to pick this book up—but I can't assume they know *too* much about me. If they knew everything, this book would be a useless dud. I assume that most people know that I'm a volleyballer of some renown. In fact, for a long time, volleyball became as big a part of my life as basketball once was. I helped to start an international league of players from around the world, even behind the Iron Curtain (when there was an Iron Curtain). The volleyball organization was called the IVA (International Volleyball Association). I was president of the league, a team owner, *and* the star player. One of my most cherished feats was being chosen MVP in an All-Star volleyball game that was nationally televised by NBC. It was extra sweet because the sportswriters and media had intimated that I didn't deserve to be playing in that game. (These were the same people who voted for the MVP.) I have to admit, a few players felt the same way—though they felt it anonymously, which I always feel is chickenshit—even though they knew that without me the league had no chance to survive. After I retired from the league to take a four-man volleyball team on a worldwide tour, the league *didn't* survive. It folded. I am proud to say that those media people who voted me as the MVP of that All-Star game congratulated me afterward and apologized for doubting my ability to play the game of volleyball as well as I'd played basketball.

I am also proud to say that before my involvement in volleyball, our country could not even qualify to send a team to the Olympics, but my team and I helped to give the game new meaning in America and the U.S.A. has since won two Gold Medals, in 1984 and 1988.

I started playing volleyball very late in my athletic career, around age thirty-three or thirty-four, but I became quite proficient. It's a highly skilled and very fast-paced game. Being able to hold my own against the best in the world, on the beach or indoors, is something I am very proud of. I can *still* do so—even at the tender age of fifty-five.

☞ WILTISM 🐟

The problem with doing nothing is that you never know when you are through. That's why it's so easy to *keep* on doing nothing.

With all my traveling, one could wonder how I find time to keep in any kind of physical shape. Well, about two years ago I started playing tennis. Now, with business ventures in Florida—my restaurant chain in Boca Raton—I get to play this frustrating but satisfying sport a great deal in the warm Florida sun on their great clay courts. Volleyball is also still a part of my routine and gets a lot of my attention. Wherever I find time I work out with free weights.

My strength has always been a popular topic of conversation and I have always enjoyed shocking people with my feats, like lifting cars front-end and back-end and putting them up on sidewalks. I loved to do this in Europe, and did it often as people stood and stared in amazement. When I worked out with Schwarzenegger, I benchpressed 500 pounds and did "reps" the way most people do with 150 pounds. Long arms are a negative in lifting, yet I have never seen anyone who can curl more weight than I could.

I also do aerobics, which are a blessing in disguise, because they give me a chance to build up my cardiovascular system, yet keep the pressure off my knees and the other joints in my old, aching body. If I'm in L.A. I find a lot of time to ride my mountain bike in the hills of southern California and on the bicycle paths of Santa Monica beach. Whenever I can, I ride downhill, because I really hate pumping uphill. From time to time you can find me at Drake Stadium on the campus of UCLA, running track or throwing the discus. I still find track and field a very exhilarating way to relax and get a workout.

I have no set time for any of the above workouts, because the one thing I have no time for is regimentation. I like to do what I feel like doing at that time, and I always make time for that.

I *have had* two major operations post-professional basketball. One was on a ruptured tendon in my right elbow, suffered after being kicked by a polo pony in a pileup during a game. And a year ago I had a knee operation that was done to alleviate the pain from a worn-out knee that someday may have to be replaced by an artificial knee joint. But with a great doctor, and the Wilt to play, I'm still pretty active every day.

Unfortunately the playing of games is like the living of life. Sooner or later you have to pay the price. No one leaves here alive. If you play long enough, the body does break down—no matter how well you take care of it and prepare it for those games. Normally you would think that games, because they are physical exercise, would build your body up rather than tear it down, but that is just not true. Our bodies were not made to play these games, and eventually, they take their toll on all of us.

They say a house is the largest investment the average person makes. His car is the second. What is the third—and often the last? You guessed it, your funeral. (It's not always the last, though. Remember, there are people who think ahead. I don't know why, but they pay before they die.)

We're always complaining about the fact that living expenses are too high. But now it's expensive to die. It's pretty costly for the average guy, so imagine what it will cost for me! You know the undertaker will charge me for the two extra feet on the casket. He'll make me buy two burial plots because one won't be long enough. Then there's the cost of putting the extension on the hearse, because my casket won't fit in the average one. All that extra embalming fluid will probably cost me an arm and a leg (unless they don't do my arms and legs). Then there are the extra pallbearers, and since good friends are really hard to find I may have to buy a half-dozen. And what about all those extra flowers that will be needed to cover my oversize casket? With so much to say about me I'm sure I'll have a minister who will be very long-winded, and he'll charge me extra. The wailing women I plan to hire will cost enough to make anybody cry.

But ah! I didn't go to the University of Kansas for nothing. I plan to be cremated. Since one match can start a forest fire and burn down all those tall trees it shouldn't cost me that much for me to be burned down. And since I plan to donate my organs to help others live longer, maybe since there will be less of me to burn up I can get a price break on that, too.

My ashes will be put into a little jar with the following inscription:

I BET YOU WONDER HOW ALL OF ME GOT IN THIS
LITTLE JAR. WELL, THE SAME WAY I GOT INTO
THOSE LITTLE CARS WHEN I WAS ALIVE.

EVEN IN DEATH, WHERE THERE'S A WILT, THERE'S
A WAY.

THREE

On Athletes: Jockularity

As everyone knows, I am a fan of all sports. More than that, I am a fan of all athletes. Here is how I see the state of athletes—and athletics—today.

The word *"unbelievable"* only begins to describe the world's most unbelievable athlete I've ever seen. I know many of you have seen the acrobatic moves capped by the aerial show of Michael Jordan. We have also seen incredible passes and three-point shots at the buzzer by the Magic Man time after time. Whether playing in the rigorous NBA or the casual showmanship style of the Globetrotters, what is required is basketball wizardry. And since I played both,

I am here to tell you that a thirty-foot shot in front of twenty thousand fans is tough for anyone no matter what league you're in.

That's why watching Meadowlark Lemon, when he was the star for the Harlem Globetrotters, throw in a half-court hook shot night after night after night, with such consistency that people thought it was just part of the act, as if he had a magnet drawing the ball to the basket, is the most unbelievable thing I have ever seen. He gets my vote as the most incredible athlete far and away.

I watched the man walking away from the basket, never looking at it, and make a basket by flipping the ball over his head time after time, to the amazement of everyone, players and fans alike. And the only time Meadowlark seemed to be affected was when he'd miss one. To be able to make one of those incredible shots in a game just once in my life is all I would ask for. And he made them every night—while making a joke of it.

The Globies had a lot of tricks, but Meadowlark's shots were for real. Don't ask me how. My only answer is, Wow!

A reporter in Rome once asked me, "Does Meadowlark practice very much?" I said to him, "You can't practice those things. How do you practice a once-in-a-lifetime shot, even though you're asked to make it every night? It's like practicing drowning."

If *you think* the Globies were clever with that basketball on the court, you are, of course, right, but, boy, how we used that cleverness in ways people will never guess. One ploy that was often used was the Dropping of the Bomb. It goes like this: Before the game, during our introductions, we would scan the arena for good-looking girls. When we found the finest one, we marked her position and made it known to Meadowlark, the center and funny guy of the Globies. During the second quarter we'd give Meadowlark a piece of paper with our telephone numbers and room numbers written on it. Also on the piece of paper was a request to call us after the game. (We did the best we could with the foreign languages, but luckily numbers are the same in most languages.) We called this note a "bomb." One of us would then proceed to point into the crowd and shout, "Meadow, she's not laughing! Go see what's wrong with her." Of course no one could do this better, so Meadow would amble up to where the pretty lady was seated. If she was not with a guy he would ease into something to make her laugh and while he was doing this he would slip the note into her hand. When he returned to the court we'd ask, "Did you drop that bomb, Meadow?" He would, more often than not, reply in the affirmative, something like, "It will go off thirty minutes after the game." For some odd reason, if he could not get the note to her, he would say, "The bomb blew up in my face."

The Globies had all sorts of their own rules. They even had a Globie language that was only understood by the players. But there was one thing they were totally death on—and they would never ever let you forget it. And that thing was if you were caught entertaining, talking to, walking with, or even looking at an ugly girl. In Globie talk, an ugly girl was a "mulion." All Globies thought of themselves as Don Juans, irresistible to all members of the opposite sex. To deface their image by consorting with a mulion was unpardonable. It was hilarious to watch grown men hide their dates, or scan ahead looking to see if any other Globie was watching before they invited a mulion into their hotel rooms or the hotel lobby. If caught, the guilty Globie would desperately try to bribe the player that caught him. If that didn't work, he would lie like you can't believe. But usually never to any avail. The team would do whatever it took until the guilty party confessed and swore never to do it again.

I *have often* been asked to pick my all-time basketball team. This seems to be a question that's asked of basketball players more often than football or baseball players. Maybe it's because there are only five on a team, rather than eleven or nine. I find picking a basketball team almost impossible to do today, because professional basketball is so much different now than it was twenty or thirty years ago. There is no way to honestly compare players. So what I have done is come up with something you might have a little more fun with. It's my all-athletic team, translated into a basketball team.

My all-athletic team is composed only of people who were either the best in their sport or so close to it that no one can argue about it. Most of these athletes are of my period, simply because I just don't know many of the contemporary players as well.

Having already said I thought Meadowlark Lemon was the most unbelievable athlete I ever saw, you might expect him to make the team. However, unbelievable isn't quite the same as being the greatest, so I'll pick him as my sixth man. I'll also pick Michael Jordan as a sixth man. (It's my team, so I can have two sixth men if I want to. Who's gonna argue with me?) I pick Michael because I've seen him *kill* people on the basketball court. He's also a great golfer capable of making a hole-in-one, a baseball player who can hit home runs in major league ballparks . . . and he can deliver six-packs of Coca-Cola to a tree house without a ladder.

As for my starters, I pick Rick Barry first. In my opinion Rick was as good a forward as ever played basketball. As an athlete, well, even today, at forty-six or forty-seven years of age, he's in good enough shape to play. He is also an incredible golfer, plays a great game of tennis, and could play a number of other sports on a world-class level.

My second choice is the great Jim Brown of the Cleveland Browns football team. Of course, Jim was also an All-American lacrosse player at Syracuse University— some say he was the best lacrosse player ever. Today he is a superb roller skater, plays a lot of basketball, and could basically play any sport that requires power and speed. Plus, Jim has a competitiveness to him that is second to none.

Jim Brown is *so* competitive and proud he has challenged me often, even at parties, to race him. I have raced him, and I've beaten his butt—but afterward he would claim that I never won, even though many people watched us. One of the greatest conversations I've ever heard was between Jim Brown and O.J. Simpson at the *Playboy* mansion in Holmby Hills. They were in the living room arguing about who was the best running back in the NFL and I was eavesdropping. Of course, both of them thought they themselves were by far the best. And each was telling the other why that was so. O.J. told Jim that he, O.J., though he had not run for as many yards as Jim, was a much more clever runner. Jim was insisting that, since his rushing average per carry was better than anyone's who ever played, *he* was the best. And O.J. replied, "Yeah, but you had to run *over* people and get all bruised up like a big dumb type of runner." Jim said, "Well, you know, I was so much stronger than the rest of the guys, I just ran over them—the shortest distance between two points," etc., etc. "But you see," O.J. came back, "I was so clever and fast that I just ran *around* guys. No one ever had a chance to touch me."

The argument went on and on, both of them repeating the same thing over and over. I'll bet they still have that same argument every time they meet.

Willie Shoemaker is third. I have had the great pleasure of doing some work with Willie. Most people don't think of jockeys when they think of world-class athletes, but they are wrong. When it comes to heart there is no one with a bigger heart than Willie Shoemaker. I am sure that everyone reading this knows about the tragic car accident that Willie was in not so long ago. He was paralyzed—and for an athlete there are not too many worse things that can occur than physical paralysis. Yet this is where Willie showed his true heart. In my opinion, he's alive today—and, from what I hear, beginning to make some progress in his recuperation—just because of the strength of his heart coupled with his athletic prowess. In his prime—and what a prime it was—Willie was a tennis player, a golfer, and a bowler who once beat me in a bowling match on television—and I want you to know that I was a *great* bowler when I was in college.

My fourth choice is one of my all-time favorite athletes, and a contemporary one: Jackie Joyner-Kersee. This young lady was a great basketball player in high school and college, and we all know what she can do in the heptathlon. Jackie is quite capable of playing any sport she wants to.

Since we are picking five great, versatile athletes, I pick

myself as the fifth player on my mythical team. I have played a few sports. Presently I try to play tennis. I was a fairly decent racquetball and handball player, I was good in track and field, played volleyball, have done speed water skiing, and have tried my hand at sports like boxing, team handball, and some others. I qualify for my team.

For the coach, I would pick Bill Sharman, an outstanding athlete in his own right and a near-perfect guard—who might have been the greatest shooter of all time—for the Boston Celtics.

How do we make this a basketball team? Easy. I'm at center, Rick Barry is the shooting forward (he's an outside shooter supreme), Jim Brown plays power forward (who can argue with that?), Jackie plays off-guard and subs at small forward when you sit Rick down to cool the net off, and Willie is my point guard (just try to steal the ball from him). Michael comes off the bench and can play all the positions. And if I need a hook shot from center court, I know who to go to—Meadowlark.

The problem with this team is keeping everyone happy. With Rick taking sixty shots a game and me taking sixty shots a game, the others would never get to shoot the ball.

It is assumed that when an athlete retires he does one of two things:

(1) He drops off the face of the earth, never to be heard from again;

(2) He sleeps in a cave somewhere and comes out of hibernation annually, just long enough to participate in an old-timers game and show off his ever-growing beer belly.

Most people are convinced once a professional athlete is through with his athletic career he is also done with life, because his sport is the only thing he was prepared to do. Remember the gentleman in Chapter 1 who assumed I was dead? He's a perfect example of someone who thinks athletes need the limelight to survive. The average person does not want to give the professional athlete credit for being able to do anything else. Partly because the average person can only picture him or her doing that one job, and partly because it makes it a lot easier to rationalize away an athlete's greatness. It's a lot easier to say, "Oh, sure, he could do all sorts of things I couldn't do" if the follow-up is "But you should see him now. He's fat and old and broke."

When I retired I was not in the kind of secure financial position that most of the players of today will be in when they retire. I never, however, had any fear of not being able to survive in the outside world. I always knew I could enjoy my life as I saw fit.

Recently, Nat "Sweetwater" Clifton, one of the first men of color to play in the NBA (with the New York Knickerbockers), died. At the time of his death he was a taxi driver in Chicago, and had been for many years. That must have been a degrading job for Nat. Quite a comedown.

Financial preparation should only be a small part of an athlete's preparation for retirement. The really sad thing— much sadder than taking a job driving a cab—is that many ex-players simply are not ready to deal with the world as civilians, without the pomp and pageantry they experienced most of their adult life as stars in college and in professional sports. It's tough to go from being adored to being ignored. Real tough. But it's also real life.

What *really* happens to the pro athlete when he retires? Having gone through this, I can tell you in great detail. He (or she) gets his ego stomped and crushed as he is unceremoniously welcomed into the real world. He quickly finds out that we all live in little insulated areas—I call them cubicles—and that whatever happened inside his own cubicle is important to him but is irrelevant to others.

What I mean is, inside the athlete's cubicle, it's important who won the last NBA championship or how many points he scored last season. But in the other cubicles of the real world, these things don't really matter. The retired jock quickly discovers that all those personal achievements he sweated, bled, and died for, the records he took so much pride in making and breaking, mean nothing when it's time to live in the nitty-gritty of the real world. Points, touchdowns, goals, home runs, and championships made in one cubicle do not transfer to another cubicle—say the cubicle of business, or politics.

It's true on a personal level, too. In general, we are indifferent to those events that don't touch us personally, those events that take place outside our own cubicles. Test yourself. If you heard that 550 people were killed in traffic accidents over a holiday weekend, you would pass it off as just another number. But if one of those 550 people was a dear friend or relative, the pain and anguish you would feel would be so great that you could never forget it.

So the athlete who retires has this lesson to learn first and foremost: What he did as an athlete may have been wonderful and important when he played, but it isn't anymore. Maybe that's why some of them do sleep in a cave for a while. It takes a while to realize this fact, and to learn to live with it and move on.

When my contract with the Lakers was over at the end of the '73–'74 season, I went for two weeks to a friend's house on the island of Hvar, off the coast of Yugoslavia. While there, I had a chance to swim and play water polo with the Yugoslavian National Team. It made me realize there were games *other* than basketball that I wanted to play (volleyball was uppermost in my mind). I realized that if I stayed in basketball, I couldn't do any *better* than I'd already done. If the Lakers didn't go all the way again, it was as if I'd done *nothing.* If I didn't win the scoring title—or the assist title or lead the league in rebounding—it was also as if I'd done nothing.

My heroes—Joe Louis, Sugar Ray Robinson—had all gone on too long. I didn't want to go out that way. I wanted to go out on top. I was *still* the best center in the game. Some people felt that Kareem, then with the Bucks, was the best—but I didn't. He was scoring more points than I was but that's because my role had changed. I wasn't supposed to score points anymore. Besides, I didn't care what other people thought. I wanted to leave while *I* thought I was still the best.

So I retired from basketball.

And you know what? I never gave the game another thought.

I went right into something else—volleyball. I went right up against world-class athletes and took over, same as I had in basketball.

I'd had the attention and adoration that comes with being a superstar since I was fourteen years old. I'd had it long enough. Though, to tell you the truth, I didn't really give that up. It carried over into my life as a volleyballer. Hell, it carries over into my life as a restaurateur—you should try walking down the street with me if you want to see someone get attention.

So, in a sense, my retirement was easy. Partly because I was ready. Partly because I never really retired.

. . .

I *don't like* the way the athlete of today taunts his opponent. A football receiver catches the ball and immediately turns to the defensive guy, throws the ball down, and gives him an "in your face, chump!" look. The defensive player knocks the quarterback down and stands over him yelling.

It's true in other sports as well. I have no use for basketball players who, when they score, go through all these wild gyrations. I applaud the coach of Temple University, John Chaney, and John Wooden of UCLA past, men who don't let the players get too carried away. They keep their players on an even keel. Not too high when they were winning, not too low when they were losing, and always respectful of their opponent.

Where is that respect today? Many players seem to have none at all. Yet I believe it is damn important to respect the people you're playing against. If you have no respect for your adversary you really have no respect for yourself, and if you don't respect yourself your accomplishments mean nothing. I mean, if your opponent was nothing to start with, why play against him in the first place (other than just to get paid)? Beating him is worthless (other than financially) if in your eyes he is worthless.

As a competing athlete, I always tried to respect my opponent. When we won a championship I often felt sorry for the team that didn't. Hell, sometimes the winner isn't the best team. Sometimes the loser deserves to be the winner, and that deserves respect.

I believe this lack of respect today is because of those damn television cameras. Everybody wants to be on the tube. After the athlete completes his five-second play he's going to make sure he takes six more seconds with his antics, because he knows the TV camera is on him and will give him more air time. That camera has made fools out of a lot of good athletes.

It comes down to sportsmanship. When I was playing, if you were called a sport it meant you respected your opponent, you did nothing overtly to embarrass him, and you believed in fair play. Today, too many athletes are not sportsmen but assholes. Beating someone four in a row should be enough of a statement; there is no need to add to that sweep by bringing out brooms. (Remember the Knicks a couple of years ago when they swept the 'Sixers out of the first round of the playoffs? The first round! Too many teams today have championship arrogance without ever bothering to win a championship!) Dennis Rodman makes a routine basket and runs down the court throwing an antagonistic fist into the air, saying in essence, "Look what I just did to these bums." I understand enthusiasm and I'm all for it, but these things are in bad taste and should not be accepted. I don't believe these moves stimulate a player and his teammates. I think it's all just a slap in the face to a player's opponent.

In my scrapbook, I have a picture of me in the Boston locker room with John Havlicek and Russell after one of the league championship games that the Celtics won against us. God knows I did not enjoy having to go there and congratulate them. But the one thing I thought, and still do, is that being a good sport is as important in defeat as it is in winning. When Tyson lost to Buster Douglas, he was anything but a good sport. I am not sure if he apologized later for some of the crass remarks he made, but if he didn't he damn sure should have.

Being a sport once meant being a good, giving person. What the hell has happened?

☞ **WILTISM** 🖐

(sad but sometimes true)

The only way to rid yourself of a temptation is to yield to it.

The selling of autographs by our sports heroes for personal gain—even though at times signing can be a hell of a pain—is to me as unethical and unbelievable as Roy Rogers trading Trigger for a Kawasaki. The fault lies not just with the seller. Equal blame should be placed with the buyer. I equate it with the buying and selling of love. Some things lose all real value when they are bought and sold. Sure, players may really need the revenue these autographs bring (like Pete Rose claimed he did on some of those TV shows where he was selling his memorabilia). But I say if we love and respect these athletes, donate freely to their cause. Don't cheapen the act by purchasing their cherished items. It only degrades these fallen heroes; it doesn't glorify them.

This act of signing for money has infected the whole autograph business. When I was at the Goodwill Games in Seattle there were scores of people outside my hotel waiting for autographs. This seems complimentary—and once upon a time it was—but unfortunately many are now there to get autographs for commercial reasons. One guy threw eight different pictures at me to sign at nine different times. When I asked him what in the world he was going to do with all these signed pictures of me, he insisted he was going to put them on his wall. Fat chance. Later I saw him down the street selling all those photos.

This kind of wanton greed makes it hard on the true fans who seek autographs. It's also difficult for people like me who wonder whether we should continue to sign things or not. I don't like supporting an industry that is not only dishonest but dampens the spirit of true autograph collecting.

Many of you owe us athletes more than you are cognizant of. For many years, we athletes were the guinea pigs for orthopedic surgeons and other medical men. Now, when a cartilage operation is performed on the knee of the average citizen, the success rate is close to 100 percent. This is due to the multitude of mistakes once made on athletes.

Today this operation is routine. Now, a football player can have one and be back on the field in a few weeks. Not long ago, cartilage surgery meant the end of a career and usually left the athlete lame.

During my last two knee operations a year or so ago I had a chance to reap a little of what I and other athletes had sown. I was stunned to see (and feel!) how smoothly these operations went compared to those of the past!

When I was a player we didn't even know how to rehab after a knee operation. When I injured my knee with the Lakers in 1971, many thought my career was over. But I had owned racehorses and remembered how we rehabbed them. Since a racehorse is also an athlete, I did some of their same exercises. I ran in ocean water and jumped in the soft sand at Santa Monica beach. I did a lot of hill climbing on my bicycle. As a result, I returned to the Lakers in a few months and finished the season. I also surprised a lot of people.

I might not have been the first person to employ these procedures, but because of the publicity I received for returning to the lineup only three months after my injury, they have become standard procedure.

It *doesn't matter* how smart or talented you are, timing is everything. Born a hundred years earlier, Sir Isaac Newton probably would have eaten that apple that fell on his head and thought no more of it. Instead he came up with the law of gravity. All of Thomas Edison's wonderful inventions would have gone for naught if he'd been born during the Ice Age and had to spend all his time keeping dinosaurs from chewing on his butt.

Born fifty or a hundred years earlier, most of the tall, strong, fast athletes of today would not be million-dollar superstars but attractions at freak shows. That's something for them to think about.

E*arlier I said* that no one roots for Goliath. I was wrong. Today many people are rooting for Goliath, because they don't realize who he or she is.

In the world of gymnastics, for instance, the smaller the participant is, the easier it is to do all the tremendously demanding things the sport requires. So in gymnastics the Goliath is that tiny, seventy-five-pound, four-foot, nine-inch girl, not the big strong, imposing woman.

Y*ou often hear* coaches say that a particular player is hard to handle. In those cases the problem is not with the player, it's with the coach.

In my pro career I was labeled as someone who had problems with coaches. This was an unfair rap. Other than

Dolph Schayes and my very first pro coach, the only other coach I didn't get along with was Butch van Breda Kolff, and only recently did it all come out in the wash why this was so—at least on his part. A friend of Van Breda Kolff's, a fellow player named Hot Rod Hundley, was interviewed by an L.A. radio sportscaster. He let it be known that, more than one time and usually over a few drinks, Butch would say to him that he didn't know why but he just couldn't stand Wilt Chamberlain. I think *I* know why: bigotry. Plain and simple.

Most of my other pro coaches, Frank McGuire, Alex Hannum, and Bill Sharman, were and are dear friends of mine. I'll remember Dolph Schayes most for the statements he made about my ineptness at the foul-shot line. He was a great foul shooter and took exception to people who weren't. He made a statement to the press after my second year in the pros, "Anyone can make fouls shots if they just practice." He was making a definite dig at me, intimating that I was not working hard. When he became my coach, he took up the gauntlet; we spent many an hour shooting foul shots. As a pro, I already told you I shot very well in practice, but stunk the joint out in most games. I am happy and sad to report that under his tutorship, I had my worst foul-shooting year, percentage-wise. He never mentioned to anyone how hard we had practiced or that hc failed as a coach in that particular regard. Which just goes to show you, practice doesn't always make perfect. He never did apologize to me, either—even though he knew I was working very hard to improve that aspect of my game.

I *am often* asked why men of color dominate in our major sports, especially basketball. And especially at the high end, meaning the NBA. People are hesitant to deal with this question because of the various racial implications. Not being an anthropologist, I suppose my answer to this question can be held up to a bit of ridicule, but nevertheless, here goes . . .

Men of color seem to be blessed with specific physical attributes that benefit them in several sports, particularly basketball. They have explosive muscle power that translates into speed, quickness, and jumping ability (three major ingredients needed to be a good jock, a good basketball player in particular). And there is another element that makes men of color tend to stand out above the rest. For lack of a better word, let's call it "flair"—which translates into showmanship. A perfect example of this can be seen if you examine the playing styles of the two best passers in the game of basketball today, Magic Johnson and John Stockton. At present, Stockton outassists Magic—on a per game basis—by approximately one assist. But Magic has that flare and Stockton doesn't. It makes Magic appear as if he's doing so much more than Stockton. It's not ability, it's style. And in basketball, men of color have all the style. Think about it. Think of the good (even the great) white players. Who's better, Kiki Vandeweghe or Gerald Wilkins? One thing's for sure—Wilkins has the flair. Even Larry Bird, a consummate pro, great in every single phase of the game, doesn't have nearly the style that Michael Jordan has. I suppose this flair can be traced back to environmental conditioning or heritage or even to the Harlem Globetrotters, the true forefathers of all the showmanship that has become the trademark of so many stars—all men of color—in the NBA. The one exception I can come up with is the late great "Pistol Pete" Maravich. I don't know where the hell he got *his* flair, but he sure had it.

. . .

You *hear some* so-called smart announcers say, "That player is unselfish." But often, when a player passes a ball to a teammate he is not being unselfish; he's doing his damn job. Guys like Magic Johnson get *paid* for making assists.

What announcers fail to realize is that many players are afraid to take the responsibility to do what they are really *supposed* to do, so they pass the ball instead of taking the shot. In this case, passing the ball is really being selfish— looking out for himself instead of contributing to the team like he should.

That's why I like Larry Bird over Julius Erving. Bird takes the big shot in the clutch. Dr. J. passes off.

Many *times there* are accomplishments that are more impressive than the records in those particular events. Do you realize that Hank Greenberg once hit fifty-five home runs? Not quite the record Babe Ruth and Roger Maris had, but do you know that many teams would not even give him a chance to hit a home run? Some opposing pitchers would not pitch to him at all, and not because he might have hit the ball out of the park. Yeah, you got it—because he was Jewish. It makes me wonder what his total *might* have been.

As I said earlier in this book, I do wish I were playing today so I could get some of the incredible money the players are getting. But I'm also troubled at what these salaries are doing to athletes and sports.

What I can't figure out is why the owners can't wait to tell the other members of the team and the media, "Yeah, we just signed player X for three million dollars." Not only does the player now have to live up to the money he's getting—big money puts big pressure on an athlete—but the moment his production slips the other players on the team want the same amount of money, prorated to what *they're* doing on the court or on the field. It also ticks off all the fans because they have to pay for the higher salaries in the form of higher ticket prices.

The whole thing is an ego trip for the player. He can't wait to say, "Yeah, I'm commanding three million dollars." It's an ego trip for the owner, too. He can't wait to stick his chest out and say, "Yeah, I can afford to pay my player three million dollars."

I don't get it. Other businesses don't broadcast their salaries. Do you know what your boss makes? Or most of your co-workers? Of course not. It's not good business practice.

It all has to stop. Sports is no longer about what a player does, it's about how much he makes. Not only do exorbitant salaries create resentment and animosity between players and fans, they send out the wrong message to the kids. Kids want to play pro sports for the money. They should want to be a professional athlete—or a professional anything—because they love doing that thing and they want to become the best at doing it. This change in kids' attitudes toward sports is, to me, terribly sad. With true love of a sport, even if they don't make the pros, they will at least have enjoyed playing it.

Perhaps sports should adapt the payment system of the motion picture industry. They pay the major stars a great many millions of dollars, but most actors are paid scale. If the average players think that people pay to see them, they are in for a shock. People pay for the stars, the marquee players. All the journeymen, the young and the old and mediocre players, should play for scale. And they would if they had to, just like nonstar actors have to.

TWO ATHLETES I LIKE TO WATCH

Jackie Joyner-Kersee

The athlete I like to watch the most is Jackie Joyner-Kersee. She may be the best athlete in the world—regardless of sex. Jackie competes in the grueling seven-event heptathlon, which is the equivalent of the men's ten-event decathlon. As I said earlier, the winner of the decathlon is considered the greatest athlete in the world, but what many people don't realize is that in the individual events the decathlon champ usually couldn't beat many high school track stars. For example, a world-class decathlete will run the 100-meter in 10.7 or 10.6 seconds, while a good high school runner will run the same event in 10.3 seconds. Just by the fact that he can even compete in the ten events together, the world-class decathlete is certainly a good athlete—but he is not world-class in any single event. Jackie Joyner-Kersee, though, is world-class in *five* of her *seven* competitions—she is one of the top ten in the world (in some, she's the very best in the world) in those events.

Greg Louganis

Greg Louganis is the best ever in diving (both springboard and platform), which I think is the most graceful and demands the most body control of all athletic events. Anyone who is the best ever at a sport so difficult and underappreciated is going to get my attention. Also, the things we do the worst in are often the things we marvel at the most—like me and diving.

I *would travel* the world to see these two people perform—and I have. But why don't more people care to watch these two great athletes (and the many other great athletes in their fields)? I don't understand why some sports get so much attention and these fine athletes are too often ignored by both fans and the media.

When I think of what some baseball, basketball, and football players with no talent are making in comparison with these people, I wonder what we—no, I mean you—are looking for when you take your family to a sporting event. Obviously, you're looking for hype rather than pure athleticism. And as long as we—I mean you—keep buying tickets at higher and higher prices and sit in front of the TV long enough to justify near-obscene television revenues that trickle down from owners to mediocre athletes, a lot of great athletes in wonderful sports will have to remain amateurs—because they don't get that kind of financial support. And you'll miss some of the truly great sports performances of all times. (At prices, by the way, that are most reasonable.)

A*t the opposite* end of J.J. and Greg's spectrum are those overpaid athletes in the big sports. I get particularly furious with the nonstars. Great amateurs project such love and devotion onto their sports. It's wonderful to see. But I am always amazed when I watch professional ball games and see bench warmers and nonstarters looking as if they couldn't care less about what's going on in the game. The only time they show any emotion or get involved is when they're selected to play. Why is it that those who are paid the least enjoy what they are doing the most?

Sure, I understand that seasons are long and sometimes you're just not feeling it, but brother, when you're getting paid the dollars these guys are making you sure as shit should realize how fortunate you are and show some enthusiasm for your game and your team. Let's face it, most players would have a hard time earning the salaries made by most blue-collar workers if it weren't for their special athletic gifts. Before an athlete makes a team, he'd give anything and everything just to be a part of it. But once he's there, that changes. People don't want to play anymore, they want to *star*. It's one of the curses of our time—no one cares about being good at what they do. They just want to be (take your pick): 1) famous; 2) successful; 3) rich. And the quality of the work—or the play—be damned.

These unprofessional-acting bench warmers project a very bad image. They're living a dream that most people would give their right arm to be a part of. As a result, they should be into every goddamn facet of the game and enjoy every fucking moment! Can you imagine getting paid great money (the average salary in the NBA is $1 million as of 1990!) for watching a game you love from the best seats in the house and being "pissed"? I can't.

Players today, they don't have the fun we had. Man, I was a basketball *junkie*. I played—for free—on nearly every playground in the country every damn chance I had.

And do you know what the Globetrotters were making the year I played with them? How about three thousand dollars for an eight-month season! Plus a giant three dollars and fifty cents per diem! In Europe, the Globies weren't paid *at all*! The European team was the *honor* team. Pros were only making nine thousand or so then. But we played for love of the game, something the players today don't know a lot about.

All *right, while* I'm on the subject of contemporary athletes, how does the likes of an Andre Agassi get to be such a favorite and make millions from commercial endorsements? Whether his image is manufactured or not, it's a despicable image. Does any mother or father want their kid to be like Agassi off the tennis court? I would hope not. So why do we make these characters heroes? Is it because silly thirteen-year-old girls are screaming for them and telling us how much they like them? Maybe. But we shouldn't cater to that. Athletes have a certain responsibility. Maybe not to be heroes . . . oh hell, why *not*? Why *shouldn't* they try to be heroes? Who else do we have? In Agassi's case, all his bullshit, like calling people "bimbos," as he did at the French Open when officials questioned his tennis attire, and faking injuries to get out of tournaments, makes you wonder whether this kind of athlete could *ever* be a hero.

I think we fans and the companies who seek endorsements should be a lot more discriminating when choosing a hero.

There are *athletes* I admire today, in all sports. In basketball, I'm always asked, "If you were under seven feet tall, who would you want to play like?" Well, one or two of my choices may shock you. Let's take Bill Laimbeer of the

Detroit Pistons. As I mentioned before, there is no substitute for using your noggin. I *love* the way Bill rattles the opposition, gets them out of their game and playing his game. He does whatever is needed. His "rep" of being the dirtiest player around is way overblown. He's just good.

Danny Ainge is another of the same cut. Not only are both these guys talented, they're heady. They could play on my team any time. So could Magic, of course. And Bird.

Dave Winfield is an athlete I admire—except I would have never taken all the bullshit Steinbrenner said about him. I don't know Steinbrenner, but from what I've read and heard, I don't want to know him.

I have great admiration for Magic on and off the court. More like him are needed. We also need more strong coaches like Bobby Knight. Bobby could coach me or my son any day.

I used to be very careful about comparing the athlete of yesterday with the athlete of today, because I'm clearly of the yesterday vintage and I always wanted to give the athletes of today credit for what they are doing. And I do give them their due. Having said that, I don't believe the athletes of today are better than the ones of the past. In fact, in many ways they're a lot worse.

There are certain positive things the athlete of yesterday had that are being bred out of the players of today. I've already talked about toughness, respect for your fellow athlete, and a true love for the game. The one other important thing that must be noted is that there is an acceptance of a *style* of play today that was not tolerated in my day. If you were a hot dog when I was playing and did things like dribble the ball between your legs or take three-sixty dunks, your teammates would look at you like you were crazy, the fans would say you were a showoff, and the coach would bench you. You would not be considered a professional-type player. Only the Globetrotters were allowed to do things like that, because that is what they were getting paid to do.

Nowadays, it's considered normal to go down the court and do a cartwheel three-sixty; the more you can turn a simple play into something acrobatic, the more the fans like it. Fans don't care if you're ten points down and you should be conserving that energy to get back on defense—and, apparently, neither do the players.

But just because the fan has accepted a different style of play does not mean that today's athlete is a better athlete than his predecessor. The guys I played with could do all the things the guys are doing today. I could have done three-sixty dunks myself, but I wouldn't do them. I wasn't into showing off. Believe me, twenty years ago Michael Jordan would not have been *allowed* to do the things he is doing now.

The acceptance of this new style of play is primarily because of television. All the major sports are now a part of show business. I, for one, am sad to see it.

☞ WILTISM ☜

In show business, the more show, the better the business.

It is my opinion that, given the same conditions, training equipment, and facilities, the athlete of yesterday would be far superior to the athlete of today. Why? Because huge numbers that follow dollar signs—the ones that are flashing in front of today's athletes like neon signs—seem to be much more important than playing the game. This has to distract from performance. When I was young, players never thought about making money if and when they ever got to be a pro. Today's young athlete has "pro" on his mind first, last, and always. Even before high school they are thinking of being another Michael Jordan—not as an athlete, but as a spokesman, a sneaker salesman, and as a millionaire businessman.

I must admit, though, there are things contemporary players have to fight off and deal with that we in my time were not saddled with. I am talking not only about drugs and all the peripheral stuff surrounding that problem but also the availability of so many women who are attracted by all the available cash.

When I played back in the '50s and '60s, the drug was beer. Only a few athletes used pot; it was still more prevalent among musicians than athletes. There was very little of anything else. (Unless I was being naïve, which is possible. There were two guys I played with, and I could never understand how they could be so inconsistent—scoring thirty points one night, four the next. I never could figure them out, until much later, when I found out they were into coke. But I believe they were very rare cases at that time.)

As to the women in my day, hell, yes, there were groupies, but everyone knew who they were, and there was a stigma about being seen with them. People would say, "Oh, there's that girl, she's with Wilt tonight, she was with so-and-so last night." And there was no time to meet ladies except at the undesirable nightspots in town—that is, if the town had a nightspot.

In my day, we weren't as *famous* as today's athletes. The media coverage wasn't comparable. There was no cable TV, no ESPN, no marketing experts figuring out how to turn us into one-man industries. Fame makes people desirable, even more than money does. It almost doesn't matter if you're a criminal—as long as you're famous. Take all that money floating around, add the cachet of celebrity—and it's no wonder women are throwing themselves at today's athletes. I think the only surprise about cases like the Wade Boggs/Margo Adams incident is that there aren't a lot more of them. Nowadays an athlete can even fly his ladies into town with him. What's a five-hundred-dollar ticket to fly a girl in Chicago to a game in Denver? It's meaningless and the athletes of today do that a lot. In my day no one could afford to do it. Also, almost no one was famous enough for the lady to *want* to do all that flying.

I was, by far, the most famous basketball player of my time, so, of course, I was desired. Other players saw this and envied me. It was very obvious when the team traveled from city to city. In those days, stewardesses had to be pretty and reasonably intelligent and many of them made passes in my direction. This did not endear me to a lot of guys, players and referees, who were along on the flights. Since almost all the girls were white, I knew some of these guys were particularly unhappy about all the attention I received. I remember once these two stewardesses got on the intercom and wished us good luck in Cincinnati. They concluded by saying, "Good luck, especially to number thirteen." Sitting across from me were two refs and I could see their faces contort in disbelief and anger. I'm not saying they had a hard-on for me—but I find it hard to believe that they were not a *little* bit affected in some of their judgment calls that night.

. . .

I *'ll tell you* one strange tale about fame and women—and the dangers of combining the two. If you think this life isn't dangerous, then explain the following trap that was once set for me.

Once, during the basketball season, I got a long-distance call in my hotel room in Buffalo. A male voice said he was an agent for a new up-and-coming movie starlet whose dream it was to meet me. He asked if he could set up a date with the young star and me when my team came to L.A. to play. (I was with Philadelphia at the time.) That same day, she called from Los Angeles to tell me how happy she was that her agent had reached me. I made no promises, but she said she was going to send me some information about her and some pictures so I wouldn't think she was just some nutty young kook. She floored me by knowing our road schedule and said she'd send the photos on to our next stop. She even knew the hotel I'd be staying at! Sure enough, when the team checked into our hotel, there was a parcel waiting for me. One of the photos of her was a large portrait (a head-and-shoulder shot) of the most beautiful woman of color I have *ever* seen. Being a movie buff, I sure didn't remember ever seeing or hearing of her, which made me suspicious. There were almost no women of color in the movies—and I couldn't believe I would have missed one as gorgeous as this creature. While I was being mesmerized by her picture, the phone rang. She was calling me from L.A. again. I agreed to see her.

It was a month before I got to Los Angeles and she called me every single day. I began to wonder if this was going to turn out to be my true love. When the big day arrived, she offered to have her limousine pick me up after the game and take me to her condo for our dinner date. I told her it wasn't necessary. I would use my father's car, meet her at her place, then we could go out for a late dinner.

When I arrived, she was dressed in an outfit befitting a fashion queen. As I walked around her spacious, beautifully furnished apartment, I noticed a full-length mink coat lying conspicuously on the bed. She suggested we stay there rather than go out to eat. "I'll cook dinner for us," she said. Needless to say, I agreed, and she retreated to the bedroom to change. When she reappeared, she was in a more casual but just as stunning outfit. She was no gourmet cook—the meal she prepared was only half-decent—but I was polite and forced most of it down. Food was not uppermost on my mind by this point. After dinner she changed again, this time into a seductive, peek-a-boo nightgown. We immediately began a close encounter of the sexual kind. In the middle of our thrashing about, she whispered, "Now, be careful, Wilt, I have no protection and I become pregnant easily."

Well, immediately, everything became extremely clear. I withdrew, reached for my clothes, and hurriedly got dressed while she lay there mumbling, "What the hell is going on?" I coolly said, "My mother's calling me," and I got the hell out of there.

She tried many times to reach me after that, but I wouldn't speak to her. I had a friend in L.A. who knew everything about everybody check her and her agent out. The real story was that she and her "agent"—who was really her boyfriend—made investments of long-distance calls like the one I got, renting a condo and fur coat, and limousines when necessary, all in hopes of catching a big fish in a paternity suit. If they got *really* lucky, they'd catch some poor sap in marriage, a quick divorce, and half his money—California laws being what they are. They had the nerve to talk about their schemes to other people, which is how my friend got his information.

There are a million stories like this in the big city—and especially in the NBA.

FOUR

On Basketball: Hoops du Jour

Recently, HBO aired a show called *The History of the NBA,* and many people found it to be a nice piece on the history of the game. I didn't find that at all. I was interviewed for the show, and I gave them three to four hours of my time. It wasn't something I wanted to do personally, but I felt it was my responsibility because it was the NBA that helped me to be what I am. I talked about a lot of things concerning the NBA and how I felt about many of the players, past and present, but when I viewed the final show all I heard was a piece of my interview—less than one minute long—about how well I think I could do if I were playing in the NBA today. Which once again makes me seem like I'm only into myself and totally egotistical.

But that wasn't the worst thing about the show. *The History of the NBA* was not very good to me and my peers because the tape was 75 percent about the 1980s. They highlighted guys like Darryl Dawkins, just because he broke a couple of basketball backboards—big deal! You don't think we could have broken backboards?!—and forgot to show you the greatness of Elgin Baylor, Oscar Robertson, Chet Walker, Jerry West, and many other superb players and Hall of Famers. It can't be an important documentary when they ignore so much of the league's true history.

For people who are very young and only remember the '80s, it was a shame that they didn't get to see some of the older players really playing. I know there are not a lot of films and tapes of the '50s and '60s, but there are enough to do a historically respectable show.

Until that happens, you'll have to take it from old-timers like me. In this chapter, I would like to give more of my thoughts on basketball—the game of today, and the game of my day.

I *have often* been compared to other centers, past and present. Sometimes this comparison makes me angry.

Leaving myself out of the competition for the moment, here, in my fairly knowledgeable opinion, are the five best centers of all time:

Bill Russell has to be number one. Possession of the ball is the single most important element of the game of basketball and Russell was the best rebounder I've ever seen. He gets a lot of credit for his shot blocking and defense, but rebounding—*getting the damn ball*—is what counts. Russell got the ball better than anyone else, so he's the best. He also created something that didn't have anything to do with his athletic ability—harmony with his teammates. He did the work that, at the time, was not considered glamorous. Scoring was what got you the glory and the dough. Russell was content—and secure enough—to let others score (it helped that he was not what you'd call a great shooter). He never infringed on the other Celtic stars.

Number two: Bill Walton. I like Walton because, like myself, he played every single phase of the game he was supposed to play. He scored, he passed, he rebounded, set picks, filled lanes. He didn't dribble or take the ball up— but neither did I. We weren't supposed to.

Kareem is number three. I might have my problems with Kareem personally, but he was a great, great offensive weapon. He was also capable of being a big defensive force as well as a rebounding threat, though he didn't excel in those areas as I feel he should have.

One huge negative for Kareem: He never pushed his body to the limit—certainly not the limit necessary for rebounding and defense. He pushed his body for scoring, but that's it. He was never willing to work that hard, which is why he was relatively injury-free. All racecars that run at full speed eventually break down. Kareem never did. That's one reason why the all-time leading point scorer only had one or two games in which he scored over fifty points.

Number four is probably a surprise: George Mikan. He can't be overlooked just because he's not really of the modern era. For the type of basketball that was played in his time, George was supreme. He did what he was supposed to do and did it better than anyone else.

My guess is that my fifth choice will also be a surprise. It's Robert Parish. He was the best center of the '80s. If I'd played sixteen or seventeen years the way Parish has, until my late thirties, I don't think I could have played any better than this man is playing at that age. He's better today than he ever was. He's a hell of a center.

Whenever I omit someone in lists like this or say something bad about someone's skill or ability, people always think it's because I dislike the player. Sorry, but that's pure bullshit. This list is based on ability only. I might like Russell less than some other guys but he's the *best*. Russell never had the talent to score fifty points—but he sure as hell did what he could do.

Where do I fit in?

Look, I think it's obnoxious for me to write that I was the best ever. But just look at the numbers. Look at photos where there are three Celtics guarding me. You never saw three players on my team guarding Bill Russell. At various points in my career, I led the league in scoring, rebounding, assists, and blocked shots. Show me one other player in the history of the game who did all that—and *maybe* I'll admit that you've found someone better than or as good as I was.

There may have never been a star athlete used as a yardstick by which to judge other athletes as much as I have been used. No single basketball player has ever done so many different things better than anyone else. The record books prove this. That makes me unique, in a class by myself. It really pisses me off when every center that comes down the pike is compared to me. Maybe compare him to Russell if he can block shots, or Kareem if he has a hook shot, but whenever a Patrick Ewing or Ralph Sampson comes along, he's not only compared to me but the so-called experts always find something that the young chargers can do better than I could—or at least that's what they say. When these so-called phenoms' careers are over, the experts realize that they don't compare at all. Some, like Ralph Sampson, are actually disgraceful flops, according to standards used by the "experts" who extolled them.

People are always saying to me, "How do you feel about Kareem breaking your record?" I say, "Which record is that?" He broke *one* record—total number of points scored. Believe me, I've got plenty of other records neither Kareem nor anyone else can touch.

—Do you know that I went my whole career never having a game in which I didn't get double figures in rebounds? Not *one* game with fewer than ten rebounds. Nowadays, ten rebounds a game practically leads the league.

In my third year, the year I averaged fifty points a game, I scored in the twenties only three times. (I *never* scored below twenty points a game that year.) Every other game was thirty points or more.

My greatest feat: In my third season in the NBA, I only missed seven minutes the entire season. I went fifty-one straight games without missing a minute, then came out for three minutes. In one other game, I sat for four minutes. Think Patrick Ewing or David Robinson could ever match that?

People find it hard to let me stand on my own athletic prowess. All the great athletes I know were given their due, win or lose, but I have always had to deal with being judged by things I *didn't* do. No one ever talked about what Babe Ruth could *not* do. (What kind of fielder was he? Could he bunt?) In the case of Bill Russell, people always talk about how many championships he won. They speak of Kareem's poetic hook shot. Do you ever hear critics speak of Russell or Kareem or other centers in the league not being very good because they never fouled out of a game like Wilt? Or never even got twenty-seven rebounds a game like I *averaged* for an entire season? Of course not. All those other centers were and are measured on their own merits, not what they could *not* do.

I am always amazed how, when Bill Russell is mentioned, it is always in connection with me. People forget that, early in Bill's Boston career, the star of the Celtics was not Bill but Bob Cousy, who was voted the basketball player of the half-century over both Russell and yours truly. It's funny that later, in the late '70s, the Boston fans picked John Havlicek as the number-one player to ever play for the Celtics. And now I'm sure if they had a chance to pick the best player to ever play for the team, they'd choose Larry Bird.

If you're going to compare me to Russell, you've got to take into consideration the genius of Red Auerbach, whom many consider the best pro basketball coach ever. Add all that formidable talent the Celtics had over the years and I think my team did bloody well to even *challenge* those guys.

One of the reasons I was the villain and Russell the hero was that I was this young brash man of color doing great things in a basically lily-white sport. *Outside* of basketball, I was dating white girls, making large sums of money in various businesses, owning racehorses, restaurants, and nightclubs, and receiving accolades from all over the world. This was all a bit too much for a lot of the people involved with and playing in the league. What I find strange now, though, is how the man picked as my antithesis has fallen from favor. I wonder if it's because that stable married man, who, when we were playing, was raising a family of color and was married to a woman of color, has turned out to be more like what they really thought *I* was. He's been surly to the media, certainly hasn't shown that he can handle an executive (or even a coaching) job, and I think the public now perceives him as somewhat arrogant. Bill even went and married a white lady! As long as I'm on the subject, I may as well get this all off my chest. It's not that I'm that competitive with Bill—believe it or not, I haven't even seen him in twenty-two years, so I have nothing to be competitive about. I suppose, though, that underneath my gruff, insensitive exterior, I'm still a little resentful of the hero/villain roles that were thrust upon us. You *never* heard anything negative said about Russell's basketball game. It was always about him blocking shots and winning championships. There was *never* anything said about his foul shooting—when in fact it was often worse than mine.

Since I am talking here about great centers I would be remiss not to mention some personal feelings I have about number 33, Kareem. I will not use this book to answer any of the negative things he said about me in a recent book he wrote. I don't like that kind of game playing and I don't think the things he said are even worth responding to. What I will say is that it must be noted that he has always felt that I am the only one who stands in the way of his being considered the premier center of all time. I say that because when I played against him he always made a much greater effort to shoot many more times than he did against any other center. I guess I'll also add that his shooting percentage was *much* lower against me (and, to be fair, against Nate Thurmond). Because he fired up a lot more shots, his scoring would usually be impressive—but his percentage was always way down. The thing I remember most about number 33 was his insistence, early in his career, that he wanted to play in the NBA only three or four years. No more than that. Those three or four years somehow stretched to twenty years. Whether you think this is sour grapes or not, I must tell you that all the farewell nights they held in all those various cities around the league for him were ridiculous and insensitive. Those are the best words I can use to describe the whole fiasco. How could he allow those cities to give him motorcycles, tennis courts, Rolls-Royces, and so much material bullshit? And why did so many teams do it? Believe me when I say that many of them *really* felt like Doug Moe of the Denver Nuggets. Moe said, "What a waste it all is—and the feelings are so contrived." My beef was that all the sentiments and ceremonies and gifts were indeed contrived—and were all done with number 33's knowledge and approval. Hell, that farewell tour was a moneymaker for him! I would have thought that a guy making $3 million a year would have opted for gifts that benefited the less fortunate, like scholarships given in his name and what have you. This would have had a lot more appeal for me. From the comments I heard from other stars around the league, they hope and pray that this type of farewell tour will never happen again. So do I, brother.

. . .

Since my retirement in 1974, some things have happened that make me think I was regarded in a much *higher* light than even *I* thought I was.

In the past fifteen years no fewer than half a dozen NBA teams have tried to get me to come out of retirement and play. The most recent offer was made, believe it or not, in 1989. Dr. Jerry Buss, the owner of the Lakers, offered me a high salary, plus revenue from Prime Ticket, the television station that carries the Lakers (and that he also owns)—and I only had to play home games.

I was first asked to play in 1976 by one of the owners of the Chicago Bulls, William Wirtz. He offered me a substantial salary plus full return on all the tickets sold over their current average. At that time they were only drawing eight or nine thousand a game. If I was able to fill the stadium my cut would have been a couple of million dollars a year.

The New York Knicks tried for years to get me to play in the late '70s and early '80s, and I must admit that this was tempting. I would have loved playing in New York, because the fans are so knowledgeable.

The New Jersey Nets made a very strong offer, up in the millions of dollars plus a percent of the gate, if I would play for them in the mid-'80s, around 1985–86.

Dr. Buss actually tried for a number of years to get me to play for the Lakers alongside Kareem. I felt secure enough to handle being his back-up, but I don't believe it would have worked too long. People would have demanded more playing time for me. If I did as well as I think I would have, it's possible there might have been a clamoring for Kareem to back *me* up. Number 33 might not have been able to handle that at all.

At the time, the L.A. Clippers' owner, Donald Sterling, said to me, "You don't belong with the Lakers, you belong

"DON'T JUST WATCH IT... LIVE IT."
—Wilt Chamberlain

INTRODUCING
THE ULTIMATE HOME THEATRE
SHARP▼ISION™

It's big. 100" big. And it's unlike any projection system you've ever seen. SharpVision's revolutionary LCD technology brings movies, sports, video games, and TV shows to life.

ZOOM FROM 20" to 100"

What size picture would you like? You can enlarge the SharpVision picture from 20" to 100" with a simple twist of the zoom lens. And you can enjoy the crystal clear image on one of Sharp's retractable wall screens, or elegant console furniture screens.

MODELS SHOWN: XV-100 LCD PROJECTOR (31 lbs.), RS-100SP 100" SCREEN
SCREEN SIZES MEASURED DIAGONALLY. PROJECTED PICTURE SIMULATED.
© 1989 Sharp Electronics Corporation

TAKE IT ANYWHERE

The SharpVision projector can be moved easily from room to room, or even outdoors. Set up is quick and easy. Select from multiple video sources such as a VCR, laser vision player, camcorder or video game.

Turn any room into the Ultimate Home Theatre with incredible new SharpVision. For details call 1-800-BE-SHARP.

SHARP
FROM SHARP MINDS
COME SHARP PRODUCTS™

Who better to advertise a 100-inch TV screen than the man who scored 100 points? But the ad agency never thought of that approach. I always wondered why those guys got paid so much money.

With Eddie Gottlieb, who owned the Philadelphia Warriors and was one of the founders of the NBA.

A typical night on the job. I also blocked seventeen shots in this game... and they talk about triple doubles!

NATIONAL BASKETBALL ASSOCIATION
OFFICIAL SCORER'S REPORT

HOME PHILA	MIN	FGM	FGA	FTM	FTA	REB	AST	PF	FTS
WALKER	42	9	14	8	9	12	4	0	2
JACKSON	30	3	8	1	1	9	1	2	
CHAMBERLAIN	47	10	16	9	17	36	13	2	2
GREER	47	12	28	8	11	2	4	2	3
W. JONES	28	10	18	3	6	2	6	5	2
CUNNINGHAM	23	5	12	11	12	8	2	4	2
GUOKAS	23	1	7	0	0	4	5	5	2
Team Rebounds Total	240	50	103	40	56	79	35	20	140

FG% 48.5   FT% 71.4

VISITORS BOSTON	MIN	FGM	FGA		FTA	REB	AST	PF	PTS
HOWELL	26	7	14	1	1	8	0	4	15
HAVLICEK	48	16	36	6	8	6	2	5	38
RUSSELL	42	2	5	0	1	21	7	5	4
S. JONES	38	9	25	1	2	3	6	1	19
SIEGFRIED	42	8	18	8	9	6	8	4	24
SANDERS	4	0	0	0	0	1	1	2	0
NELSON	11	3	8	0	0	3	1	3	6
EMBRY	6	0	4	0	0	2	1	3	0
K.C. JONES	16	2	4	0	0	4	6	4	4
BARNETT	7	2	4	2	2	2	0	0	6
Team Rebounds Total	240	49	118	18	23	64	24	38	116

FG% 41.5   FT% 78.3

Date 4-11-67   Place PHILA   Attendance 13007

Refs NORM DRUCKER + MENDY RUDOLPH

Score by periods	1	2	3	4	OT	OT	OT	TOT
PHILA	26	39	35	40				140
BOSTON	37	33	24	22				116

REMARKS: CROWD TIES RECORD SET APR. 5

Thanks to **NASA** for the front-row seats.

The Cleo-winning Volkswagen and TWA ads.

"Why I'm so big on TWA."
— by Wilt Chamberlain

You don't have to be 7'1" to be big on TWA. You just have to like being comfortable.

Take their planes, for instance.

The only widebodies TWA flies are the 747, the L-1011 and the brand-new 767—big, roomy widebodies even a tallbody can love.

A fast break.
TWA's Airport Express.
Another nice thing is how TWA can get you to those widebodies without making you run through the airport.

You don't have to rush to make sure you'll get the kind of seat you want. TWA's Advance Seat Selection lets you reserve it up to 30 days in advance.

Coming home, you don't even have to check in.

With TWA's Round-Trip Check-In, you can get a boarding pass for your flight back when you check in for your flight out.

So instead of standing in line, you can spend your time doing something else.

Even if it's doing nothing but relaxing.

Taking care of business.
TWA's Ambassador Class.
From where I sit, flying on business ought to be a pleasure. Which brings me to TWA's Ambassador Class.

It's a separate business cabin where the seats are bigger and wider than coach. With fewer seats per row, so you're never more than one seat from the aisle.

Then, to go with all the extra room, lots of extras. A special check-in desk in the airport. Complimentary cocktails and wines in flight. Entrees served on china and linen (little things mean a lot—even to a big guy).

Even the service is relaxing. Friendly, attentive. But TWA's always been pretty good at that.

Fact is, I could go on and on about how great TWA is. But you get the idea.

Besides, I promised to keep it short. Call your travel agent or TWA.

You're going to like us TWA

© NURY HERNANDEZ, *NEW YORK POST*

We're both standing. No wonder they used to call me "Stud."

The only basketball game I ever played after I retired from the Lakers. I did it for Meadowlark Lemon and his Bucketeers.

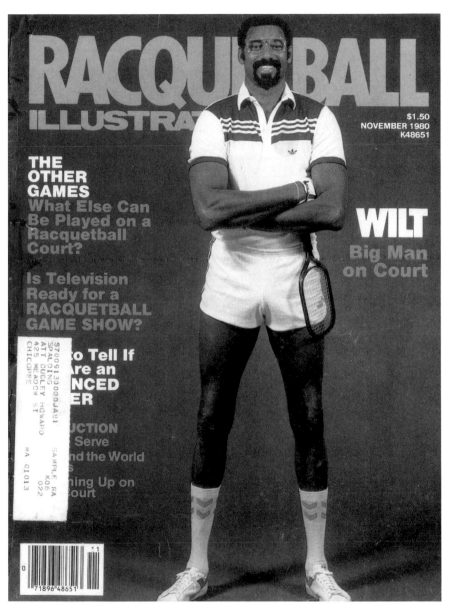

RACQUETBALL
ILLUSTRAT

$1.50
NOVEMBER 1980
K48651

THE
OTHER
GAMES
What Else Can
Be Played on a
Racquetball
Court?

Is Television
Ready for a
RACQUETBALL
GAME SHOW?

WILT
Big Man
on Court

o Tell If
Are an
NCED
ER

UCTION
Serve
nd the World

ning Up on
ourt

S7009130000JA81
SPALDING
ATT DUDLEY HOWARD
425 MEADOW ST
CHICOPEE

SAMPLE RA
K06
022

MA 01013

11

0

71896 48651

As a seven-footer, I had every possible disadvantage playing
racquetball. But I was able to play competitive doubles with
some of the best players in the world.

#85171 #85170 #678577

LeTigre's Big and Tall acrylic crew neck jacquard sweater
looks and feels like a winner. Lead the way when you
team it up with our Encore canvas pant.

I was the first man of color to represent a full line of clothing.

With Dan Gurney, professional race-car driver. Believe it or not, I once held the record for driving nonstop from New York to L.A. in thirty-six hours and twelve minutes. Dan broke the record. He did it in a Terrain in thirty-five hours and forty-three minutes—but he had help. Dan had another driver with him. I did it *alone*!

With the Globies on our European tour.

© WILLIAM SAVARIN

Doing my job at Kutsher's Country Club in the Catskills. I made over $3,000 in cash that summer. I was proud of being captain of the bellboys—and I ran a tight ship.

I still believe that Richard Nixon is the one. He made mistakes—but I think being a great politician is not something that would necessarily make one's mother proud.

A portrait for my fiftieth birthday.

SPORTS ILLUSTRATED

With my two cats, Zip and Zap, named after Guy Rodgers and
Al Attles, two fast little guards who used to zip and zap around
the court.

© NURY HERNANDEZ, NEW YORK POST

I've been involved with horses for years. At one time, I owned
the second-fastest pacer in the world.

In *Conan the Destroyer*. You can see why I might have been a little intimidating, even to Arnold.   P.S.: I had to do my own stunts. It's hard to find a stand-in for Wilt Chamberlain.

People will always say Bill Russell guarded Wilt. Is this Russell guarding me or the rest of his team guarding me? You'll never see a picture with three guys guarding Russell.

With my hero Joe Louis, when he was honored in Vegas in the early seventies. They brought in Max Schmeling from Germany for the awards ceremony.

© PETER C. BORSARI

The top of the net is around eight feet above the ground. Note that my waist is *over* the net.

DID HE MAKE IT? Remarkable action shot shows Wilt (The Stilt) Chamberlain, seven foot star of the Harlem Globetrotters, so high in the air on this drive-in shot that camera couldn't bring in the rest of his arm, hand, ball and basket. But as his smile and anguished look on faces of rival Hawaii 50th Staters attest, it was a perfect two-pointer.

This 1959 caption says it all.

here with the Clippers because the Lakers already *have* a center." For a while the Clippers made an annual offer.

The Houston Rockets also inquired if I wanted to come back and play. The Phoenix Suns' owner made an overture through their coaches to see if I wanted to try it with them.

The team that made the strongest offer was my original team, the Philadelphia 76ers. They tried at two different times, once in the late '70s and again in the mid-'80s. A whole campaign was launched. Many articles were written on the subject of my return. They had a fan participation campaign about bringing me back to Philly. I had two or three meetings with owner David Katz when he flew out to California.

I was intrigued from time to time by these offers, not because of the money but because it would have been the first time a person who was already in the NBA Hall of Fame came out of retirement to play again. Obviously, all the people in the Hall are retired; in fact, most of them are dead, so it was a unique situation. Coming back would have been a great, fun challenge for me. I had a feeling I could help these teams, and I will always wonder "What if . . ." There is no doubt in my mind I would have led the league in rebounding. It's not even a question. But it would have been at a cost, an emotional strain I no longer needed.

In the end, I simply didn't have a strong desire to play again. That's the only thing that stopped me. I would have needed this strong desire because of my absolute need to represent myself properly and give the fans who buy the tickets their money's worth. I felt it was better to remain something special in the fans' eyes than to come back and be less than what was expected of me. And less than I expected of myself.

The thing I find so gratifying is that other centers with

whom I have been compared have *never* had these offers to return to the game; Bill Russell was certainly never asked to play in today's setting. I wonder if anyone will ask Kareem to come out of retirement and play in the year 2004—fifteen years after his retirement? Or even five years from now, for that matter.

If I can be so presumptuous—which I am, of course—I will answer the question many people ask, which is how I feel about today's pro game and its contemporary players. Well, without beating around the bush or hiding my feelings behind a "pick," I am here to say that today's game is a better show, and I do mean show. As Ed Sullivan used to say, basketball today is "a really big show." Showmanship and the clever use of PR by the NBA to sell the game to the media and the fans has elevated the game to its greatest popularity.

But, to make a musical comparison (and as I suggested earlier), is a hard rock concert that attracts a hundred thousand fans better music than what we used to hear at a Frank Sinatra or Sam Cooke concert, which drew only two thousand fans thirty years ago? Is Bruce Springsteen a better singer than Frank Sinatra? Just because more people are watching doesn't necessarily make the product better. More people have seen *The Beverly Hillbillies* than have ever seen *Hamlet.* Does that mean that, as a literary creation, Jed Clampett is superior to the Melancholy Dane? I don't think so.

What I've noticed about the game today is that to a great extent it parallels the Globetrotters. I am not saying this in any demeaning way, because I had a chance to play for both entities and I enjoyed them both—in different ways.

What I am confused about here is, do fans come to see a show with some good pro basketball thrown in, or basketball with a lot of show thrown in? I knew when I played with the Globies what they really came to see: It was the show, no doubt about it. Fans today can watch the Bulls or Hawks win by twenty points and come away disappointed if Jordan or Dominique have not put on an aerial act.

One of the big mistakes we tend to make is believing that everything is better as time goes on. Are today's athletes better than yesterday's because today's cars are better or faster than cars of the past? Obviously, I don't think so. I believe that conditions and equipment and playing fields and arenas make it easier to play and make it all more comfortable for player and fan alike. *That's* why everything appears to be better.

O*ne of the* ways I draw conclusions when I evaluate various players is to take two players—let's say Magic Johnson and Michael Jordan—and ask myself if one of them could do what the other does if he had to, and vice versa. To break that down, ask yourself: If Magic had to, could he fly through the air and dunk the ball like Jordan? My answer, of course, is, "No, he couldn't." If Jordan had to control the game and hit the open man in the same manner Magic does, could he? My answer is, "Probably, yes."

There are many other attributes of a player's game that you can evaluate in the same way. If you are talking about Bill Russell and Wilt Chamberlain, ask: Could Bill ever score fifty points in a game? Draw your own conclusion. Could Wilt Chamberlain have blocked the shots Bill Russell blocked? He blocked more.

When you are making comparisons and asking, "Could this guy do what that guy did?" you also have to remember that many players are forced into a certain role; given a chance to escape that role, a lot of those players can be very proficient in other areas. Other players do superbly in the role they are asked to play, but if called upon to perform other aspects of the game they are *not* nearly as proficient—and in some cases they become a liability.

In this era of sports there are many more specialists, which prevents an athlete from becoming a complete player and getting a chance to use all his natural or learned abilities. That was never the case during my era.

One guy who had no idea how to use his natural talents was Ralph Sampson. I say "had" and "was" rather than "has" and "is" because even though Ralph is still on the Sacramento roster, his career really is over. Ralph was taken in by sportscasters, sportswriters, and sycophants who applauded him for doing things like bringing the ball up court on a fast break. Well, guess what? He shouldn't have been doing that! He should have been scoring inside and using his size to his best advantage. His own talent was his downfall. He'd be my number-one pick for biggest waste of ability.

In many ways the players today seem bigger and faster, seem to jump higher, throw trickier passes, but this does *not* make them better basketball players than the more fundamentally sound players of the past. I suppose until we figure out a way to put the players of yesterday, today, and tomorrow on the court at the same time, we will never be able to make an honest judgment or a fair choice.

Still, there are many players today that I feel could have played in any era. Players like Charles Barkley, Magic Johnson, Larry Bird, Michael Jordan, Kevin McHale, and

Joe Dumars, to name just a few. Sometimes you might think that Barkley is *not* sound because of some of the things he does—silly fouls, many turnovers—but his approach to the game, which is to give everything he has when he's out there on the court, is *very* sound. We all know how well Larry Bird plays, how he's able to adapt and give the team whatever it needs. Kevin McHale shoots his little three- and four-foot shots and plays his position as well as any player today. Magic Johnson is the ultimate architect of a team; he keeps all his players happy by giving them the ball at the appropriate time. Dumars is sometimes overlooked, but he is the perfect combination of great shooting ability and defense. He can guard the Michael Jordans and still make the pressure shot at the end of the game; the last person I saw who could do all that as well as Dumars was Jerry West. I am also a big fan of Johnny Stockton, who controls the ball perfectly. Without very much flair, he gives it up with pinpoint passes at just the right times.

In my opinion, most of the coaches in the NBA are wimps. They let the superstars get away with murder, too terrified to take things in hand because their job is at stake. They're afraid of the media, which scrutinizes everything they do, and they're afraid to bench a player or tell him he's not getting the job done. When they are upset, they choose a rookie or nonstarter to berate.

Doug Collins, when he coached the Bulls in Chicago, exemplified that type of coach to me. He never said or did anything negative toward Michael Jordan, but he sure as shit gave tough tongue lashings and benchings to lesser players. That's wimpish. Don Nelson, on the other hand, has never been afraid to treat his stars any differently than he does any other member of his team.

If NBA coaches benched their stars when the stars were not carrying their share of the load, it would help the entire team. I guarantee it. The other players would have to say, "If he's willing to bench the *star*, the coach must be *all right*!" The nonstars would work even harder. Trust me, players know when they are being used as scapegoats because the star is not doing his job.

I had coaches who told me what they thought of my game and what I should be doing to help the team. I didn't always like the things that were said, but some of the coaches who reprimanded me are today some of my best friends. And none of my best friends are wimps.

Speaking of coaches, the retirement of Lakers' coach Pat Riley was not what it appeared to be. I think Pat was actually fired. I know firsthand from people who would know these things that Pat was not quite the guy who many in the Lakers organization wanted him to be. Actually, he was *more* than people wanted him to be. He became too hard a taskmaster, and he became bigger than his job. Pat started to think he knew more about the way players should be medically treated than the team doctor. Also, believe it or not, he began deciding where and with whom players should sit on airplane trips. That's overstepping one's coaching responsibilities, don't you think? What coaching techniques do *seating arrangements* affect, for God's sake?

As a result, the people he worked with, for, and around didn't want him around anymore. It's too bad, because I remember Pat, from the days we played together on the

Lakers, as a good man. It's strange what power can do. In Pat's case, it seemed like it went straight to his head.

What is also strange to me is that the media *never* focuses on these things. Instead of reporting the truth about Riley's job change, the headlines in the papers said things like the one on June 12, 1990: LAKERS CHANGE A SMOOTH ONE. The papers just went along with the lie the Lakers were presenting. I can understand the Lakers lying—they just wanted to protect the organization and Riley. But why would a newspaper want to protect anyone? Why doesn't the media pick up on the truth?

There have been other examples. When Boston coach K. C. Jones announced his retirement in midseason a few years back, not much was said when he turned up a while later in Seattle as an assistant coach—which happens to be as far as you can get from Boston and still be in the continental United States. You think that's a coincidence? Who do you think was really running the Celtics, K.C.? Hell, no. It was Larry Bird, because superstars run franchises today. The same thing happened to Chicago's coach, Doug Collins. How can a successful coach who leads his team to its greatest season in years and almost knocks off the world champion team (the Pistons) get fired? Two simple words: Michael Jordan.

We've *all* heard the rumors that Bird had Jones fired, that Jordan had Collins fired, and that Magic had Riley dismissed. Well, you know and I know how things really work. So how come the newspapers never talk about it?

We *need to* have a better sense of history. Not just in sports. In everything. If you know your history you're more able to relate to what's happening today. Knowing what transpired yesterday gives you a hell of a lot better feeling for what and how things will be tomorrow.

A lot of basketball players today have *no* sense of history, of how the game evolved and how and why they're able to make two or three million dollars a year. All they seem to know is that that kind of money is being paid and their agent better get them some of it. They have no idea that basketball players thirty years ago were guys making only a few thousand dollars a year.

In my first year, 1959, four or five grand was a perfectly acceptable salary. I was told that the highest salary in the league was $22,500, and only Bob Cousy and Bob Pettit got that much. I was told I would have to come into the league at less than that and that I'd have to prove I was worth as much as those stars. I told them NFW—No Fucking Way— it would never happen that way, and demanded four or five times as much as Cousy and Pettit got. I eventually got it, too. My first salary was announced at $65,000, but with bonuses it came to $100,000.

If players today knew these things, they would have a better appreciation, and they would be better for it. They would be more willing to produce and they might be much happier if they would reflect on: What a lucky guy I am, a few years ago I would be making only $5,000, and not be riding first-class (where would I put my legs?), and be forced to play on the same day I flew across country, and always be saddled with some roommate I wouldn't even pass the ball to, much less live with.

He should also know that in the old days there were no places to eat after the games. In 1960, even in a city as big as Detroit, places didn't stay open late at night. There was no all-night room service in hotels. Things closed down at 10:00 P.M.—except for maybe some greasy burger joints.

Players today wouldn't be caught dead after a game in the places we were forced to eat at.

The gyms were so old and antiquated back then, there was no ventilation. It was always either too hot or too cold. You couldn't give your best because of the conditions. Now conditions are always first-class. Players perform in multi-million-dollar domes where the temperature's exactly seventy-two degrees no matter how large the crowd is. The lighting is perfect. You also have breakaway rims, not rims that are all bent out of shape.

People talk about the players being better—hell, it's the conditions that are better, brother, not the players.

You must know history to understand today. As I asked earlier, how far could Jesse Owens jump on a Tartan track? Give Doc Richards a fiberglass pole and how high would he have vaulted? That fifteen-foot limit of his may have gone to twenty feet. What would Wilt have done in a pair of Nikes? Most of my career we never even had trainers to wrap our ankles—we wrapped our own damn ankles! And when things went wrong with our bodies while we were playing, who did we call on? Mommy, if she was in the stands. If she wasn't, tough luck.

I am not complaining here. I just think people of today—players and fans—need to remember their yesterdays.

People always want to know who I thought my toughest foe was, who was the toughest person I had to play against. No matter how candid I am they never seem to be satisfied with the answer. Nevertheless, I will try to explain it once again. As far as I am concerned, it doesn't come down to particular guys when you're playing a team game. I was never played against by a single person during my entire basketball career, from grade school to the pros. It took a team effort, and that is the way it should be.

Many centers had a lot going for them, but I never considered myself to be playing against just centers. I played against teams. And without a doubt the toughest team I played against was the Boston Celtics. That's why they won so many championships—because they were the best. The New York Knicks of the late '60s/early '70s were formidable, but they were more fortunate than great. The Celtics dictated the odds. The Knicks won in spite of the odds.

What makes teams really strong is their intelligence. This is what gave the edge to Boston and New York over the rest of the teams I played against. Forget about all the talent you possess. There's a *lot* of talent in the NBA, always was, always will be. What makes you a little bit better than the rest is the gray matter.

A*fter viewing the* Gold Medal game between the American basketball team and the Yugoslavian team at the Goodwill Games in 1990, which the Americans lost, I focused on the difference between the two teams. The Yugoslavians had learned their basketball, as did the Russians, from the days when I played, back in the '60s, and they are still pretty much playing in that style. More than just playing a '60s style, they have '60s types of players.

The Europeans who were killing the Americans were the six-eight, six-nine, six-ten shooting forwards who could hit the three-point shot and also rebound. We Americans seem to have lost that kind of player. We've lost the Bob Pettits, Dolph Schayeses, Jerry Lucases, Dave DeBusscheres, Chet Walkers, Luke Jacksons—big, strong, great outside shooters who could also pound the shit out of you under the boards. Now, the guards have taken over the game—the U.S. team was led by a guard, Kevin Jackson—and the forwards try to play like Julius Erving, swooping to the basket and dunking balls. They exemplify contemporary basketball in America. Exciting, but not effective. This is why Larry Bird has been such a standout player over the past decade—he's a throwback to basketball of the '60s.

The Yugoslavs reminded me of the teams of the '50s and '60s, and their winning reaffirms my belief that there was better basketball back then. The guys may be more exciting today, but the brand of ball is not better. So when they go up against a team that plays '60s-style ball with '60s-style players, they lose.

A*s I said* in the HBO show, I think I would be even more dominating in today's game. Here's why.

First of all, the rules of the game today definitely favor a player like I was. Zone defenses are now illegal—it's called four or five times a game these days and that would strongly favor a Wilt Chamberlain type of basketball player. They did consider a zone defense illegal when I was playing, but back then they never enforced it. Before I even got my hands on the basketball when I was on offense, there would be two or three opposing players all around me. When I played against the Celtics, Bill Russell would be behind me, K. C. Jones would drop down from the weak side, and Tommy Heinsohn would come over from the other side of the court, all before I even *got* the ball. Today, that would be called; those guys could not triple-team me in that fashion.

(By the way, I think the no-zone defense in the pro game is stupid. I think pros should be allowed to play any defense they choose. If all five guys want to stand in front of the basket to keep a guy from coming and dunking the basketball, then they should be allowed to do that. It's ridiculous when a player has to be told what part of the floor he can stand on, where he can go, and when he can go there.)

Without zones, I would be allowed to go head to head with other centers. In my day, there was no one player who could contain me one on one in the pivot position. Today there is *definitely* no center who could contain me one on one. I once averaged fifty points a game for the season; today I could probably average seventy-five points a game. I'm not bragging, I'm just telling you how I think I would do if I were guarded by one guy alone, whether that guy's Bill Russell, Kareem Abdul-Jabbar, or Patrick Ewing.

H*aving said all* that, I must now say that there are some things that an opinionated guy like me has a lot of trouble understanding. I don't understand why all of you out there view people in the limelight, especially jocks, who from time to time are asked to comment on themselves, as arrogant and conceited if they answer honestly.

We're all familiar with Muhammad Ali calling himself "The Greatest" throughout his illustrious boxing career. Many took him seriously, others thought it was a ploy to get attention. Some considered him a braggart, or a man of poor taste. What Muhammad really thinks is a mystery to most of us. But my point is that from time to time I am asked to evaluate my game—how I feel about what I accomplished in basketball and how I feel I would stand up against today's competition.

As I've said before, I am an extrovert, so when people ask

me these questions I'm willing to talk about them. I'll give the real story, not a bunch of tired clichés, because I feel I owe that to the people asking the questions. I also believe there is no harm in expressing one's honest opinion. But when you give honest answers, it reinforces the belief many people have that you are full of yourself.

I have never claimed I am *the* best or *the* greatest at any sport—and, as I've said, I play a lot of them. That can only be determined by how others feel about what one has done relative to his or her sport. But, like choosing a great dessert from an array of many, the best is often predicated on what you like best and how you feel on a particular day. It's too subjective to have much importance.

I have *no* problem talking about what I'm capable of doing at my age now. This comes from a strong belief in myself. It also comes from knowing what I can do and am doing today. Basketball may be one of the toughest team sports to play physically—if not *the* toughest—but if I say that I can go out there and lead the NBA in rebounds today, don't smirk. In fact, if I tell you a mouse can pull a house, hook him up.

During the summer I work out with guys who play in the big leagues. I know what their capabilities are and I know what my capabilities are. Up to a couple of years ago, I played with guys like David Greenwood, Marques Johnson, Kiki Vandeweghe, Mark Eaton, Kurt Rambis—and I took them all. *Six years ago,* Greenwood told me I couldn't play the pivot in the NBA—it wouldn't be fair to the other NBA centers. I don't play anymore, but I still work out with them in the summer. I work with *me* every day, all year long. So I know. And I get tired of people telling me what they think I can or can't do when they really have no clue.

I personally don't see the difference between someone

talking about himself in an objective way and sending in a convincing résumé for a job. A résumé points out abilities and credentials, which are backed up by certain credits. Is having a good résumé bragging? Isn't it just stating the facts so a person can get a job? The only ones who would think a person with a good résumé is bragging are the people who are vying for the same job.

Likewise, I get more than a little miffed, as I've said, when I hear announcers rave about some of the moves and abilities of today's players. They make it seem as if these things have never been done before. Take the body movement of David Robinson, the genuinely sensational center for the San Antonio Spurs. When he runs down the floor leading a fast break, the announcer shouts, "God, did you ever see anything like that?! A seven-footer running up the floor like that?!" Well, yeah, damn it, I've seen a seven-footer do that a lot, more than thirty-five years ago! He wore number 13. So of course I get a little annoyed when I hear "experts" insisting that seven-footers never led fast breaks before.

I'm proud of my accomplishments, as any athlete should be. As an artist with ability would be. Some of my talents are God-given, like speed and agility; others I worked very hard to attain, like strength and endurance and patience. I am proud that I was one of the first, if not the very first, to use strong weight-lifting programs along with my basketball training. Weight lifting was frowned upon when I was a player. I was told never to mix the two. As you can see today, all great athletes, especially at the professional level, now have strong weight programs.

It was not by accident that I never fouled out of a game, either. I was taught early in my career by an old Philly coach that my value was on the court, not on the bench, which is where I'd be if I was in foul trouble. So I worked *extremely* hard to keep from making dumb over-the-back fouls. I worked damn hard trying to do things that were not a true part of my game.

I was an innovator in shots like the finger roll and the fadeaway jump shot from the pivot. The hook shot, which Kareem used with great proficiency, has been around since the game's inception; all centers used it. I used it very effectively.

I am sure salaries would have escalated in time, but I didn't wait for time. I made it happen by demanding it—and that was when the owners claimed that the game could never afford the high salary I was asking for. (Ha! What a joke that was.)

I even made them change some of the rules of basketball. Offensive goaltending was a rule created only because I was able to do things with the ball in flight that others couldn't do. So they made what I did illegal. My first year in the NBA, you were allowed to touch your teammate's shot the instant it left his hands and could touch it anywhere along its flight path until it reached the basket. You could guide the ball into the basket, touch it over the rim, whatever you wanted. This was to my advantage because I could jump so much higher than most of the other players on the court and I possessed great timing for intercepting the ball and guiding it into the basket. I had so much success guiding my teammate's shots and turning them into two points that the powers that be—the rulemakers—decided I had an unfair advantage over the rest of the players. So they terminated that part of my game. They created a no-no called offensive goaltending, in which no one can touch the ball on its downward flight to the basket or over the rim after it has been shot.

(This new rule did hurt my game, I guess; my scoring average, 37.5 points a game my rookie year, only went up to 50 points a game by my third season.)

They also widened the lane to keep me farther away from the basket. The rule makers made it illegal to throw the ball over the backboard on an out-of-bounds pass because I could jump so high, catch the pass, and dunk it so easily. When I was in college, the NCAA immediately outlawed dunking the ball from the free throw line when taking foul shots when they heard I could do it. I can only wistfully speculate as to what my free throw percentage might have been if that rule had not been written.

These and a few other rules were legislated specifically against yours truly. I of course take all this as a supreme compliment, but I never hear the boys on the mikes explain how these things came to be. All announcers seem to pretend that this is the way basketball was since its inception.

When people talk about things that are being done today as if they have never been done before, of course I feel cheated. I am sorry that video was not perfected during my early career so that more people could view for themselves. I must admit that I don't know any other sport that changed the game because of a single player. And I don't know of another athlete who dominated any phase of his sport like I did with scoring and rebounding. Nor have I heard of anyone else who was asked to give up the most dominating part of his game (in my case, scoring) because they thought he could be even more dominating if he concentrated on other aspects of his game. (In my case, it was passing. And that year, 1968, I led the league in assists. That would be like asking Joe Montana to switch to defensive back—and have him lead the league in interceptions.) In some ways it was very flattering that they were so confident. I could dominate in any aspect of the game I wanted. On the other hand, would you have asked Babe Ruth to go back to pitching after realizing how great he was at batting? I don't think so.

Perhaps anger is too strong a word to describe my feelings on this matter, yet the more I reflect on this aspect of my career, the more I bristle.

In my first four or five years in the NBA, I so dominated the scoring that even my strongest detractors had to concede that I could score almost whenever I wanted to. An example of how I dominated was brought to light on January 9, 1991, when Michael Jordan scored his fifteen thousandth point. All the papers praised his achievement and related that he reached that milestone in his 460th game—faster than anyone in NBA history *except* yours truly, who did it in 358 games. That's right—102 games quicker. I mention this to illustrate the point that it was only after I was besieged by many bullshit factions that I started to score less and less. I did it only to appease my detractors, not because of any inability to keep scoring. There is no doubt that if I had *chosen* to keep scoring, I could have, and just as easily in my last years of play as in the beginning of my career. I became a smarter player as I got older and my field goal percentage started to climb to unreal numbers. Also, the center competition, in my mind's eye, became less and less formidable. Russell was getting old. Kareem was not strong enough to stop me from going to the basket (which I did more of in my later years than I was allowed to in my early years). I want you to realize that I dunked the basketball about *half* as many shots a game when I was really scoring points as Michael Jordan does now. I mainly used fadeaway jump shots and finger rolls to score my shots. The point is, I could have put the scoring record so far out of reach that Kareem would have had to play thirty years, not twenty, to break the record. But I sacrificed all that scoring ability for whatever my teams wanted of me. I call that *real* unselfishness—not like that crap you hear announcers say when a player gives off a pass to a teammate. My last game in the NBA was indicative of what I had allowed myself to become as a scorer. I took one—that's right—*one* shot during the entire game. There were many games during the last four or five years of my career when I took one or no shots. But I led the NBA in rebounding and blocked shots, and I established a shooting percentage record that may stand for many a year—72 percent.

What would *you* have done if you were the greatest scorer the game has ever seen? Would you stop shooting and pass the ball to some guy who on his best day couldn't score in an entire game what you averaged for one quarter? For better or worse, that's what I did.

At times I got a little angry when I read that I couldn't score any more. So I would go out and score fifty or sixty points just to show people that I could still do it; then I would go back to role playing, scoring twelve and thirteen points a contest.

Like any artist, we all want credit for our paintings. And when you were the innovator and terminator of a great many things in your chosen field, some credit is due you. I am sure that if Leif Ericsson were alive today he would not enjoy hearing about Columbus discovering America.

But my getting credit for these events is not that important. Making people realize that the game was not always as it is now, *that's* what's important. The hows and whys of that change, that's what matters to me.

. . .

Since I retired, I have begun to receive more recognition for my accomplishments than when I was playing. Writers, ex-players, and contemporary players are now saying they think of me as the greatest this or the greatest that—compliments they never gave while I was an active player.

I am, of course, honored by this, but to tell you the truth, I always wondered why the hell it took so long. Finally, I realized that when someone is no longer a threat, more positive things can be said about him. It's like what happens when people pass away. They become much better in other people's minds after death than they ever seemed in life.

This really bothered me until I figured it out. Now I can rest a little more comfortably. When I was out there doing my thing I was too intimidating, too threatening. Now that I am no longer an adversary on the court or to the media, everyone can relax and be more open and honest.

Recently, Larry Bird said I was the greatest player ever to play the game, which I appreciate. But notice he's not picking a contemporary like Magic or Jordan, someone he can be compared to. *They* are threats to him, I'm not. So, though I appreciate his compliment, I wonder how sincere it is.

Shooting percentages are higher in the pro game today than they were in my day, which would lead you to believe that the players of today are better shooters. This probably won't shock you, but I don't think so. I think that because of the enforcement of the no-zone defense rule, the defense today is *much* softer than it used to be. Having no zone leaves the court much more wide open, and once a player gets the ball he has easy access to the basket. That's what allows players today to shoot tons of lay-ups and fly through the air to jam in their 360-degree slamaroos. All these lay-ups and dunks are the reason shooting percentages are so high. The shooters in my day were far superior. Bill Sharman, Jerry West, Jerry Lucas, Oscar Robertson, and Hal Greer, to name a few, were never allowed to get in and shoot lay-up after lay-up, so their percentages were in the mid-forties. But if you ask my humble opinion, which I am going to give whether you want it or not, today's shooters (with a few exceptions, like Bird and Dumars) could not compete with the shooters of yesterday.

The game has changed in a few other ways, too. Most of the great contemporary basketball players do not stress defense nearly as much as we did in the past. A lot more players want to be great shot blockers these days. (Mainly because the shot blocking stat now exists and players love to accumulate high totals in that stat. I'll talk about the phenomenon more in my chapter on "things that piss me off.") Although few can truly be great shot blockers, they sure continue to try. The result is they weaken their defensive posture—and the team's overall defense suffers.

I think the game has shifted in one area that *does* improve its appeal. The NBA today has become much more guard-oriented. This brings more excitement to the pro game because guards are normally faster and quicker than the big men on the front line. Also, fans can relate to a small guard since their size is closer to the norm.

. . .

When *the three-point* field goal came into the NBA, I thought, "How dumb to reward a shooter an extra point for a lucky shot." The object of the game is to get into position to make the easiest shot, not the toughest. But I have changed my opinion. It has added excitement to the game. All things that appear bad are not necessarily so. I now enjoy the three-point goal. (But please, no three foul shots for a guy who is fouled in the act of shooting a three-pointer. That's going too far.)

The game of basketball has peaks and valleys, and as far as the play of centers is concerned we are now in a valley. In fact, we're in Death Valley. The demise of the center as *the* force in basketball is due to the fact that the guards are controlling the ball more and more, dictating when and where the ball goes to the other players. More often than not many of the guards hold the ball for almost the entire twenty-four seconds, looking for their opportunity to do whatever they decide to do (in many cases, shoot). They often give up the ball at the last second, which gives their teammates no time at all to do their thing, unless their thing is tossing the ball at the basket or getting called for the twenty-four second violation. This keeps the ball out of the center's hands and diminishes his offensive value a great deal.

The idiotic zone defense rule forces the centers who are not so mobile to go out away from the basket and guard their man, who may be just standing around doing nothing. Still, the center has to come out and guard him. It's ridiculous! If you want to get rid of the defensive-minded center, all you have to do is send the offensive center out to the half-court line—the defensive center has to go and stand there with him. What are you supposed to do, go out there and dance? It makes no sense. The defense is there to keep the other team from scoring easy baskets. As I stated earlier, this rule makes it easy for players to make uncontested lay-ups and gives the average fan the idea that players are great shooters. Only in the playoffs are players not allowed to get in for uncontested lay-ups. As a result, shooting percentages go way down. (Defense is played so much tougher in the playoffs because most players are not concerned with offensive charges. Also, the refs allow more lane jamming and overall physical play.)

Announcers today always seem amazed whenever a big man scores from the outside. They make it seem like something new and incredible when a Bill Laimbeer scores from twenty feet. And yet from the beginning of the game many big men, like six-ten Dolph Schayes and six-ten Clyde Lovellette—who was recently inducted into the Hall of Fame—had velvety soft touches. They were *great* outside shooters. Jerry Lucas, a *center,* was one of the best shooters ever in the game of basketball. Not only could he shoot from inside and outside, he led the league in free throw percentage one year.

Some people think the height of the basket should be raised from ten feet to eleven or twelve feet because the guys are getting too big. Well, let me tell you that the average pro basketball player's height has not gone up more than an inch in the last thirty years. This thought that players are bigger is a lot of BS.

If the average height *has* gone up an inch it's because of

guys like Chuck Nevitt, who is seven-five, Manute Bol, seven-seven, and a few others. These supertall guys have confused the viewer, because they are considered in the team's average size stats, even though they don't play all that much. These guys, whose basketball skills—to be polite—leave much to be desired, would be a joke playing in my day. Take these guys out—and I wish someone would—and you'll find the average size would be close to the same as when I was playing.

Many people want to raise the basket because dunking is too easy. Well, it was easy in my day, too. We just didn't do it. As I have explained elsewhere in the book, dunking was considered hotdogging.

Thinking that big men don't and shouldn't have great shooting touches is like saying someone is too big to have feelings. Get one thing straight, please. Foul shooting is one kind of shooting and field goal shooting is another. Many great foul shooters are only fair to middling from the field—and, of course, you know the other side of that coin. The point here is that the sensitive touch it takes to be a great shooter does *not* have anything to do with size. Look in the record books. Many big men were and are great outside shooters *and* foul shooters.

I do believe, though, that the court could be widened to give the players more room to maneuver. But leave the basket where it is.

A *few more* thoughts on Manute Bol: I get bent out of shape when Bol—or Nevitt or other seven-footers who can't really play—take up space on a roster. They're not professional basketball players. They're sideshows. As a former player and a seven-footer, I feel this is exploitation.

It cheats everyone—fans, other players on the team, players who are kept off of rosters because of these no-talent seven-footers.

Who needs to see Bol stand with his hands in the air on defense, and hiding in the corner so he doesn't have to get involved in offense? Who needs to see fans laugh and giggle when he attempts any kind of shot? Not me. Not any of us. It's ludicrous.

One question I often get today is how I would fare in today's game playing against so many more tall players like Bol, Mark Eaton, who's seven-four, and Sampson, also seven-four. For me, the taller the competition the better I would like it, although that doesn't mean I always played better against taller foes. There were many I would feel sorry for and actually ease up on—empathizing with them and some of their shortcomings on and off the court. I never really wanted to embarrass them any more than necessary. An example: There was a guy named Swede Halbrook of the Syracuse Nationals. He was seven-three, about three inches taller than I was, and I would allow him to do things I would not give others the same privilege of doing. I sometimes didn't block shots I could easily have blocked. And when he would put the ball on the floor to dribble, I could definitely have stolen it—but I'd choose not to humiliate him. I just couldn't stand to see guys like that look awkward and foolish—and be the goons that everyone thought, at that time, that seven-footers were. In a way, I was protecting my own image. There were and are almost no men of my size blessed with my agility, strength, and stamina (stamina has always been a shortcoming for big men). My vertical jumping ability set me apart from all the other really tall men. Only much shorter men could *begin* to get off the floor as high as I could. I had *all* the advantages against tall guys. The one thing I love about the Mark Eatons and the Bols is that it proves to the world that height's not everything and that all those rebounds I got were not only because of my size. (Manute is not even among the leaders on his own team in rebounding.)

I always found it more difficult to face a good percentage shooting, mobile six-foot-eight center than an awkward seven-footer. I truly believe that with my physical gifts—excluding my height—I still would have made an excellent basketball player. However, if I were shorter, pro football would have been my choice of sports: my position would have been quarterback, where I could have shown off my athleticism (like Randall Cunningham of the Philadelphia Eagles).

I can't fathom being only six feet tall, but if I had to be a "munchkin" like that and still wanted to play basketball, I wouldn't mind being—and think I could have been—a Johnny Stockton type.

A *lot of* today's players, like Vlade Divac, the new center from Yugoslavia who now plays for the Los Angeles Lakers, are readily accepted with point and rebound totals that are far below what one would think a good team is looking for. Now, ten points and five or six rebounds a game are considered awesome feats for these young, rookie players.

When I first came in to the NBA I was expected to get forty points a game, and it stayed that way until the end of my career. If I didn't have superhuman stats, people thought I was dogging it. Young players today don't have that kind of burden to carry. In fact, the fans seem quite happy with *any* contribution that some of these guys make.

This thinking is more readily apparent with players who are on winning teams. It's only when their teams start to lose that what these players are *not* doing becomes a point of discussion—negative discussion.

What has become obvious is this: As long as you are in a winning situation you can get away with anything. It doesn't make any difference whether the team has any real harmony, whether they like each other, or whether they fight and bicker on or off the court. Nothing is said even if a guy misses a dozen foul shots as long as the end result is a victory. Winning is all the fans and press seem to be interested in.

On the other hand, a guy can work his heart out, but if the team is losing, people will always dwell on the negatives of his game. They make statements like, "If Wilt would work on his foul shooting more, the team might not have lost." It doesn't matter that Wilt got forty points and pulled down forty rebounds and tried his damnedest to make those foul shots.

I guess my point is that expectations of players' performances have changed, and not for the better.

Here is an example of the previous statement. When most people talk of me as a basketball player they remember my scoring prowess—my hundred-point game, and all my other offensive records. But when I came into the NBA from college I was known more for my defensive expertise—blocking shots, altering shots, intimidation, etc. Defense is what was expected of me. In one game in the NBA I blocked the first ten shots taken by the great Walt Bellamy. People left that game *raving* about my defense.

They forgot to mention that, by the way, I also scored fifty-three points and had thirty-six rebounds. I guarantee you that if any of today's centers ever had even one game like that, it'd be front-page news.

Now *that I* think about it, I bet most of you contemporary fans don't know who Walt Bellamy is. Maybe a few sports announcers do, though I never hear them mention his name. Yet his credentials are quite imposing, especially in his rookie year, when he posted numbers that almost no one else has ever come close to posting (with the exception of me). His rookie year was *far* more impressive than David Robinson's—and Robinson was the NBA rookie of the year in 1989. When the media talk about Robinson they make it sound like no one else ever did that well in their first year. Well, Bellamy did. Even now he is among the top five leading rebounders in the game's history and is up there in scoring as well. His records are only twenty years old, yet he is almost forgotten.

When talking about players of the past, announcers only mention five or six guys—Russell, Robertson, West, Cousy, myself—like they were the only good players then. That's bull. Basketball needs to be put into the proper perspective. Great players of the past—like Walt Bellamy—need credit for making the game what it is today.

Specialization *may be* in order when you are looking for a certain type of lawyer. If you have just been accused of murder you sure don't want a tax lawyer—that's obvious. But in sports this specialization has gone way too far. In baseball you not only have the relief pitcher, you have the *short* relief pitcher, the *long* relief pitcher, the pitcher who comes in just to throw to the left hander, the hurler who comes in just to throw the fastball, etc., etc. Today you have every type of pitcher possible. In the old days you just had a pitcher who was on the mound to do his thing—and that thing was to win the game and go the whole nine innings. Today, in the American League, the pitcher isn't even allowed to hit! That same pitcher hit pretty well, I guarantee you, before he got to the pros, but now he isn't even allowed to swing the bat. In football it's so specialized that they have special teams *within the team*—people who are put in the game on third down just to rush the passer. That's their only damn job. On defense there are people who just defend "short" and others who defend "long." It's become so specialized that soon there'll be people who just come out to tie the quarterback's shoestrings.

In basketball you have a point guard, a defensive guard, a three-point shooting guard, a guard who penetrates. In the good old days you just had a guard, like Jerry West, and he did it all. There were others, like Walt Frazier, who played great defense—but they also were great offensely. In other words, they did whatever you wanted a guard to do. I think what's happened with all this specialization is that fans have not only been cheated out of seeing great athletes doing *all* the things involved in playing a game— whatever game you choose—but they (the fans) no longer *expect* all-around greatness. Fans seem quite content to watch a jock do just one thing. What ever happened to the Willie Mayses of the world, guys who could run, catch, throw, and hit? When you get a player now who can do all of that, he is truly a super-super-star. Everyone knows that Bo Jackson plays two sports (or, at least, did before he got hurt). We talk about him like he's a miracle man. This only shows that people don't expect anything out of the ordinary athlete anymore. Remember, *most* pro athletes played two or more sports when they were amateurs. During my day there were many guys who played two professional sports. Gene Conley, who played backup center behind Bill Russell (he also played forward on some of the Celtic championship teams), also pitched for the Boston Red Sox. Not only wasn't he considered anything special, he wasn't even considered a particularly good athlete. Today he'd be front-page news! Another one who comes to mind is Dave DeBusschere. He was a good basketball player and a decent baseball player. The fact that he did both wasn't particularly newsworthy, though. I wonder what people would think if Jim Thorpe were around today? He'd probably be considered the brother of Jesus Christ.

The point I am trying to make here is that we fans have come to accept a lot less than we used to need to satisfy us. Or am I being too subtlc?

The real thing that bugs me today is when I hear people say, "Let's get this guy to play like Bill Russell." What they *mean* is they want someone to be a defensive stalwart as Russell was during his playing days. These people don't realize that Bill Russell also averaged seventeen points a game for his whole career—which is only about seven points less than the great Kareem Abdul-Jabbar did, and Kareem is the greatest scorer in NBA history! Bill Russell is also among the all-time leaders in assists in the NBA. *This* is why he was so great—he did *many* other things in addition to blocking shots. Sure, his defense was his strong suit but he was a *complete all-around player.* Damn! That's what's needed today—all-around players. Today we have the Bols and the Eatons who can block five shots a game for you, but the rest of their game makes them a liability to their team. Many NBA rosters are *full* of guys who are liabilities because they can only do one thing.

Look, we all know that you're only as strong as your weakest link. That doesn't necessarily mean just your weakest player; it means that if a player has a weak part of his game, he has a weak link.

In sports, an athlete should learn the game he's playing and learn every phase of it. This was the way it was when I grew up. If you wanted to be a basketball player, you learned to play defense, rebound, run, shoot, and *all* the things that made you a complete basketball player. I'm sure it was the same if you wanted to be a pro-baseball player. We need to get back to those simpler ideas of what sports is all about. The players will enjoy it more, I promise you, and the fans will *definitely* enjoy it more.

Magic, Bird, Barkley, and Jordan are stars because they can play every facet of the game. We are dumbfounded when we see those guys play because we are no longer accustomed to seeing complete athletes. I think this has evolved because of overcoaching. It started way back when football went to the platoon system—offensive teams, defensive teams, and special teams. All of a sudden, the theory got developed that if you played defensive you couldn't play offensive. Honestly, I don't see much difference in the two—it's strictly a mental thing.

WILTISM

They say nobody's perfect. They also say practice makes perfect. I wish "they" would make up their minds.

I like facts and stats and things like that, but sometimes facts and stats can be misleading. Some examples: Michael Jordan now has the fourth highest scoring season—total points in one season—after my three. But it is not mentioned that early in my career we played twelve fewer games per season. Back then a season consisted of only seventy games, as compared to eight-two nowadays. That's a fact.

Kareem is the shot-blocking leader of all time. That's a fact, too. But it's also a fact that when Bill Russell and I played, shot-blocking stats were not kept.

 WILTISM

Sometimes you have to have all the facts before a stat becomes a *meaningful* stat.

I'd like to make a suggestion to the NBA:

I was often denied the privilege of playing for the world championship because when I was with the 76ers I was in a tough division, the Eastern Division, and we were often knocked out by the Boston Celtics. The two conferences in the NBA, East and West, are not usually equal. In the '80s the Eastern Conference was usually the strongest and many of the teams that could have played for the championship were knocked off in the preliminary rounds. Here's a way to solve that, and bring parity to the playoffs. This very simple maneuver would also allow fans to see teams in playoff situations that they only saw once during the regular season. Have cross-conference playoffs in the early rounds, not just the finals.

As it stands now, the eight teams in the Western Conference with the best record play each other for the right to represent the West in the championship series. Likewise in the East. I say that, instead, let the top teams in the East play the bottom teams in the West. And vice versa. Say Boston is tops in the East; let them play the number eight team in the West. The Lakers win the West and play the East's number eight team.

This would give balance to the playoffs. If all the strong teams were in the West, they wouldn't knock each other off. The two strongest teams would reach the finals whether they played in the same conference or not. You wouldn't have one team arriving at the finals from the weaker conference fresh while the other from the stronger conference is beat up and tired.

Television ratings would be higher, because the two best teams would be playing each other. No one wants to watch a strong team from the East against a lousy team from the West. If the two best teams are Boston and Detroit, believe me, the TV ratings will be high.

Many men of color, including me, owe a lot to the game of basketball. The game has given us great opportunities; more so, I think, than other sports. Professional basketball has many successful coaches of color. In other pro sports that either doesn't exist at all or is an oddity. That's a pity, because basketball has flourished from our efforts. It is well documented how the sport has prospered from the likes of the great Bill Russell, Elgin Baylor, Oscar Robertson, Magic Johnson, the sensational Michael Jordan, and now David Robinson. These players have helped make the NBA into a first-class league and America's most popular sport.

But even before men of color were allowed to play in the

NBA—which was six or seven years after the league's inception—the league got a big boost from, perhaps was even able to survive because of, men of color. And one Caucasian man who was small physically but huge in foresight and enthusiasm. His name was Abe Saperstein, and his team was the world-famous Harlem Globetrotters. Abe loved the game of basketball and had friendships with many of the NBA team owners, when NBA teams were still struggling. Abe and the Globies graciously played the opening games of doubleheaders—and when the Globies played the arenas would fill up. After the Globies played some of the fans would stay to watch the NBA contest. And this was the major reason many NBA teams were able to survive financially and gain recognition in the first place.

So when you see huge crowds cheering on those tall NBA men of color today—men who, ironically, now play the brand of basketball the Globies made famous—a fast-paced, showboating kind of game that the fans love—I think you should remember a small white man who helped make it possible.

When I was a young boy first learning the game of basketball, the ultimate dream for players of color was to play with the Globetrotters. The NBA meant zero to us at that time. When you had a chance to go see the Globies play in person and be that close to them, it was like a dream come true. In my eyes and in the eyes of many others, they were the best basketball team in the world. As I said above, men of color were not playing in the NBA at that time—but the Globetrotters often played games against NBA powerhouses and all-star college teams. The Globies were always the ultimate winners. To be that good *and* that funny, what could be more desirable? So when I was offered a chance to play for them I forwent my last year at the University of Kansas and joined them. How could I not? I was so damn intrigued. Even though at that time I was considered the best player in the world, I was in awe of the Globies. The chance to play with men I dreamed about, the opportunity to wear those red-and-white shorts, was more than I could refuse. The icing on the cake was all the world traveling I was going to get a chance to do. I craved that. It was a new world opening its arms to embrace me and I've never been able to resist that.

So there I was playing to "Sweet Georgia Brown" and becoming a part of the greatest basketball show on earth. I never thought of the hardships: traveling ten to fourteen hours a day, mostly on a rinky-dinky bus; eating one good meal a week—*maybe*. Before I came along, the Globies were the greasy-spoon kings of the world. A greasy spoon is a place that a roach would not venture into for fear of dying from the greasy food being served. My contribution to the team was teaching my teammates to shop at local supermarkets like I had learned to do as a kid, when I used to shop for my family. The food in the supermarkets cost much less than the same food in the bad restaurants they frequented. I taught them to buy good canned goods, lunch meats, breads and fruits, and a can opener. Soon they were all expert shoppers, eating gourmet meals from tins.

The hotels, with few exceptions, were of the lowest possible class. Management saved money this way. It was actually better and more comfortable to sleep in the bus than in some of those ridiculously short, lumpy beds and in the rooms that smelled of whatever it was they smelled of. I never really wanted to know.

But the hotel rooms and the beds were nothing when

compared to the most irritating part of being a Globie: caring for your clothes was the real aggravating problem. On our American tour, which lasted seven or eight months, we were literally stranded on the road. Every single day we had to travel and play two, sometimes three games. We were only allowed to carry two bags, one large suitcase for personal clothes and one small bag for our two Globie uniforms and playing gear. The problem was we had only two uniforms, yet we played up to three games a day. We never had time to wash and dry our tops, shorts or jocks. We never stopped at a laundromat. At that time, there weren't too many laundromats where we were playing.

Our uniforms got so crusty and hard that they could stand on their own—they didn't need us to hold them up. We tried to doctor the odor with various colognes we bought in Europe, but after a while that only enhanced the stench of our perspiration. We were disgusting. But for some odd reason, when it came to dressing for a date, all the Globies managed to look like men from *GQ* on their way to a debutante ball.

On and off the court, the Globies were consummate pros. No one could play a sport and make a show of it as we did night after night after night. You can't imagine how tough it is to play a strenuous game of basketball and perform tricks to create laughter—and all the while pretending it's all as easy as one-two-three.

My regular seat on the bus was in the very back over the rear axle, where every bump was even more pronounced. On long trips I would shout at the top of my voice to whoever was listening, "And to think I used to dream of being a Globie!" With that my teammates would whistle "Sweet Georgia Brown" in unison.

Still, they were great times. Hardships shared with

friends often make the bonds of friendship grow stronger and stronger. That's why we were good when we hit that court; we knew all the things it took to get us there—from those early dreams to those very long bus rides.

Let me tell you one of my favorite stories about the Globies, which is also about Abe. Now, Abe was a big fan of Napoleon. I mean, a *really* big fan. Undoubtedly he thought he was Napoleon reincarnated.

As happened on many occasions while I was in Europe with the Globies in the '60s, I was coming home from a night of adventure in Vienna about 5:00 A.M. Dawn was just breaking. I was a mile or two from my hotel, walking down these strange streets trying to find my way, when I saw a shadow three blocks away. As I walked closer, the shadow looked a little like short, pudgy Abe Saperstein. A few steps more and I discovered it was indeed Abe, all five feet six inches of him. He was standing there on the corner with his hands thrust into his suspenders, rocking back and forth, looking up at the sky, totally mesmerized.

I said, "Abe, what the hell are you doing out here this early in the morning? It's only five o'clock."

It took about two minutes for him to give me an answer. He finally said, "Oh, Wilt! I can't believe it. I can't believe it."

After he said "I can't believe it" about twenty times I said, "Hey, Abe, what is it you can't believe?"

Abe replied, "I am staying in the same hotel that Napoleon Bonaparte stayed in." Abe always stayed at the first-class hotels, even though the Globies didn't.

"No kidding?" I said.

"And guess what? I am *also* staying in the same suite that Napoleon Bonaparte stayed in."

"I can't believe that," I said.

"Yes I am," he insisted. "And Wilt, the topper is . . . I am sleeping in the *same bed* Napoleon Bonaparte slept in."

And to that I replied, "Abe, did they change the sheets?"

I *first joined* the Globetrotters in Milan, Italy, arriving around six o'clock in the morning. Mr. Saperstein picked me up at the airport and drove me to the hotel. We got there about 7:00 A.M. As I was walking into the hotel, one of the Globies was walking out. He was immaculately dressed. I was introduced to him, then he said, "Excuse me. I have a date." And he left.

That night, after I finished playing in my very first game, I went up to him and asked, "How did your date go?"

"Oh, wonderful," he said. "Wonderful."

"Did she speak English, or do you speak Italian?" I wanted to know.

"She doesn't speak a word of English and I don't speak a word of Italian."

Needless to say, I didn't think that would make for much of a date and I told him so.

"Oh, no," he said. "It was perfect. I met her in the park. She is a baby-sitter and she sits on a bench and watches her baby. I sit on another bench and watch her. That's the extent of our date. But she looks at me and I look at her and I know that she wants me. And she knows that I want her. This has been going on for three days. Tomorrow, I think we will finally say hello to each other."

When *the Globies* traveled in Europe, sometimes we'd be in two or three countries in the same day. We had one Globie who always liked to think of himself as a language expert. His actual knowledge of foreign languages was a complete zero. He had one famous statement he would make whenever we went to a restaurant. He would say to the waiter, "Would you bring me *ein* Coco-Cola *bien cuit?*" Now *ein,* of course, is German for "one." His uniform number was one, so he was quite familiar with *ein.* We all know that Coca-Cola is Coca-Cola in any language. But *bien cuit* is French for "well done." He got the expression from his teammates in France, who would order eggs well done in the morning. He thought that *bien cuit* meant "in a hurry." So he always ordered his Coca-Cola well done—in German, French, and English.

We also got a kick out of his response to a French waiter's question. The waiter, knowing that Americans like ice in their soda, would ask, *"Avec glace, monsieur?"*

The Globie would respond, "Forget the glass. I'll drink it out of the bottle."

The highest honor or laurel a Globie could receive was the accolade "Thirty Years on the Road." It was like being knighted or given the Order of the Garter. It was the ultimate respect; it showed that this guy had seen it all and learned how to deal with it. To receive this tribute you had to spend a great many years out there with your eyes and ears open, learn from what you saw and did, and in essence make it work in your everyday life. Only the Globies gave this kind of honor—I never found it with any of the NBA teams I played for. Only the Globies had that sense of family, of traveling thirteen hours a day playing two or three games a day, eating at the same places, experiencing the same hardships (which were many).

The only thing that comes close to this is the circus.

Circus performers live in a world only they know about. They share this isolation, this camaraderie from town to town, city to city, under all conditions. No one cares where they came from, or where they are going, or what they endure to make the opening night show.

When we traveled in Europe we lived for four and a half months out of a suitcase and a half. In that suitcase were the uniforms, sneakers, and all our personal clothing and grooming needs. We had to look like fashion plates in France and Germany, know how to order food without knowing the language, and exchange money when the currency changed every day. If you couldn't learn to deal with this quickly, you didn't last.

But once you have mastered it, and you can handle it with style and guile, you earn the title Thirty Years on the Road. I am honored to have the title, particularly because once you receive it you never lose it. When ex-Globies see me, now I am greeted: "That's my man, Wilt. Thirty years on the road."

I *am often* asked what was the best team I ever saw play. It happens to be one I was associated with. The Philadelphia 76ers of 1967–68 were without a doubt the greatest ever. Luke Jackson was the epitome of the power forward. Our guards were Hal Greer, who could shoot the lights out; Wali Jones, who played defense like a madman; and Larry Costello, an awesome outside shooter. Chet Walker was the ultimate one on one player. Billy Cunningham was the greatest sixth man in the game and was a coach on the floor. Alex Hannum, our real coach, rounded out this outstanding group.

The team that did the most with the least amount of

talent would be the Los Angeles Lakers of 1972, who won thirty-three games in a row and the world championship. That was truly a team of destiny because we did not have a great array of players. Jerry West was on his way out, as was I. Gail Goodrich was a super scorer who did his job well. But basically we had nothing else going for us. We did have a camaraderie, and each guy did his job. I was the whole defensive backbone; except for West, we were very weak on defense, yet we went over two and a half months without losing a game, setting an all-time consecutive game winning record for *all* of professional sports. And that, my friends, is pretty great.

One of my more amazing stories of my basketball career revolved around that thirty-three-game streak—and it's a story that got no press at all.

For many years the Lakers, with the great Elgin Baylor and Jerry West, came close to winning numerous NBA crowns, but every year they lost to the Boston Celtics in the finals. When I joined the Lakers and we didn't win the crown those first two years, as usual the fingers pointed in my direction. The other two superstars' contributions were never questioned. Then, early in my third season with the team, a very strange incident occurred. "Elge" was asked to relinquish his starting role to Jim McMillian, a young, so-so small forward. Instead of adhering to the wishes of the coach, Bill Sharman, and management, Elgin decided to retire right then and there rather than finish the season out. So what do you think happened to the Lakers without their oldest and most beloved superstar? Starting with the very next game, the Lakers went on a thirty-three-game winning streak! We ended the season with a record-breaking sixty-nine wins and thirteen losses, an NBA record that still stands, and we capped this with the Lakers' first NBA crown.

I say all this still with disbelief. There was *never* a word mentioned in *any* of the media about how and why all this came about—after Elgin's retirement. I wonder, if I had retired and the team had accomplished what they did, how kind would the press have been to me?

A*bove all*, *I* am remembered by many for one special thing I did in life. Grown men still point me out and tell their kids I scored a hundred points in an NBA game. The question I'm most often asked is, "How did it feel to score a hundred points?" Truthfully, I'm only sure about one thing: by the game's end, I was completely exhausted. And not just from the game itself, in which the New York Knicks threw everyone and everything they could at me. Since it was near the end of the season and our place in the standings was unchangeable for the playoffs, I took some time to enjoy myself the night before the game. I was playing for the Philadelphia Warriors but living in New York City. I had to be in Philly by 1:00 P.M. that day to catch the team bus for Hershey, Pennsylvania, where we were actually playing the game. Because I'd been kept busy by an "encounter" or two (or three), I took the train to Philly having had absolutely no sleep the night before. I didn't sleep on the train, afraid I might miss my stop and end up in Washington, D.C. On the bus ride from Philadelphia to Hershey, about a two-hour trip, I spent the whole time talking to my best friend, Vince Miller. We arrived at the arena in Hershey at 3:30 P.M. and I spent the rest of the time before the game shooting a rifle at a penny arcade. I

completely destroyed all existing shooting records there—
an omen of things to come.

I give you this scenario leading up to the game and the
follow-up after the game because these events are more
vivid in my mind than any of the game itself. Afterwards,
the Knicks, who had come in cars (about a three-hour
drive from New York City), were of course driving back
home. Our bus was going back to Philly, since we never
stayed in hotels on short trips like this one, to save money.
I asked Coach McGuire if it would be okay if I rode with
some of the Knicks back to New York. The player I wanted
to ride with was a good friend of mine, Willie Naulls.
Willie drove and I took the front passenger seat. In the
backseat sat two other Knicks. Within a mile, I was fast
asleep and snoring. Every now and then I would stir and
hear the same conversation: "Would you believe that son-
of-a-bitch scored a hundred points against us?! A hundred
points!" They kept telling each other all the things they did
to try to keep me from scoring. Then they'd repeat, "Can
you believe that son-of-a-bitch scored a hundred points on
us!" I'd go back to sleep with a smirk on my face. When
they let me off at my apartment on Ninety-seventh Street
and Central Park West, I said to them, "You guys are sure
nice to this s.o.b. Letting me score a hundred points, *then*
giving me a ride all the way back to my apartment. Thanks,
fellows."

F I V E

On Other Sports: Games People Play

love all sports, not just basketball. And I have strong
opinions—no surprise there—about some of the things
that go on in sports, about winning and losing and competition, about women's sports, and about sports history.
Allow me to share some with you.

It is amazing to me how primitive we still are, especially
in sports. I was watching a television show about Africa
recently, and I noticed that on the headdress and shields
of the African warriors there were markings. These markings tell the tribesmen how effective the great warriors are.
On the shield, the markings denote the number of lions or

people the warrior has killed. I realized that this is no different from what we do with football players' helmets today. We put markings on them to show the number of quarterbacks sacked, or tackles made, or passes caught.

For some reason, we like to portray in some way what we have done. Soldiers display campaign ribbons and medals of honor on their uniforms. This "lettuce," as they call it, tells you what wars and battles they were in and what merits they received.

We are basically a show-off society. We like to show people what we can do. Actually, when we buy expensive cars we are in essence doing the exact same thing. The car is a campaign ribbon to show the world that the driver has achieved some status. It's also a way to establish position in society's hierarchy. While animals fight to establish the positions of hierarchy within their community, man shows his by displaying his accomplishments. If you are a primitive man, you wear markings on your shield. If you are a soldier, you wear ribbons on your chest. If you are a football player, you wear decals on your helmet. If you are a businessman, you have expensive cars and homes.

One of the dumb things coaches and other sports managers do is measure only how tall a guy is. It seems that the taller a player is the better they like him. But that's all wrong. The important thing about a player is not his height but his arm length and his hand size. Of all the sports, only boxing has it right. In boxing they measure the reach, because they know how important it is. Well, in every other sport arm length and reach are just as important. Consider this: One player might be six-eleven and with his arms up he reaches nine feet. The second player might be six-five but with his arms up reaches nine feet, three inches. The second player definitely has the advantage.

For this reason, I am always amused when people talk to me about Jerry West. They say, remember what he did against this guy or that guy, as if they can't believe a guy Jerry's height could dominate against taller players. The people talking about West fail to realize that West has extremely long arms. I am about nine inches taller than Jerry but we both wear about the same length shirtsleeve.

Large hands are also important in sports, especially basketball. Michael Jordan, Dr. J., and Connie Hawkins all have large hands. Elgin Baylor has the best hands I have ever seen for the game of basketball. Each can comfortably hold a basketball in one hand. This allows them to be more flexible on the court. Can you imagine Jordan doing what he does if he had to hold the basketball with both hands?

I *watch football* a lot, and there is one thing about the game that I have never been able to understand. I would like to ask all the brilliant football coaches jointly: When you are winning by the score of fourteen to seven with two minutes to go in the game and the other team has the ball, why in God's name do you go into a "prevent defense"?

I mean, you've held the opposing team to a single touchdown playing your regular game for almost four quarters. Now you're going to drop your defensive backs back and willingly give up ground at fifteen yards a pop to the other team, which is allowed to go out of bounds on every play or take time-outs?! The end result is that the opposing team is able to move the length of the field in less than ninety seconds. You have prevented nothing—except your own certain victory.

The prevent defense should be called the giveaway defense. It has to be one of the dumbest strategies in all of sports.

If *Magic Johnson* wants to represent his country by playing on the Olympic basketball team he should be allowed to do so. I believe that any professional who wants to play for his country should be allowed to, because the distinction between amateur and professional is a total joke.

Athletes like Carl Lewis, Jackie Joyner-Kersee, and Roger Kingdom are considered amateurs—and they make more money doing what they do than a lot of major league ballplayers. Tennis players like Chris Evert and Pam Shriver represented this country in the last Olympics, and I don't think we need to talk about *their* professional salaries.

The rules are finally changing in favor of what I'm talking about, which is as it should be. "Amateur" status for the Olympics should be completely abolished.

Besides, the fact that you are a professional doesn't mean that you can beat a world-class amateur anyway—or that you can even qualify for the Olympic team.

The Olympic Committee defines a pro as a person who makes money from his or her sport, even indirectly. Well, if that's so, it's time the Olympic Committee pulled their collective heads out of the sand. Edwin Moses, Carl Lewis, and Ben Johnson (three of *dozens*) have made *millions* from so-called amateur track and field events.

Amateur sports have always been controlled by dollars and cents. Even in *my* time, money was given under the table to players to entice them to go to various schools. Is this wrong? Look at the revenue athletes generate for those schools. Star quarterbacks, Heisman Trophy winners, an NBA number-one draft pick can bring in millions and millions of dollars to a university. It was said that I helped to build the Kansas Turnpike—they needed it, so people could come to Lawrence to watch me perform at KU. If this is true, they didn't pay me *nearly* enough money for my three years as a Jayhawk.

Basically, *the only* thing a third-base coach does in baseball is tell his players to stop or go. It's elementary—how much knowledge does it take? Al Campanis, when he was running the Dodgers, never had any black third-base coaches. Hey, Al, was that because niggers can't say stop? Or because they don't know when to go home?

I *used to* own polo ponies. I got involved in polo because I was not a great rider, and I thought riding polo ponies would help me to become a better equestrian. It was the single hardest thing I have ever tried to do in sports. Polo ponies are small, about fifteen hands—so I was bigger than any of my horses. This made me feel like the horse should have been riding me. Riding these ponies, I did learn to appreciate the art of polo, but cruelty to the animals drove me away from the sport.

It was amazing to me how harshly the horses were treated. In case you've never seen a game, a polo match is divided into periods called chukkers. These are like quarters in football and basketball. A chukker lasts seven and a half minutes, and the horses are driven so hard that no horse can play two successive chukkers, except in an emergency—like if one of your other five horses is too tired or too hurt or too dead to go on. The horse is 90 percent of the game, so you'd think the players would have more compassion for them. But polo players don't have the same attachment to their horses as Roy Rogers had with Trigger. The player's major concern is not the horse itself, but strictly how sound the animal is and how well he performs.

I guess it's a lot like professional sports. But I tend to feel we should treat animals better than we treat human athletes. Humans can, at least, make the choice to compete or not.

Have you checked out the route some winners have taken to win that brass ring? If you did, you would realize that everything imaginable can and does happen in sports competition. People will do *anything* to win these days, from cheating with steroids, which seems to be routine now, even accepted, to a lot more creative cheating. Take the case of Boris Onischenko, a soldier in the Russian Army, who was considered one of the very best fencers in the world. Boris was caught with his épée wired—an illegal electronic device was implanted in the tip of his épée so that he did not have to touch his opponent with it before scoring a point on the electronic scoreboard.

Sure, it's despicable. It perverts the entire concept of sports. But you can't just blame the athletes. Whole countries cheat nowadays. They put tremendous pressure on their judges and refs to favor their own contestants in the quest for Gold Medals. It's gotten so out of hand I can hardly believe what I've recently read. Before a recent Olympics, the Russians approached an American diving official and offered to have their official judge American divers favorably if the American judge would reciprocate for the Russian divers. It's sad, this belief that winning the brass ring is the ultimate reason for competing.

Sometimes the route to victory is based on luck. First, there's the luck of the draw. Look at the NBA or NFL playoffs. More often than not, one division is a lot stronger than the other. The winner of the stronger division has a real dogfight in every round while the winner of the weaker division breezes through its opposition. By the time the two teams meet for the championship series, one is plagued by injuries and overcome by fatigue while the other is raring to go. It seems unfair, but that's the way the ball bounces.

Then there is just plain luck—good or bad. It's not just injuries that make it impossible for a team or an individual to win. After the holocaust perpetrated by the Arab terrorists at the 1972 Summer Olympic games in Munich, the entire Israeli Olympic team withdrew from the games. One of their athletes was the favorite to win the women's 100-meter hurdles, the great Israeli runner Esther Rot. Johanna Schaller of East Germany won the event without any real competition. Good luck for one, and tragic bad luck for the other.

Sports heroes are today's gladiators. Almost from the beginning of time we seem to have had this need to see physical specimens do battle. Today it's in the name of sports; centuries ago it was in the name of something else. But it was and is still the same thing: the big guys knocking each other around, whether it's with a tennis racket, a hockey stick, a lance, or a spear. It's a slugfest out there, and we all live vicariously through it.

Why do you think the heavyweight boxing champion of the world is the most popular of all sports figures? He embodies what all athletic events are about: the biggest and the baddest punching out a weaker opponent.

Coaches have become bigger stars than the players and teams they represent and I think this has gotten way out of hand. The Tom Lasordas and Pat Rileys—and in some cases even owners like George Steinbrenner—can create a lot of animosity among players, other coaches, and management.

If the coach is wearing a five-thousand-dollar suit on the sideline, everyone starts wondering how much the suit cost, where he bought it, how it's cut, was it worth it, etc. The media hypes the coach's ensemble and the players consciously or subconsciously compare their threads with his. This is a distraction players don't need. The *good* coach—a Larry Brown or a Don Nelson—knows he shouldn't do anything to distract the team, especially at game time.

Nelson, the head coach of the Golden State Warriors, and Brown, head coach of the San Antonio Spurs, have proven to me that, with or without the best talent, they can produce competitive teams. Both coaches have strong beliefs and systems and they seem to get the best out of their stars, when they have any. If they don't, their team concept seems to work well in the pros. I would like to have played for either of them.

In college, John Wooden did an incredible job. He knew what to do with his talent. I do think he tended to close his eyes when it came to *getting* talent, though. John always claimed he didn't know about the payments his kids were getting under the table. Uh-huh. Hell, college kids *should* get paid to play sports. They bring in a lot of money to the school. A *lot* of money!

I went to the University of Kansas just because I respected their coach so much. He was Dr. Forrest C. Allen. He learned his basketball from a guy named Naismith—perhaps you've heard of him? Dr. Allen also taught Adolph Rupp and other great coaches. But I never had a chance to play for him. He reached retirement age after I picked the school—and the school forced him out. So I played for Dick Harp, who was a hell of a nice guy but someone who had no idea what top-level basketball was all about.

For me, coaches should be like referees. The less conspicuous they are, the better it is for all concerned. Nobody watches a sports event to see a coach. It's the athletes people care about. Somehow, in the past ten years or so, coaches—and even announcers—have gotten to think *they're* the stars. I promise you, the Lakers won't lose one fan because Riley left, CBS won't lose one viewer for their football games because Brent Musberger moved to ABC. Now, if Magic Johnson or Joe Montana retires . . .

B*oxing is the* one sport I love and hate at the same time.

Why do I love it? Because of the craftsmanship that all great fighters must have. A master boxer is an artist, a disciplined and creative artist. But the price they have to pay for their art is much too great, which is why I hate it, too. When I look back at my old boxing friends, I see them as magnificent creatures. To see them now, the way they are forced to live, not in control of all their faculties, I can only feel real pity. God rest the great Joe Louis and the late Sugar Ray Robinson, who were close friends of mine; in their latter days they had lost control of their own lives because of what boxing had done to their bodies and minds. Thank God they had people to love and take care of them in their time of need.

I find it hard to face the once so graceful and gifted Muhammad Ali and the sturdy, unmovable Joe Frazier. It's clear to me they stayed in that ever-demanding yet alluring ring much too long.

I know no one should be told not to do what they love when it's their choice and their body, but whether sports heroes like it or not they belong to us all. Nothing is more depressing than seeing someone who was once so magnificent reduced to mumbling and stumbling and, in the case of Ali, moving practically in slow motion. I hate to see greatness after it's fallen.

I don't know how many of you remember, but I was once supposed to fight Ali. A lot of people think that the proposed fight was a lot of hype, but it really almost came off.

The idea was put into my head by a guy named Jack Hurley, who did PR for the Globetrotters and also managed a few boxers. Hurley was a hustler, a dealmaker; he always had his finger in one pie or another. Well, Hurley thought I'd be a great pie for him to have a piece of and he was always telling me I should quit basketball and become a boxer. He managed a club fighter named Pete Rademacher, and Hurley actually got Rademacher a chance to fight for the heavyweight championship. Hurley said to me, "Rademacher couldn't beat my grandmother and I've got him fighting for the championship. Give me two or three fights—I promise no one'll lay a glove on you—and then you'll fight the champ."

It *sounded* great. But I had too much respect for the game of boxing to think it could possibly be that easy. I believed I could get the fight—but it would take a lot more than that if I was going to *win*. Also, I never really had any desire to hit anyone. *Getting* hit didn't bother me. But hitting someone to hurt him—shattering a nose, cutting a face—wasn't anything I ever wanted to do.

When Cus D'Amato (the man who guided Floyd Patterson and, later, Mike Tyson) became interested in me, though, that was different. Cus was well liked, well respected and he had respect for me and athletes in general. If Cus took me on, *his* rep would be on the line as well as mine. Cus didn't want a sideshow, he wanted the championship belt. And Cus thought I could beat Ali.

Cus always believed that basketball players had the right foot speed and agility to be good fighters. He also thought he could teach me how to fight and beat any single boxer in the world. He wasn't egotistical enough to think he could teach me the whole fight game, just how to fight one guy. In this case the one guy was Muhammad Ali. Cus said to me, "Remember, Ali will know *nothing* of what you can do and what I'm going to teach you to do. You'll know *all* of his strengths and weaknesses." That intrigued me, but there was some fear on my part. Not fear of pain or even losing, but fear of being embarrassed. When I related this to Cus he immediately told me that if I had no fear of fighting, he would not have wanted to coach me. So I decided to go ahead with the fight. My athletic ego decided for me. I wanted to beat Muhammad Ali and become heavyweight champion of the world.

In a closed room at the Houston Astrodome, Ali, his entourage, my lawyer, my accountant, and I sat down to sign contracts while close to a hundred press and television reporters waited outside for the announcement. That announcement never happened—we could not settle on my percentage of the ancillary rights. We were talking a *huge* amount of money for those days—five to ten million dollars apiece. *Everybody* wanted to see this fight—big, bad villain Wilt, maybe the world's best athlete, against "The Greatest," Muhammad Ali.

Who knows what would have happened? Perhaps I would have been the heavyweight champion of the world. Perhaps I would have had more fights, and perhaps it would have led to one of those bad endings I mentioned. If pushed to answer the question of who would have won, I think I would have. Ali may have been in over his head— and I wasn't the only one who thought this way. His manager, Herbert Muhammad, told him that I was "no palooka" and that he thought I could hurt Ali.

Of course, my father, that boxing expert and great Ali fan, contended that my best chance to beat Muhammad Ali was to challenge him to a free throw shooting contest—but only if I went out and practiced shooting right away.

Many *rules have* been changed to make sports seem safer today. Some people think these rules make the game better. I think they are absurd.

The "in the grasp" rule, created in professional football a few years ago to protect the quarterback, makes the quarterback look like a sissy. Football is one of those games that require a man to be a man in every sense of the word; installing that rule takes away from what the game is all about. A lot of the great quarterbacks of the past, and certainly some of them today, respond when they are in the grasp. They become elusive; their strength and agility, the things that helped make them great quarterbacks, come out stronger than ever. So when they are being held for a split second by a lineman and not given a chance to break free, elude that lineman, and throw the ball, it takes something away from their performance. It also takes something away from the game. I believe that until the quarterback is knocked to the turf, play should continue.

The "breakaway foul" is another rule that was adopted a few years ago, this one by the National Basketball Association to protect a player on a fast break. And it's another rule I dislike. It was conceived to protect the player with the ball from being hit from behind. If the offensive player is ahead of the defensive player on a break and has crossed the half-court line on his way to the basket, the defensive player cannot hit the offensive player. If the defensive player hits the offensive player, the offensive player gets the basket, if he makes it on his follow-through shot; he also gets one free throw—*and* his team gets the ball out of bounds. That gives an insane advantage to the offensive team, and completely stops the defensive player from trying to make any defensive move from the rear, like a block or steal. I remember chasing plenty of guys down and blocking a shot from behind, but the defensive player today has much too much to lose to try a maneuver like that. What that rule does, in my view, is keep potentially fantastic plays from ever happening.

What are they really saying with this rule, anyway? If they are afraid of the player getting hurt, then maybe you shouldn't be allowed to guard him from the front, either; you might put a finger in his eye. Guarding a player—from any side—is all a part of the game. A foul from behind is no different than a foul from the front if it's done in the spirit of the game. What difference does it make if the player is hit on his rear or on his belly?!

The only thing that doesn't belong in the game is when someone deliberately tries to hurt another player with a dirty, mean-spirited play. If a foul is flagrant and is done in an unsportsmanlike way, it doesn't matter *where* it comes from. And that's up to the ref to call.

And finally, please, please, *please* let's do away with instant replay to review calls. Think about how dumb it is, when you are allowed to review some plays and not others. You are allowed instant replay when a receiver or ball carrier is called out of bounds; then, another official far from the playing field tells you whether the call is good or bad. Anyone who knows anything about football knows that most of the action takes place on the line of scrimmage, where an infinite amount of things are going on, things that have at least as much to do with the outcome of the game as a receiver stepping out of bounds. Yet there is no instant replay allowed on the line play.

If in any game you can't run *everything* back, then why run *anything* back?

What makes instant replay even worse is that we viewers are forced to listen to all these announcers killing time during these delays, giving us their mostly idiotic opinions and telling us over and over again what we have just seen. I have been on the wrong end of a lot of calls but I still believe that human error, which goes with having a referee make a decision on the spot, beats any other choice. It definitely beats the second-guessing that comes with instant replay.

. . .

A *lot of* people think that the toughest thing to do in pro sports is to hit a baseball. That might be true, especially since I can't hit a baseball in batting practice—even though I fill up the entire batting cage and the ball is coming toward me at no miles per hour. So I can imagine that trying to hit Nolan Ryan's hundred-mile-per-hour fastball is pretty damn tough.

However, if I had to choose the toughest sport, bowling and golf included, it would have to be auto racing, the Indy 500 type. By far! Those drivers, my man, take their lives into their hands every time out. You need nerves of steel, reflexes of a cat, the concentration of *The Thinker* and— believe it or not—*tremendous* body conditioning. How else do you think you can deal with the heat and the uncomfortable position you're forced to sit in for the long period of time it takes to run a race?

Can you imagine going two hundred miles an hour, mere inches from a car going the same speed, and approaching a turn? You can have it! I'm chicken. Those guys definitely get my vote for bravest athletes.

It's *unfortunate what's* happening to kids today in the world of sports. More and more of them are watching sports and reading about sports in the papers, and because so much emphasis is put on the great amounts of money the Michael Jordans and the Magic Johnsons are making, the kids become enamored with the money. They fall in love with the money, not with the sport they're following.

I suppose it's natural for young people to dream of making millions of dollars and buying big cars and doing all the extravagant things they see on television. But they lose something when they do that, because if they only have love for the money and not the game itself, then when they don't make their college team or never get to the pros (and we know the odds are very high against that), they are double losers. They don't make the money and they don't experience the love that goes along with being a participant in a chosen sport. At a young age, the focus should be on the game, not the rewards. So if a kid doesn't make it along the way, whether it be in high school, college, or the pros, at least he won't feel like his efforts were wasted. At least he'll have spent his youth doing something he loved.

WILTISM

Love of money may come later on in life, but love of sports should come first.

It is amazing to me that people take it for granted that, when it comes to sports, if you're big you're able to do things better. Never has a thought been so far from the truth. Let me tell you that unless you are a seven-footer you don't have a *clue* about how things like body control, quickness, stamina, and speed are usually lacking. Those are *small* people's attributes.

And I haven't even mentioned the natural physical laws that totally work against you, like center of gravity. If you know anything about geometry and physics, you know the levers that so often work for you often work against big people. Can you imagine the force it takes to stop a falling redwood and how much easier it is to stop the falling of a small Christmas tree? Well, that's part of the problem a bigger person has to deal with in sports. If he makes the wrong move or loses his balance, correcting this is infinitely harder than it would be for a smaller athlete. That alone is enough to give a big edge to a smaller player or opponent.

There are so many more advantages in being of lesser body size in most sports.

Let's start with the sport that needs the ultimate in body control. What did I hear you say? I hope it was gymnastics, because the various gymnastic events require the use of almost all your major muscles, plus balance, strength, coordination, flexibility, reflexes, timing, and stamina—not to mention physical beauty. All of these are more often found in abundance in smaller body types. In gymnastics, we all know that if you are a female, being five feet tall is almost too tall. An ideal size for a male gymnast is about five feet, four inches.

Diving is another sport that requires a tremendous amount of body control. Tucking those arms and legs can be a hell of an obstacle if you are extremely tall. Skiers need that low center of gravity to negotiate those slalom courses; once again the great ones are never too tall. Most professional hockey players are well under six feet tall. Very tall baseball players have too big a strike zone to be effective. Wade Boggs and Kirby Puckett, two guys around five-eight, are the ones getting the most hits. (While checking my facts for this book, I found out that Boggs is actually six-two, not five-eight. The bad news is that those six inches don't make that much difference to me. From my vantage point, anyone under six-five *looks* five-eight!) In football your great running backs are more like the all-time leader in yards gained, Walter Payton—five foot eight or so, where their center of gravity is low.

It seems logical that if you have long legs you'd be able to cover distances more quickly, but you never see a marathon runner of any size at all—too much body to move, easier for muscles to fatigue. Look at the size of Joan Benoit. Some of the great male African runners barely weigh 115 pounds. That's just about what one of my *legs* weighs! All racing events seem more suited to smaller body types; even milers and sprinters are small and slight. I'd bet anything that if some seven-footer won a marathon you'd hear comments like, "Well, in two steps he's halfway around the course." They wouldn't realize he had just accomplished something that was far more difficult for him than for other competitors.

I consider ballet dancers to be the greatest of athletes. Check out the size of the tallest.

Now you ask, "What about basketball? Don't tell me the big guys don't have the advantage." It's all relative here too, my man. Take my old standby, Manute Bol, now of the Philadelphia 76ers. As I've said, he's seven feet, seven inches, the tallest player in the NBA. You would think at that size he would be, if nothing else, a good rebounder, but almost every man in the league, some close to one and a half feet *shorter* than Bol, outrebounds him. Bol possesses few of the physical attributes that make a good athlete; for him to get up and down the court is a real hassle. Michael Jordan is half a foot to a foot shorter than many of the guys he plays against, but he's gifted with all the attributes he needs to make him one of the very best ever at his game. Though he may be a physical giant in the world outside of professional basketball, in the confines of his game he is relatively small. Therefore, to many, his feats seem even more amazing than they are—and are more appreciated than if these feats were done by someone a lot taller (like me, for instance).

I believe the real underdog in sports, the one that is not truly appreciated or given his or her due, is the person with the awesome size who is not blessed with the right physical attributes. He or she should be the one cheered the most. These tall people are handicapped more than the average person can see or know. Not till you are a seven-footer can you really understand how hard it is to do an "iron cross" on the gymnastics rings, or to negotiate a slalom course on the hills of Aspen, or even to just roller skate. How about a simple pull-up on a chinning bar? Which do you think is easier—lifting 150 pounds the length of a two-foot arm span or lifting 300 pounds over four feet? The next time all your applause is given to the 80-pound, four-foot, eight-inch bundle of dynamite on the balance beam, remember that *she* is the one with all the advantages, not that five-foot, five-inch gangling young lady having a hard time doing those cartwheels.

WILTISM

There are not enough people in the world who are willing to give you a lift without taking you for a ride.

Do you ever wonder why the guy who possesses the best jumping ability or is the fastest or strongest—or, in the case of basketball, the tallest—is not always the one to produce in the manner you would expect? It's because these special attributes, which seem to be favorable for his sport, can sometimes be a negative.

When the athlete is faster, stronger, or taller than his

opponent he depends on these attributes; more often than not the athlete relies on them *too much*. As a result, these natural attributes keep the athlete from becoming more diverse, more of a complete player. When the athlete moves up against stronger competition, which usually happens when you move from high school to college and again from college on to the pros, he finds that he needs more than one or two of the attributes he's always coasted by with. He finds himself at a loss. On the other hand, a person who was not so blessed hones all of his skills from the beginning of his career. Without ingenuity he would have never made it from high school to college—never mind the pros.

These are the things that give parity and sometimes the edge to those lacking in natural ability. Larry Bird and Dominique Wilkins are classic examples. You would think that the high-flying Dominique would have a rebounding edge over the nonjumping Bird. The opposite is true. Bird has a far better rebounding average than Dominique. Why? One of them always thinks his jumping ability is enough; the other knows he has to do something else to get that ball.

In football the fastest guy is not necessarily the best receiver. Just look at Steve Largent of the Seattle Seahawks. He holds many receiving records yet was one of the slowest receivers in pro football.

When no one thought he had a chance, Muhammad Ali beat a much stronger Sonny Liston for the heavyweight championship of the world. Ali had to be a more complete boxer because Liston was as strong as a gorilla. (Ali called him that, not me.)

The most important thing in sports is not necessarily

being faster, taller, or stronger. By being creative and wiser you'll last much longer.

Maybe the Olympic motto should be changed from *citius, altius, fortius*—which means swifter, higher, stronger—to extol ingenuity, intelligence, and perseverance.

Perhaps you will translate that into Latin for me. I can't do everything, my friend.

T*o me, baseball* players seem to have lost the magic. There are many players with credentials that should make them more embraceable stars, players like Wade Boggs, Darryl Strawberry, Dave Stewart, José Canseco, and on and on, but none of these guys seem to have fun while playing the game. If they *are* having fun, they sure as hell don't pass that enjoyment right off the playing field and on to us, the fans. Not the way Willie Mays and Mickey Mantle did.

I believe money has changed the game and taken the fun out of it. Baseball has become *such* a big business there is simply no room for it to be a fun game anymore. What does the word "game" represent? The dictionary says a game is a way of amusing oneself, a pastime, a diversion. The players today get so much money for what they do and have so much pressure on them that they cannot be light-hearted. The only time you ever see smiles is when they win that last big game. And that smile is more a smile of relief than of joy.

I*t should be* obvious, but to many it's not, that the accruing of big numbers in sports, like rushing yards in football or rebounding and scoring in basketball, takes more of a concentrated effort than those glorious numbers imply. Often the label of being a selfish player—a gunner—is given to players who amass large totals. It is assumed that if you are a great scorer you must be a gunner. Well, what about the label "hard worker" rather than gunner? To consistently attain big numbers takes a great effort. If you are a scorer for your team you must outplay the defenses that are put up against you, sometimes two or three men on one. It would be easier for many of the scorers to just pass the ball off to someone else, but they take it upon themselves because they know it is their role to put the ball in the basket or the end zone. This requires a great deal of energy and effort on their part.

This can be seen clearly when watching a football game. A running back who normally carries the ball fifteen or twenty times a game must carry it thirty or thirty-five times when the game is on the line, the way O. J. Simpson did. When they carry the ball that many times their body and their will takes a great beating, because the defenses key on them. The same is true in basketball, but the player who is carrying the load usually gets the reputation of a gunner.

The next time you hear a basketball player scored fifty points, remember it's not just gunning that got the guy his points. In most cases he was just doing a lot more work than anyone else on the court. Give him credit for being a hard worker, not a gunner.

After all, many athletes will not work hard on offense *or* defense to give their team a lift. They just coast along with numbers that they can live with, numbers the fans are happy to accept as the best the athlete can do. Only the athlete knows he hasn't given his all; unfortunately, the greater the talent, the harder this is for us to recognize.

After a game you look at the stats and see a star player got twenty-five points and ten rebounds and you think he did a good day's work. But *did* he? When these numbers are put in the context of what he can really do, is he really doing enough?

I *say Division I* universities should offer vocational training for scholarship athletes. I also think that technical schools should be allowed to play on the same level as the NCAA Division I schools.

There is a great need in this country for more master plumbers, electricians, carpenters, etc., and this kind of education would be a lot more beneficial for many of these athletes who have no desire to become lawyers, doctors, or Indian chiefs. Besides, these vocations earn more money than your average lawyer, anyway. You've got to be realistic and practical. Athletes are now forced to take curriculums they care nothing about and, realistically, a lot of athletes attend major universities only to play sports and to get in a position to make it to the pros. They are not really interested in what is taught and they will never ever have a chance to use the abstract education they had no desire for in the first place.

Vocational studies, either at a Division I school or at a technical school playing at the Division I level, would give them some real meat, so when they don't make that professional team—which 99 9/10 percent won't—they would truly have something to fall back on. If they could come away from the university as a master plumber or electrician or contractor or carpenter they would truly have marketable skills and a chance to make a decent living.

. . .

We generally make too much of winning. Let's face it, someone always has to win; that is the nature of competition. But the mere fact of winning doesn't make you great.

We've had a Kentucky Derby each year since 1875 and each year we've had a winner. Does that mean all the winners were great horses? No. It doesn't even mean the winner was the best three-year-old of that crop. It just means for that moment in time (about two minutes), at that track, that horse was the best. Every horse in a particular race could have been lousy, but the winner still gets his name in the record book. And that winner is compared to all the winners of the past and will be compared to all future winners.

How do you compare past and present winners? Well, in horse racing, running times, track conditions, how many lengths the horse won by will be brought into the equation. The ultimate winner is usually the horse that holds the track record. But what does that really mean? The track record could have been set in a four-horse field, while other races that were timed close to the track record could have come in a twelve-horse field—where there was a lot of bumping. Track records don't take gate positions into consideration either. So things that *seem* definitive and objective aren't always.

A horse might be the winner of the Kentucky Derby and the Preakness, but if he becomes a lousy stud horse he may not be considered as great as one of his contemporaries that didn't win at all but in later life became a magnificent sire.

One year's winner may not have been able to beat the last-place finisher of years gone by, even when the clock might show otherwise. In an Olympic mile the contestants might decide to run a tactical race, emphasizing pacing and position. Let's say the winner wins in four minutes and two seconds, a slow race these days. Well, that's not indicative of how fast any of the contestants can run. He might not be a fast runner at all, but he won and he'll go down in history as the winner. He might not have been close to the last-place runner in the previous Olympics, yet that man is looked on as a loser.

The same is definitely true in team sports. Is the 1972 Lakers world championship team better than the 1988 Lakers championship team? If you compare them, one of those teams will have to be a loser. The Boston Celtics may have won eleven world championships, but when they were comparing the best NBA basketball teams of all time recently, two teams that I was fortunate enough to be on were voted one and two: the 1967 76ers and the 1972 Lakers. Ultimately that makes me the winner. Or does it? You may be a winner today but by tomorrow you may be just an also-ran. And vice versa.

Society is too quick to say that certain winners are great or even the best ever. The best competitor does not always win. On any given day a miracle can happen; the worst can actually beat the best. Winning a game or series does not necessarily mean anything more than this: *Someone had to win.*

What I am trying to say is that too much is made of winning, and contrary to what a lot of us think, that's not what sports is really all about. How do you really gauge what a winner is, when there are so many variables that determine who won or lost? Simple! The ultimate winners are the ones who are doing the best they can do all the time. Yesteryear you were asked, "How did you play?" Today, more often than not we now hear the bottom-line question, "Did you win?" I say the real question is, "Did you give it all you had?" To me, that is the only criterion that makes you a winner.

Here's another example of the variables that determine winners. I can't help wondering how far Jesse Owens would have jumped on a Tartan track at an altitude of five thousand feet if he'd made enough money from his sport to keep him in training all year round. Would the record books show how superior he really was? They sure don't now.

The majority of people enjoy watching men play various sports more than watching women play the same sport. That's because most events were invented to showcase a man's greatest attributes: speed, strength, quickness, and size. But I can get as much—and sometimes more—from watching world-class females competing.

To those who think women's sports are inferior because the pace is slower, I say at least you're able to see what the hell you're watching. I mean, do you really get ecstatic watching Nolan Ryan throw a fastball a hundred miles an hour that neither you nor the batter can see? I love it when people say, "Did you see that fastball?" Of course they didn't, but they won't admit it. In men's sports, all we see is the end result, the umpire calling a strike, the red light flashing behind the goal in hockey, the scorekeeper changing the totals as the tennis players switch to the other side of the court.

Watching women's tennis and women's volleyball, you

get a chance to see what the game is all about. You get to appreciate the nuances of the game.

When a player like Boris Becker serves at 130 miles per hour, the guy he's serving to can't see the ball, so how the hell can you see it from twenty rows up? You have a hard time trying to figure out what's going on, because before the play starts it's over. You can enjoy tennis *much* more when watching the women. You can watch their techniques and learn from their styles and shot selections.

Am I saying that men's games should be slowed to be better? No. I am saying that some things are better enjoyed at a slower pace—sex and food are two examples that come immediately to mind.

My suggestion is that some of you smart women who have your Ph.D.'s in physical education invent a game that gives the edge to the female. Create a game that would incorporate grace and style instead of speed. Instead of strength, balance. Instead of jumping ability, flexibility. Use endurance, something women have an abundance of. Their greater threshold of pain has been proven, so use that. Now just add a twist or two like gymnastics did with the balance beam and you have the makings of a sport that men may have to take a backseat in, yet would still be as entertaining to men as games like football and baseball.

Come on, women, do some thinkin'. It's out there.

Allow me to say one more thing about women and sports:

Women in general should give more support to women athletes. If women would go see Steffi Graf and Martina Navratilova in the same numbers they go see Boris Becker and Andre Agassi, women tennis players would receive their due. Until women go to the women's events, the men will always be in the forefront. Women should say, "Hey, I want to go see the women's NCAA basketball finals or swimming finals." Have more confidence in yourselves, ladies!

As *I said* earlier, basketball has peaks and valleys. Well, other sports do, too, and boy, right now my favorite specta-tor sport, women's tennis, is at a peak. The females are getting better and better and better. I thought Billie Jean King was the best that would come along during my time, but before I could turn around came the unflappable Chris Evert, who was so steady and so good that she made the game look as easy as one-two-three. She attracted millions to the game as players and fans.

When Chris gave way to the dominance of Martina Nav-ratilova, I'm sure most tennis buffs thought no one *but no one* would ever dominate the game like she could. Well, say hello to the number-one player in the world today, Steffi Graf! She's young, strong, ambitious, and has a desire to win like few athletes I've ever seen.

And yet, as I'm sitting here writing this, I'm watching the Berlin Open, and Steffi Graf is being shellacked by sixteen-year-old Monica Seles, who is all of 115 pounds. And guess what, Monica? How are you going to like playing fourteen-year-old sensation Jennifer Capriati in another year or so?

I find it gratifying to know that these incredible athletes are getting to the top by virtue of their own will, hard work, and good coaching. You know that drugs have played no part in their development; you know that there were no steroids or other drugs involved in making Monica Seles or Jennifer Capriati what she is, even though they both now hit the ball harder than many men. The same sure can't be said when you look at the bodies in track and field, football, and wrestling, where steroids are practically as much a staple as Gatorade.

There is no room in sports for drugs of any type. The sad thing is that many athletes were and are administered these banned substances by their coaches and doctors and other authorized officials with their teams. It not only is dishonest, it can be a real tragedy for the clean athlete who's forced to compete in the shadows of these drug users. The clean athlete has only two choices: become a drug user and compete on an equal basis, or quit and never have a chance to realize his dream. It's sad.

Steroids are used to grow larger muscles; they strengthen you and give you quicker, more explosive power. Most of your star basketball players don't need and don't use this kind of strength. They use quickness, agility, touch, footwork, and hand-to-eye coordination. These skills are not enhanced by the use of steroids; hence few, if any, basketball players use them.

In the old days people would have said, "All this just for a Gold Medal?" But today, Gold Medals often lead to a golden life—commercials, endorsements, jobs, hundreds of thousands, even millions, of dollars. There are people who will sell their souls to win one. Compared to your soul, I guess taking drugs is nothing if you think you can get away with it.

One of the things I've felt proudest about since my stint in the NBA is my involvement in volleyball and track and field. I helped to form the IVA, the International Volleyball Association. I toured the United States and the world with my four-man volleyball team. We challenged six-man teams all over the world and helped bring recognition to the sport. Since then, team volleyball has become very strong in this country—we won Gold Medals in the last two Olympics. I'm not trying to take any of the credit for that, but I do know we gave some of the guys on the Olympic team inspiration and the desire to become better players. I feel very good about that.

I also feel good about some of the track and field teams that I had a chance to sponsor and be involved with, from coaching to cheerleading. I had a team that we called Wilt's Wonder Women, and then I sponsored a team called Wilt's Athletic Club, which boasted a roster of Gold-Medal talent like Jackie Joyner-Kersee and the now-famous Flo-Jo, Florence Griffith Joyner. Some of the guys on the team went on to win medals in the Olympics, like André Phillips—gold in the 400-meter hurdles—and Greg Foster, the great hurdler. Bob Kersee was the coach. (He's the one who created the slogan "Where there's a Wilt, there's a way.")

Track and field has always been close to my heart, and to see these great people go from hard-working, relatively unknown athletes to world-renowned stars has been gratifying and heartwarming.

We have all heard these would-be cute announcers and color commentators say about a one-sided game, "It's a massacre" or "They were scalped." "Put all the wagons in a circle," is another one they use, like they're witnessing a frontier war with the Indians. I think these phrases overreach the limits of good taste.

To insensitive announcers using Indian metaphors such

as scalping and massacre, I say, what if we started using images and terms of the Holocaust when describing how teams get beaten? That would sure as hell be considered bad taste, wouldn't it? If you agree, then you've got to agree that using terminology of Indian massacres is also in bad taste. There's no place in sports for that.

I *have spent* a good deal of my life traveling the world to watch sporting events, venturing to six continents to get "up close and personal" at great events. I've been to the Australian Tennis Open in Melbourne, the first world track and field championships in Dusseldorf, the World Games in Finland, the great summer basketball leagues in Harlem and Philadelphia. I went to Boca Raton to watch Jennifer Capriati play her first professional match. I've been fortunate to watch some of the great fights of our time, from bullfights in Spain to the wars between Sugar Ray Leonard and Thomas "Hit Man" Hearns in Las Vegas.

(If being famous has any benefits it's that not only have I been at these events, I've gotten the best seats in the house. Even when there weren't supposed to be any seats left.)

At the Goodwill Games in Seattle, I was reminded of the single greatest athletic performance I ever saw. I attended the gymnastics event and was seated next to none other than Nadia Comaneci, the legendary Romanian gymnast. Yes, I was one of the lucky ones to be at the Montreal Olympics in 1976, when Nadia scored the first "10" in Olympic history. That was the greatest performance I have ever witnessed. In any sport. How could it not be? How often do you see perfection?

. . .

While *I was* at the Goodwill Games I also got involved with a sport that I only knew a little about and had never seen in person, but I immediately fell in love with it. It's called team handball, and it's not anything like the handball we Americans play, hitting a small ball against a wall. Team handball is played on a court about the size of a basketball court and the goal is like the one used in ice hockey. There are six players to a team plus a goaltender. The object is to create a mismatch by constantly dribbling and passing the ball. When you get an opening, you fire the ball at the goal. Because the ball is much smaller than a basketball it can be held in one hand and thrown overhand, very hard, or bounced at the net. The size of the player is not relevant. There is a line about ten feet from the mouth of the goal that the player cannot cross if he has the ball. The ball may be fired at the goal from anywhere behind that line. The player may, when making his shot, dive at the goal if he releases the ball before he crosses the line. Team handball is similar to soccer, it has a lot of basketball elements to it, and it has the toughness of water polo. I love its perpetual movement and contact. If you've ever seen Australian football on TV, that'll give you an idea of what this sport is like.

I am told that team handball is the second most popular sport in the world behind soccer. Consider this an announcement that I am personally going to get involved to make it better known in America.

There is a typical Catch-22 with this game. Like me, *everyone* who sees the sport falls in love with it. It really is one of the great spectator sports of all time. To become popular, all it needs is to be viewed on television. But TV only airs sports with rich corporate sponsors, and rich corporate sponsors only lend their names to events with built-in large TV audiences.

Still, volleyball has managed to become a pretty big sport in this country over the past twenty years. Maybe we can do the same for team handball. Check for a chance to watch it firsthand in your area. I am sure you'll love it as much as I do.

T*here are a* few athletes I've never met—or, at least, never had the opportunity to talk to the way I'd really like. Here are a few questions I'd like to ask:

To John "Cadillac" Williams of the Cleveland Cavaliers (who's called, of all things, "Hot Rod") and Jon Koncak of the Atlanta Hawks: Do you guys kiss your agent every time you see him, or do you really believe you're worth any- where *near* what your contracts say you are?

To all the defenders who guard Magic Johnson: How many more years will it take for you to learn when he (Magic) looks one way he almost invariably passes the basketball the other way?

To James Worthy: Why three hours before a game with those ladies of the night? Why not *after* the game?

Buster Douglas: How does anybody in his right mind report grossly overweight for the biggest fight and pay- check in the history of sports and with the potential of making it even *bigger* on your next fight? (His manager and trainers should have been shot, unless they are all from the Ray Charles School for the Blind.)

To whoever it is that advises Muhammad Ali to make various personal appearances that leave people in a state of shock and disbelief when they see how really sick he is (and how little of what he was is left): Why not give Ali a chance to live his life out in a more dignified way and allow people to remember him as the great champ he was? I don't think these appearances are his own choice because I no longer think he can make choices on his own.

Bill Russell: Why do you find it so hard to apologize to me for that statement you made about me some twenty-odd years ago, that you later admitted was made in error? Bill, we all make mistakes—or, in basketball terms, we've all taken a shot we shouldn't have. For those of you who don't remember, after a championship series in which Bill's Celtics beat my Lakers, I sat out much of the fourth quarter—I was *taken* out. Russell was asked, in a postgame interview, why I wasn't put back in the game and, infuriated, he said, "I would never have *left* the game with anything less than a broken back." As if I *wanted* to sit down, as if I didn't *want* to play! I was furious. Years later, Bill admitted—but not to me—that his comment was out of line. Someone asked him if he'd ever apologized to me and he said, "No, I can't apologize. I'm not that kind of guy."

Kareem: I haven't read your letter to me yet, but I hope it helped you to sell a lot of books as I am sure that's why it was there. But why, if you were going to use me to make money, didn't you at least send me a free copy?

On Others: Ordinary People

In this chapter I would like to offer some of my thoughts about all you down there—the things you say and do, the trials and tribulations you endure—as seen from up here.

The respect and adulation we give people who can speak well is dangerous. The loquacious talkers of this world seem to take the forefront and become our leaders whether they are qualified or not. Hitler almost ruled the world because he could bring people to a frenzy with his oratory skills. DJs have power, pimps control girls because they can talk. It doesn't matter that they are talking shit because people are so auditorily oriented.

Remember the big debates between Kennedy and Nixon? Nixon was ahead in all the polls until they had the debates, when Kennedy passed him. It wasn't because of *what* they said, it was because of *how* they said it. Kennedy was perceived as the better speaker, even if Nixon was saying the better things.

WILTISM

Talk is cheap, but what they are saying can cost me more than I want to spend.

People will play Lotto even though they know that the odds of winning are thirteen million to one. We all believe that we will win. Yet it is a proven fact that one out of three people will suffer from some form of mental illness, and no one is willing to believe it will ever happen to him.

WILTISM

(Not mine but good)

Luck beats a shotgun.

When I get a little full of myself and feel like I'm really clever, I turn on the TV and watch the program *Jeopardy*. That brings me down real fast. I can't believe that all these average-looking people are so damn smart. They have a way of making me feel *very* uninformed.

I often wonder if this program could be rigged, but then I realize that even if they gave me all the answers ahead of

time I couldn't possibly recall them or respond in the al-
loted time. Are there *really* people out there who are that
well versed in so many areas? And if so, why do they seem
to have such mundane jobs? They should be making millions putting all that wisdom to use.

I guess wisdom isn't worth very much these days.

People often complain that they are bored. I guess I've
been lucky because I have never been bored in my whole
life. I believe that people who are bored are in truth boring
people. If you are not boring you can always find something interesting to do. Bored people should look inside
themselves.

In many ways, people are like cattle: They are easily led.
They are certainly led by the dates on the calendar. Come
the Fourth of July the beaches are loaded with people,
whether the weather is hot or not. Then Labor Day rolls
around, the official end of the beach season, and everyone
leaves the beach. It doesn't matter that September is usually the best time to be at the beach—the weather's perfect,
the parking is usually free, the beaches aren't crowded and
the bugs have gone—they'll remain relatively empty, just
because the official date for swimming and sunning has
passed.

People should not be slaves to dates, especially fab-
ricated ones. We should give gifts, have feasts, and cele-
brate whatever we want whenever the urge moves us. Like
nature, we should be more in tune with the seasons, not
dates on a calendar.

WILTISM

If everyone was as smart as they think they are, all of us would be average.

Our bodies are like great memory machines that crave whatever we condition them to. The human body wants whatever we give it, good or bad. It doesn't care. That's why we have dope addicts, smokers, people who must have coffee to wake up, people who must run five miles a day or get eight hours of sleep a night . . . all these things are filed away in the memory machine, and we become slaves to them.

Here's what I mean. To quench your thirst as a kid you wanted milk, juice, or some soft drink. Your body knew nothing about alcohol, so it didn't ask for a beer; that came later, only *after* you decided to introduce it to your body. I used to wonder how priests and nuns could be abstinent and be so happy about it. I thought such a powerful urge (or two) had to creep in sometime. I know now that if the body has never experienced sex, it doesn't crave it. Certainly not in the same way. If you can abstain through puberty you can live quite happily without it, because the body will have no memory of it. If you start running five miles a day consistently and then stop, your body will feel bad, even though you'd think it would enjoy the rest. It remembers running and that's what it craves.

As a player I would shoot around every day. When I missed a day of practice my body would feel unfulfilled; it cried out for that basketball.

The memory machine can be reprogrammed, but it is much harder to undo than to do.

Ask anyone in AA.

☞ WILTISM ☜

Everything is habit-forming, so make sure what you do is what you want to be doing.

To make our politicians better leaders, I believe we need a school for them, like medical schools and law schools. Great chefs go to school, veterinarians go to school, so if a person, no matter what age, wants to be a politician he should have to be admitted to an accredited politician's school.

I'm not talking about being a political science major at a university, I'm talking about a school that is as hard to get into as a leading medical school. The political aspirants would have to study things like summit meetings and balancing a budget, all the things that presidents and congressmen have to know.

When he gets his sheepskin we'd know whether he graduated summa cum laude or at the bottom of the class. A candidate for office could show you what he has done in school, not just talk a lot of bullshit. He could say, "My specialty was foreign affairs, and I graduated in the top ten of my class."

Doesn't that sound better? I know it would help me choose who to vote for. After all, would you choose a doctor who graduated in the bottom ten of his class? Come on, no one wants the bottom ten of anything.

You should never have your doctor as a personal friend. Doctors should always be someone you look up to, someone who you only talk to about things you know nothing about. They should be held in reverence. You should go to his office and say "Yes, sir" and "No, sir" to whatever he says, and then get the hell out of there.

If we fraternize with them away from the office, we might learn that they do stumble, that they had a bad forehand and they slice on the golf course, that they drive an automobile like they never took a driving lesson in their life. You'd say, "Wow, that's my doctor, and he has my life in his hands." Better that he retains a personal mystique. Don't cloud your opinion of him as a doctor with your opinion of the real person. Doctors should remain regal.

Lawyers, on the other hand, are a different story. Most of us are willing to view lawyers as assholes. That's because lawyers *are* very much like assholes. Both are necessary, even if both are usually full of shit. (Sorry, Sy.)

I *never could* understand how some white people can be so proud of their black and Mexican nannies, then refuse to let their children fraternize with or marry blacks or Mexicans when they come of age. Children are taught to love and respect their nannies. These children spend more time in their formative years with them than they do with their parents. Then when they reach the age to start dating, blacks, Mexicans, and other minorities suddenly become taboo. It has to be confusing and frustrating to be forced to deal with such contradictions.

Am I glad I never had to have a nanny.

A *lot of* people work very hard to be average. They don't want to be different, to stick out. I think it's a big mistake.

The most alluring characteristics a person can have are those features that makes him different from the norm and exotic to others. Most people find these differences appealing. The infatuation the Japanese have with blondes is an example. Men of color in Scandinavia have the same appeal. You hear guys say they love a particular girl's accent. What he is really saying is that she sounds different.

If you're different it doesn't matter who you are; you have a real advantage because people will be attracted to you. Opposites do attract. Being different is one of the reasons I love being over seven feet tall. I know I'm something most people are not.

In this country we don't seem to want to give anything to anyone who already has something going for them. Western man seems to allow you only one natural gift. If you're multitalented you have a difficult time gaining true recognition for anything but your primary talent.

For instance, people think good-looking women can't act. If Farrah Fawcett is gorgeous, then she can't act. No one ever questions the ability of a not-so-gorgeous girl to act.

That same mentality keeps most of us from finding good-looking people funny. We find a Phyllis Diller or some fat comic entertaining; we'll give them their due without hesitation. Most successful comedians are unattractive and we laugh at what they say because that's the only thing they have going for them; they are no threat to our ego. But good-looking people have enough going for them, so we don't want to add more fuel to their fire by acknowledging that they have talent, too. It's true of athletes, too. How many times have you heard people say, when they hear a jock sing, "As a singer he'd make a hell of an athlete"?

I find this attitude grossly unfair. If people can do more than one thing well, more power to them.

People *lie to* me all the time. Or, should I say, they lie *about* me. Sometimes I even catch them:

I once flew in from Europe and caught a cab from JFK to Manhattan. En route the cabdriver started talking to me. "Man, you're really tall, but I had a guy in my cab that was taller than you."

I said, "Oh yeah?"

The cabbie replied, "He was a basketball player. You probably heard of him—Wilt Chamberlain."

"I've heard of him," I said.

The cabbie went on: "And what a cheap son-of-a-bitch he is."

I said, "Oh?" Now, I had never seen this guy before and had never been in his cab before that day. But I didn't say anything.

Then the cabbie says, "Yeah. He talked all this big ol' stuff and when he got to his hotel he gave me a crummy fifty-cent tip."

"Wow, no kidding!" I said. When I got to my hotel I didn't have fifty cents so I gave him a dollar and asked for change. He gave me four quarters and I handed him fifty cents.

People *may lie* about me, but it's because they remember my name. Even when it's not me, they think it is. I've almost never been mistaken for anyone else, but a lot of tall people are often mistaken for me. Ask Bill Russell. He's called "Wilt" all the time, and boy, does it burn him.

The most recent example is when I was asked to do an episode of *Miami Vice* a little while back. The money was good, and the people were fine, but I respectfully declined and told them no thank you. I later heard that I was replaced by Russell.

Much later on I met an actor from the show at a tennis tournament. (Not one of the stars, not Don Johnson or Philip Michael Thomas, but one of the next level of actors.) And he tells me, "When Bill Russell did the show, I accidentally called him 'Wilt' a number of times. It was an honest mistake—I don't know about basketball, I don't know who Bill Russell is. I know Wilt. So I thought it was a natural slip. I apologized every time I did it, but it didn't help.

"Boy, was he pissed!"

People are starting to reevaluate me from a personal standpoint, not just professional. Several columnists have written lately that I'm not the villain I was made out to be during my playing years. They've also written that perhaps Bill Russell wasn't the hero he was supposed to be. I wonder what has made people change their minds, especially since Russell hasn't been in the public eye much lately. The question I have is: Twenty years after Bill retired, and seventeen years after I retired, why is this coming out now?

I am not sure I have the answer. Is it because cream always rises to the top eventually? Or that things always come around in the end?

. . .

B*ack on the* subject of lies, I admit that, on occasion, I like to tell little harmless lies. I tell them mainly when others ask me what I consider to be dumb questions, but sometimes I do it just to give vent to my sarcastic side.

Years ago when I was in Europe traveling with the Globetrotters, people, mostly Americans, would stop us and ask, "What are you doing here? Are you playing basketball?" Instead of saying yes, I'd reply, "We're musicians with the Count Basie Band." After all, if you were of color and in Europe in those days you were either a basketball player, a member of Count Basie's Band, or in the army. And as I told you earlier, we were all too tall for the army.

WILTISM

NIKE: "Just do it."
WILT: "I didn't know you needed sneakers to do it."

I am sure that in one way or another we've all been faced with this feeling. You know the one: If you're a jock and you get hurt and the team has to play without you, do you really root for your team to do well or do you hope that they don't, because in winning it may show all concerned that you're dispensable?

You may have this same feeling when you break up with a girlfriend or wife. You may wish them well, but not *too* well—because you want them to feel that you're needed and that you did count for something.

Here's another: have you ever felt guilty after you heard about a plane crash or a train wreck, and you smiled or gave a sigh of relief because you were not on that plane or train?

All these feelings come from our desire for self-preservation and our need to be needed. I'm convinced that these are natural feelings, but they are often confused with personal greed and lack of caring for others. I feel, on the contrary, that when we strive to be the best it's only another way of protecting our position. No one wants to be mediocre, yet many find it wrong to want to be better than others.

WILTISM

Equality, as it's often said, should be for all
But the need to survive will make many an equal fall.

When the television camera pans the stands at a sporting event you see grown men wearing dresses and lipstick. You see supposedly sane people doing all kinds of ridiculous things and waving silly signs just to be seen on television.

I know girls who seem shy, bashful, and introverted. But the moment you pull out a camera, "WOW!" off their clothes come. It can be a TV camera, a still camera, it doesn't matter. There doesn't even have to be film in it. It's all about that camera.

It's time we took a look at what this is all about. Whether it's sports, show business, or whatever, that camera has a way of making a fool out of all of us. It probably all started when the first photographer said, "Smile at the birdie," even though you really wanted to cry. We've been acting silly in the presence of a camera ever since.

What is the most influential thing an individual can have in our society? What do you think is the most outstanding feature a normal person can have that will get him the most attention? Fame? Power? Money?

No. It's hair.

Think about Michael Jackson before he went to the jerry-curl. What was Farrah Fawcett's most memorable feature? (That is, if you haven't seen her swimsuit poster.) The Beatles changed a whole generation, but they did it first with their long hair and bangs; the influence of their music came later.

Hair had a great deal to do with the massive appeal of Elvis, and before that who can forget Shirley Temple's golden curls?

Why is it that every major newscaster and sportscaster has a great head of hair? I mean, many of them are forty-five and fifty years old, or older, and they've *all* got great hair.

All leading men in the movies have great heads of hair, unless they purposely shave their heads, which when you think about it also makes an overt hair statement and adds to the hair mystique—Telly Savalas, Lou Gossett, Jr., and Yul Brynner are three prime examples.

All the spokespersons for major products have hair. Brian Bosworth's whole mystique was based on his hair— he was really just an average pro linebacker with a blond "high-fade" that made him a star. Would the Seattle Seahawks have paid him as much if he wore his hair like the average Joe (and I don't mean Joe Montana)? Would he have made the Right Guard commercial?

Think about rock groups and hate groups (like skin-heads). They also make statements with their hair—or lack thereof.

Even our former president, Ronald Reagan, will be re-membered for his hair.

Is no one balding out there? Or have we just kept them out of the competition? If so, that is not hair—I mean, not fair.

🖝 WILTISM 🖜

(actually, just a joke I like that happens to be about hair)

The little black boy kneeled down and asked God why his hair was so tight and matted and nappy.

The voice of God spoke, "My son, your hair is that way for protecting you against the strong African sun."

The little boy replied, "But God, I live in Cleveland."

Sometimes other people have it all wrong, as I see it.

When I go to places like Sun Valley and Aspen I see more drunk people, more dopers, more people abusing their bodies than I see in any of the large cities of this country. Yet, when these same people ask me where I'm living these days, and I say Los Angeles, to a person they want to know how I can live in all that pollution.

Who's the more polluted? Why, in the midst of all this natural beauty, would a person want to get drunk and high every night? A few years ago I read where Casper, Wyo-ming, another beautiful place, was the number-one area in the country for infidelity, alcoholism, and suicide.

Majestic natural beauty obviously isn't enough. By the same token, large cities are not so bad after all. It's not really the location that matters.

People interreacting with each other is what keeps us healthy.

 **WILTISM**

Common sense costs nothing, but if you use it you can make a mint.

On Life:
Things That Piss Me Off

Even though I have this view from above, and therefore should be above all the petty things that go on down there, there are still things that get me awfully pissed off. I'd like to get them off my chest.

The old cliché "Records were made to be broken" is wrong. The people who keep all these records should be broken.

I am so tired of all these sports records and statistics that don't mean *nothin'*. While watching a sporting event on television we hear, "This guy just broke this record or this guy just equaled that statistic." Where did all these fucking records come from? And who needs them?

One particular stat pisses me off. Announcers working basketball games these days are making a big deal out of "triple doubles." Forgive me for playing announcer and assuming that you don't know what a triple double is (that's another thing that pisses me off, announcers who assume their listeners are idiots), but a triple double is when a player reaches double figures (ten or more) in one game in three of these categories: rebounding, scoring, assists, steals, and blocked shots.

In ancient times—when I played—many of these stats were not considered important enough to keep. If they were, a triple double wouldn't be enough; they would have had to come up with better phrases to describe some of my feats, or Oscar Robertson's or Elgin Baylor's or Jerry West's for that matter. Because I probably averaged a triple double a game for the whole season! In the year I averaged close to twenty-five points and twenty-five rebounds a game, I also led the league in assists, averaging close to nine a game; a triple double was an everyday occurrence for me. And in those days they didn't even keep records of blocked shots and steals; if they had, more often than not I would have been in double figures in blocked shots every game, too. (Probably not in steals, but who knows . . . I am sure I was in double figures in that category at least once.)

In the '60s, announcers would have had to come up with all new labels, like a quadruple double, a quintuple double, and so on. On one of the nights I played, the phrase "a quadruple double with a triple" would have been born, never to be used again. Of course, that's the night I was in double figures in rebounding, blocks, steals, and assists—

and I scored one hundred points, the only "triple" in history.

To make matters worse, some announcers are now praising players who make *double* doubles, which is almost like giving credit to a guy for not going to take a piss during the game.

Who cares about all these figures, stats, and labels anyway? I don't. Really. But I *do* care that announcers and reporters don't explain to the fans and readers that certain records were not kept until very recently. When fans hear or read that Kareem Abdul-Jabbar is the all-time shot blocking leader they would naturally think he was better at this skill than Bill Russell or myself. That is about as far from the truth as someone claiming I don't have an opinion. When you see Kareem on top of the blocked shots list, remember that only after I retired did they start keeping a record of blocks.

The same is true in rebounding. They now say that Charles Barkley is the shortest player ever to lead the league in rebounding. True, but the average he leads the league with would not have even surpassed the rebounding stats compiled by Elgin Baylor, who never was able to lead the league because he played when Russell and I did. I *know* that Elgin pulled down more rebounds a game than Charles Barkley—and he was an inch or so *shorter* than Barkley.

Likewise, if a player gets 2.4 to 2.8 steals a game today he'll lead the league in that category. If the record for steals had been kept when Jerry West was playing there's no doubt he'd be the all-time leader in that department. Jerry got more steals in a month of games than today's leaders get in an entire season. And as long as I'm pissed off, what is considered an assist today is quite different from what was considered an assist when I was playing. Today all you have to do to get an assist is to be the last guy to touch the ball before some other player on your team scores a basket. It doesn't matter what transpires between the time you give the other player the ball and when he makes the basket. He can bring the ball down the court, dribble between his legs, go back to the three-point line, make sixteen fakes, move to evade the defense, and throw up a hook shot—and because you gave him the ball five minutes ago you get the assist. It's ridiculous! The rulemakers and the statkeepers should look at the definition of what an assist is before they allow people to pass them out: Assist—a pass to a teammate that leads directly to that teammate scoring a goal. The key word here is "directly." Even though Magic Johnson and John Stockton have amassed great numbers in the assist department, and Magic has surpassed Bob Cousy and Jerry West and even Oscar Robertson for total number of assists, does that make the guys today better passers than those players? Nope. It's bullshit.

In the game of hockey they give two assists on the same goal. My guess is, the way things are going, they'll start doing this in basketball. Before long they'll be giving assists for one player helping another player out on the court. Or helping a teammate tie his shoe!

These stats aren't only misleading, they often create monsters. When a player spends a great deal of his time trying to be one of the stat leaders—which, believe me they do—it often affects their game in a negative way. Take steals. Remember, you are never told how many times a player gets "burned" in his attempt to pilfer a ball. And when his attempt at a steal fails, that could cost his team. Since there are no stats for hustle, filling the lane on fast breaks, creating a mismatch that gives your teammate a chance to score, setting a pick, and all the other things that are the real reasons for a team's ultimate success, players today ignore this part of the game. Since all the factors in a game can't be counted statistically, why penalize those players who perform their job the way it's supposed to be performed—without the benefit of the glory given for piling up big stats?

These new stats, and many of the old ones too, were invented strictly to help sell the game and create stars. But we all know numbers alone can be misleading. An athlete could have played in one thousand consecutive games, but only a minute or so in each game, whereas someone else could have played in five hundred consecutive games but almost every minute in every game. Which player should have the record? Which is the more impressive?

I'm for keeping no stats at all—except for the score. This way you can decide on your own the value of each player. You won't be prejudiced by the stats he's accumulated. I know I may feel differently about all this than most, but that's never stopped me before. It is unfortunate that we didn't have videotape in my day so we could compare the great players of yesteryear with the players of today. Then fans could make decisions about who was the best passer and the best rebounder, with more important things to base it on than mere statistics.

Another *thing about* this statistics phenomenon that pisses me off: Too often these records mean nothing except as trivia for the sportscasters and color guys to jaw about. And sportscasters these days jaw far too much, as far as I am concerned. Announcers of the world, listen to Wilt: Fans are not stupid!

I can understand running commentary on the radio, but PLEASE, stop all that television chatter! It forces me to turn down the sound just so I can enjoy what I'm watching. Are we so dense that we always have to be told what just took place? Do you think we're too slow to ever figure out what's about to unfold? No, we are not. So give us some slack, guys.

There *are* some good announcers, though Johnny Most would not be among those. Most, the long-time announcer for the Boston Celtics, was always so one-sided that I am sure his underwear was green. Chick Hearn gets my vote for best basketball announcer, as Vin Scully does for baseball, and Keith Jackson for football. John Madden is my choice for most entertaining and most humorous.

Cops *hiding when* they should be riding pisses me off. Everyone knows that an ounce of prevention is worth a pound of cure. So if speed kills, why do cops wait behind billboards and exit signs to catch a speeding motorist? If cops were visible, everyone would maintain the legal speed limit. Highway patrolmen are like vultures in the night, swooping down on you, when they should be out on the highway *preventing* speeding. This tactic definitely does not help to improve their desired image as the good guys who are there to serve and protect.

Three *things about* telephoning today piss me off.

(1) I *hate* those long drawn-out messages people leave for incoming calls on their answering machines. They go on and on. You could be fast asleep before you're able to

That's president of the I.V.A. volleyball league, not, unfortunately, president of the United States.

© BETTMANN—UPI

Who would you have bet on?

With Meadowlark Lemon, my choice for Most Amazing Athlete.

Where there's a Wilt there's a way—even to fit into a
Lamborghini Countach.

Dancing in Germany. No
German was needed for this
step.

The Manhattan Beach Open—the biggest beach tournament in the world. It's hard as hell to jump in all that sand.

MEMBER OF
SPALDING
ADVISORY STAFF

I had the number-one-selling basketball for Spalding for many, many years. By the way, this is the only picture you'll ever find of me as an adult without a beard or mustache.

My car being built in the shop in England.

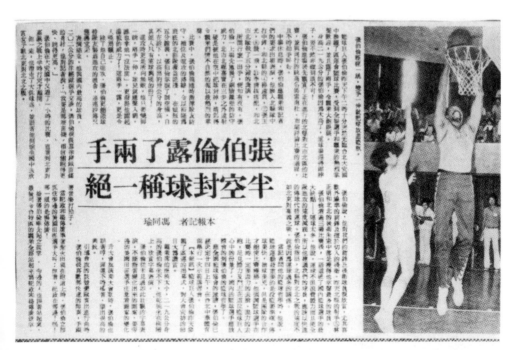

From my scrapbook: the trip to China.

High school graduation. Just to prove I made it out of the school of hard knocks.

With Floyd Patterson in 1960, when I was playing in the Maurice Stokes benefit game.

As a DJ at K.U. I was on three stations at one time—Kansas, Lawrence, and Topeka.

© DUKE D'AMBRA

Lounging in the pool in my house.

© PEOPLE MAGAZINE

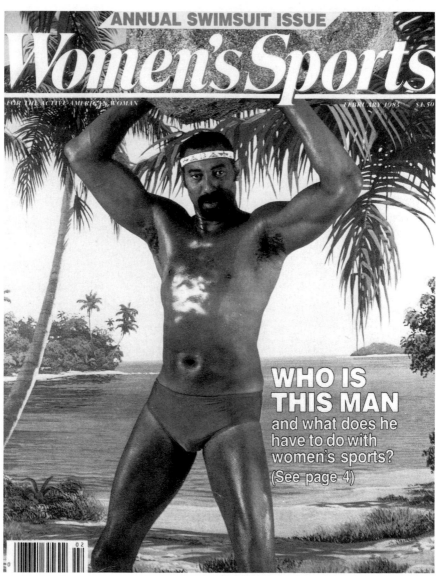

The cover of *Women's Sports*. I'm one of the few athletes who made the cover of magazines for *many* different sports—racquetball, volleyball, basketball, even *women's* sports.

A NON-STOP HIGH ENERGY FREEDOM TRIP

*with super stars
who flirt
with disaster!*

GO FOR IT

**INSANE!
MOTIVATED
MADNESS!
OUTRAGEOUS!
UNREAL!**

PG PARENTAL GUIDANCE SUGGESTED
SOME MATERIAL MAY NOT BE SUITABLE FOR PRE-TEENAGERS

A Wilt Chamberlain-Hal Jepsen Presentation
of a World Entertainment Release
Written by Neil Rapp • Produced by Paul Rapp and Richard Rosenthal
Directed by Paul Rapp • Executive Producer Wilt Chamberlain

©1976 World Entertainment Corporation

© WORLD ENTERTAINMENT CORPORATION

The first movie I ever produced.

The summer I worked and played at Kutsher's.

I was high school shot-put champion, undefeated all the way
through college. I liked this sport because I taught myself how
to do it.

Moscow, 1959, with the Globies. We were the very first people invited behind the Iron Curtain after the curtain went up.

The bellboys at Kutsher's. Bill Yule, who was an All-American with the Daytona Flyers, is next to me. Next to him was a high school All-American from Indiana named Flowers. The moral: Not every seven-foot All-American makes it in the pros.
P.S.   I was in high school when this photo was taken.

Hanging out with James Baldwin at Big Wilt's Small Paradise, my nightclub at 135th Street and Seventh Avenue in Harlem. Malcolm X worked for me there as a waiter.

© I. W. SCHMIDT

With Abe Saperstein, founder of the Globies.

The photographer won an award for this photo at the Brussels
World's Fair. I look pretty relaxed—especially since, after a
standing jump, I'm about fifty-four inches off the ground.
The bar is seven feet high. I'm not sure whether I'm going up
or coming down.

Grade 4A. Mrs. Fogarty was my teacher.

leave a goddamn message! I compose short messages for my machine that run about five seconds or less:

"Your call is pleasin' 'cause this is the season" (excellent for Christmas);

"Happy 9-1. Tell me who and why before you run";

"Tell me who and where and I'll take it from there."

I usually end each message with "peace." I welcome you all to follow my suggestions. At least, if you expect me to leave a message when I call.

(2) What is the correct protocol for an answering machine, anyway? Before the advent of answering machines, when I called someone and they weren't home, I kept calling till I got them. Now when you call, you're greeted by a recorded message. When I leave my message, am I supposed to call back or wait for them to call me? People often call me and say, "Well, didn't you get my message? I called you." My thoughts are, "So you called me. Call me back. You would have done so if I didn't have an answering machine." Just because you want to talk to me does not mean I want to talk to you—and vice versa.

(3) I hate "call waiting" for phones in private homes. I know they are great for emergencies, but how many times have you gotten a call on "call waiting" that was a true emergency? I've *never* had one. Most of the calls you get are just another nothin' call like the nothin' call you're already on. But now the last caller becomes the first and gets your attention, and the original caller is left feeling like he's not worth much. Why do we put up with this nuisance? Our egos make us think that we need and must have the latest technical gadget if we can afford it.

. . .

I *really get* a big charge—and I mean charge—from what they make you pay for bottled water. In Europe in the good old days, bottled water was put on your table for free. Now that same bottle of water costs you more than a bottle of beer, soda, milk, or almost anything else to drink. And there is no guarantee that the water you're getting in the bottle is any better than the water you can get out of your tap with a filter system—as Perrier drinkers recently found out.

WILTISM

The one thing we know that we can't control
Is how much time we have before we grow old.

Sportswriters who get quotes wrong piss me off. I've had a lot of experience with this and let me tell you, believe no quotes attributed to a professional athlete by sportswriters. None. I'm not even talking about misquotes, omissions, or misinformation. Those might be honest mistakes. I'm talking about a ploy that is commonly used by too many sportswriters. They'll interview you for hours, these guys, and during that time you may say ten good things about a guy and one negative thing about what he can't do. But the only thing you read in the article is that one thing you said he couldn't do.

And that one thing might even make the headline, with you claiming how lousy this guy is. For example, I might say that the guy—say it's Kareem—is a great clutch player, he shoots well, he defends well, he passes well, but I think he could probably rebound a little better. By the time you read it, the headline will read: WILT SAYS KAREEM IS A

LOUSY REBOUNDER! And in essence that is all you will know that Wilt said about Kareem.

Not only are these writers taking your statement out of context, they are also insinuating that you were totally negative in your comments.

The thing that really pisses me off about this type of reporting is that the writer believes the negative statement and wants to express it himself, but he's too chickenshit to take responsibility for the statement, so he puts the onus on you. By writing this way he accomplishes two things. He gets to print what he personally believes to be true without assuming any risk, and he creates the controversy he thinks is needed to make the article a success.

So, you ask, "Why give these interviews? By now you should know better." You're right. But since not every writer deals with us this way, those writers are due some professional courtesies. I give interviews because for the most part they're promoting the sport that helped make me what I am today. Yet I can't spend all my time trying to defend myself, trying to deny all these negative comments that I am always accused of making.

It's like when I choose not to put some player on my all-favorite team. As a fan, I have my favorites, just as you do. But when I omit someone, that's a signal to some writers to make an issue out of it, like it must be something really personal between me and the person I left off.

I am outspoken, but I'm not vindictive or jealous of any athlete or his accomplishments. Unfortunately, sometimes it comes out that way, because of the way sportswriters work.

. . .

I *hate when* awards are given to big-name people because they help to glorify the award itself and the group that's giving it. Most awards should instead be given to more deserving people, people who have no name recognition, status, or PR value.

I'm often chosen to be the recipient of an award, but once the sponsors of the award find out that I'm not able to attend the banquet and accept it in person they almost always choose another winner. This leads me to believe I was only chosen in the first place because the sponsors thought people would come to see me. If I was truly the "winner," why not let someone accept the award for me?

One of the best examples I know of selecting people for who they are instead of what they've done is the election of players to the NBA Hall of Fame. You are not eligible to be voted into the Hall of Fame until you've been officially retired for at least five years. Even then, only the *crème de la crème* are even considered to be nominated after *just* five years of waiting. You can name very few basketball players who were held in such high regard to be considered in five years. But one such choice really sticks out and ticks me off: Bill Bradley. Senator William Bradley was not only nominated after the mandatory five years but was voted in on his first try.

I have to take exception to this. Bill Bradley was a good basketball player in the pros, but never even close to being a great one. He only made the All-Star Team twice during his entire professional career. There were guys in the league during his time, even some of his own teammates, who made the All-Star Team eight, nine, and ten times but were not accorded the same Hall of Fame honor. His own teammates, Willis Reed, Earl "the Pearl" Monroe, Dave DeBusschere, and "Clyde" Walt Frazier, were *all* far superior players, but they did not receive the same honor as quickly as Bill did.

You can't make me believe that the people in charge of the Hall of Fame didn't know this. Nobody who can vote and nominate could possibly think that Bradley was a better player than Walt Frazier. I believe that Senator Bill Bradley got the "nod" because they thought he would bring more prestige to the Hall of Fame, because he might one day become president of the United States.

There are many athletes, especially basketball players and football players, who feel very strongly about some of the people who are *not* in the Hall of Fame. I mean, it is flat out absurd that Chet Walker is not in the Basketball Hall of Fame. And how about Guy Rodgers? He was a great guard, in my estimation the best ball handler of all time.

When it is obvious that a person is chosen to the Hall of Fame because of his outside influence, it cheapens the honor. I think the people who run the Hall should take a good look at themselves.

In a similar vein, Pat Riley won the Coach of the Year award for the 1989–90 season. His team, the Lakers, had the best regular season record. Pat was certainly overdue for the award, because his teams had won four world championships in the past, yet he had received nothing.

But in giving the award to Pat that year, they slighted coach Larry Brown, who took his team, the San Antonio Spurs, from last place to a division title. This was the greatest turnaround in the history of basketball, but of the ninety people who voted for the award, Brown got only four votes—an unbelievable disgrace. Pat Riley obviously had nothing to do with who won, but politics *did* have a lot to do with it. The writers were playing catch-up, much like they do in the Academy Awards when they give an award to someone who's about to die, slighting the younger actors, reasoning that they'll get a chance later on. Politics can ruin sports, same as they've ruined so many other things.

Stupid sports clichés piss me off. I heard a color announcer calling a Los Angeles Clippers basketball game praise one of the Clipper players. He said, "He's the kind of player a team likes. He always plays to win." Was he saying that the other players on the Clippers team *don't* play to win? I mean, I never heard such a stupid statement. Every player out there is playing to win—unless they're trying to throw the game. Now *that's* the kind of information I'd like to know.

Another thing I dislike is when people come up to me in public places and use me as a measuring stick. You can't believe the rudeness of people who want to see where their heads come in relation to what part of my body. They treat me like I am some inanimate object. Most of the time I just look at them like they're crazy and wish I could stomp on their toes with my size fourteen-and-a-half shoe.

If you're one of the people who has used me as a ruler, or is planning to, let me inform you that I'm making a poster of Wilt with numbers on it. So when you see me in public, come on up to me and I'll whip the poster on out. Then we'll have two dummies—and I won't be one of them.

. . .

I *ask all* of you out there who are fans of various teams: How in the hell can you root for one team when each new season your team is almost completely different? Each year, all the peripheral players—the guys who are the backbone and guts of the team—are traded away. These are the players we all like to root for—they're not the stars making all the money and getting all the headlines, they're the workhorses. When they're traded, you're expected to make a quick rooting switch. Joining your team are the very players that you hated the most on other teams. How can you root for them?

I guess the real point I am making is there seems to be no loyalty from players and owners any more. Not to the fan. Players don't care what team they're playing for as long as the money is right. The owners don't care who they hire as long as they (the players) can contribute. And fans not only have to put up with it, they're expected to continue to be loyal to their team.

I suggest that we not root for teams but for individuals; that seems more logical these days.

But then, can you really say you like very many of today's stars: these wife-beaters and family-cheaters, drug users and sorry losers, autograph nongivers, high-on-the-hog livers? Whatever happened to the Joe Louises of the world, athletes who had respect for their opponents, love for their families and fans, pride in their ability? What happened to great champs who hated to lose, but when they did, didn't make excuses and sing the blues?

It isn't easy to be a sports fan anymore, is it?

I *think the* paying of all that extra money for a first-class airline ticket is a big waste of money. If you can believe this, on the same plane the price of a first-class round-trip ticket from Los Angeles to London can vary with a coach ticket by as much as five thousand dollars. About all you get for that extra money is some cheap champagne. (Since it's businessmen who are the ones traveling the most these days, and mostly first-class, why would a corporate president want one of his employees to drink while going to a job?) There is not even a guarantee that you're going to get more leg room; in fact, the seat just behind the first-class bulkhead usually has the most leg room on the plane. (Trust me on this. I know these things.) Five grand seems a lot of money to pay for little more than a couple of glasses of cheap champagne—or even very expensive champagne, for that matter.

WILTISM

No matter what class you're in, you get there the same time, but by flying coach you get there a lot richer.

Written on the sideview mirrors on some cars are these words: "Objects in mirror are closer than they appear." I want to know: How much closer are they?! When you're making a high-speed lane change do you have time to read the mirror? Would a mirror with a sign on it reading, "Objects in mirror are farther away than they appear" give you more time to react?

What about making an honest mirror that makes things appear as they really are?

Who the hell needs a trick mirror on their car?

· · ·

Waiting *pisses me* off. Most of our life is *filled* with it, and that's why the thing I hate most is having to wait for anybody for anything. I mean people who are late for dates, people who seem to be insensitive about your time in relation to their time.

The one thing we really have no control over is our time. Time is our most precious commodity. When someone starts screwing with your time they are really screwing with your life. For some insensitive person to make me wait and screw up my time is, for me, like committing the ultimate crime. They say that good things come to those who wait. Well, if they don't come on time for me they are too damn late.

On Celebrity: Tin Gods

Y ou know what Tarzan said when he saw the elephants coming? He said, "Here come the elephants." But what did he say when the elephants came wearing sunglasses? Nothing—because he didn't recognize them. Herein lies the reason I often wear sunglasses.

From time to time I reflect on my life, and I am always amazed when I realize how long I have been in the public eye. Would you believe since 1946—which is forty-four years ago? Back then I anchored the 300-yard shuttle relay in the Penn Relays. No one had ever seen a tall, gangling kid like me run as fast as I did. Attention has been focused on me ever since.

It is also scary to realize that I have now been out of pro

basketball longer than I was in it—which at the time seemed like forever. Yet in all this time of not playing I am still thought of as a contemporary, or as one who could and should be playing right now. I wonder how much longer I'll carry that image; probably on to the hereafter. Like they say, "Once a president, always a president"—or, "Once Wilt, always Wilt."

Celebrity and fame is a two-sided proposition. Of all the attributes that man can possess I believe that fame is the most alluring—more alluring than money, smarts, or good looks. It manifests itself in a great deal of power. It has its perks and benefits, but it also has many downfalls. As a famous person for over forty years, I have experienced both. I've also learned a few things about our society— good and bad—when it comes to fame.

Possibly the worst thing about being famous is that people always—*always*—want something from you, whether it's money, time, endorsements, whatever. It clouds your judgment because it's hard to know who's a real friend and who's a "fame" friend. But, overall, I *like* being famous. It's a hell of a lot of fun. I like to think I've used fame to get the most out of my life.

W*e have become* a society of hero worshipers. And oh, boy, what heroes . . . We have made some of the most blasé, most average, most ridiculous people in the world our heroes. Because a guy can dunk a basketball, because a guy can hit a home run, all of a sudden he becomes our hero. Do we have such little belief in ourselves, are we so bored, that we create these tin gods so we have someone to follow? Aren't there enough worthwhile things we can get our kids and ourselves involved in and be proud of? I sure hope so.

Enough of all this celebrity worshiping! We make dolls and posters out of nothing people and they make nothing but fools out of us.

Let me tell you a little story that illustrates what I'm trying to say. A couple of years ago I was going to Europe with my doctor who, despite what I said earlier about combining friendship with medicine, is also my friend. (Hey—no one's perfect!) As I tried to board the plane I got stopped for autographs by at least fifty people. I'd take a few steps, sign some pieces of paper, take a few more steps, sign a few more slips of paper—it got a little tiresome. I finally got on the plane, slumped in my seat, and took a deep breath. But people kept coming to the section where I was sitting and asking me to sign things. Finally they had to be stopped by the stewardess. My traveling partner realized that I was a little tired of the whole thing. He said to me, "Look over there."

I looked across the aisle and saw a middle-aged, very distinguished gentleman. My doctor said, "Let me show you how screwed up the world is. You noticed no one bothered to ask that guy for an autograph."

I thought to myself, "So what? Why would they?"

My doctor went on, "That gentleman just won the Nobel Prize for medicine. What he just developed will help to save the lives of two hundred and twenty thousand people a year. And hardly anyone on this plane knows his name. Don't you think we as a people have our priorities a little screwed up?"

I knew for sure that I didn't know who he was, and my doctor's statement made me realize that I was one of those people with screwed-up priorities. The Nobel Prize winner won for his work with cholesterol. His contribution to the field of medicine had a major impact in the battle against heart disease.

As I sat there and focused on that I realized, my God, we need to take an inner look at ourselves. Why have we chosen the sports heroes and the flashy celebrities of the world to be the people that we want our sons and daughters to emulate? Unfortunately, I don't have any brilliant answers. But I do know that just asking the question is important.

I would advise parents to say to their kids: Okay, if you want to idolize Magic Johnson, José Canseco, Joe Montana, or whoever, focus on what he is doing *off* the playing field. Investigate and learn if the things he does off the court or playing field parallel his on-court heroics. If your hero's life away from the game is one to admire, then that is a great hero to have. But most people don't want to do that. If you let your kids idolize the dopers and wife-beaters without scrutinizing their lives away from the game, what do you tell your kids when they learn the truth about those so-called heroes? Fallen heroes have left many a young admirer with deep emotional scars.

I believe we should admire people who do a great job in their field of endeavor. But can we ever know them well enough to *idolize* them? Especially a sports star or a movie star. We only know what we read about them, what some writer, who only has his own interests in mind, passes on to you. Or else we know what we hear on TV in a thirty-second "sound bite." I say that's not enough to know about someone to make him your hero.

The people you know the most about as a kid are your parents. If they are doing good things, things that make you proud of them, then they are the ones who should be your heroes. If I were a parent I would want my kids to be proud of me. I would want to be their hero. I would continually try to do things that would make them feel that there is no one more important in their life than me. Even if I can't dunk a basketball or I can't hit a home run, I can say and do all the things that will make them a better person. For that I think they will eventually appreciate and understand me.

Teach your kids how to respect and admire you. Be the real hero in their world. That will give them something real to look up to and to follow.

A *celebrity today* is like a comet; he flashes across the sky and is gone, or, as Shakespeare once wrote, "struts his hour upon the stage, and then is heard no more." This is because his stardom is based on nothing of substance. All you have to do is be known by more than your immediate circle and you are a celebrity. I don't care what you do. If you sell toilet paper on television you're a star today. Somebody will want your autograph and you can make the talk-show circuit. But after you sign your name a couple of times and make that appearance on *Geraldo* or *Joan Rivers*, you are through; the talk-show hosts and the autograph seekers look for someone new to make a star for a microminute.

Potential superstars in sports fade like falling stars in the night sky these days. Young athletes are taken out of their natural environment and experience culture shock. The guy who didn't have ten dollars yesterday signs a multimillion-dollar contract and is immediately catapulted out of the environment that made him what he was and into a brand new world. Now he has more money than he ever had before—and more so-called friends than he ever had before. He's in situations he never knew existed. He is now traveling more or less on his own, with little supervision. He must make his own decisions about when and what to eat, when to sleep and wake up, when to arrive on time, when to leave. All of that makes for confusion time. And unfortunately for him, there are a lot of ladies waiting, waiting to gobble up those sweet things with all his brand new money. They are nothing like that sweet little girl he knew next door.

(These things I can say to you from experience. Even some of us old pros, whether in business or sports, are not immune from being taken from time to time by a woman who is as fine as wine. Remember that story I told earlier about the gorgeous woman con artist? That kind of thing isn't all that uncommon.)

Yes, indeed, understand that newly famous people are thrown into a deep, hostile ocean, and if they don't learn how to swim fast they will drown.

I thought, for instance, when nineteen-year-old, lovable Magic Johnson burst on the scene and into the jaws of Tinsel Town with a multi-million-dollar contract in his pocket, he would find it hard to survive. But I've got to hand it to him. It appears his magic is too strong for the vampires of Hollywood.

Most of our heroes and stars are made by public relations people, and they only last as long as the PR man is good at what he does. It's the PR man who should be the star, not his client, for he's so adroit at controlling us and our thinking via the media that the good ones have us thinking we're doing and choosing things of our own free will rather than being brainwashed.

Can you remember the hype and the money spent on the movie *Batman* long before it was released? By the time it came out you were so saturated with the hype that you were convinced if you didn't see this film you were missing the greatest entertainment spectacle in the world. If you didn't go see *Batman* you were just an idiot. The real stars of *Batman* were the PR people. Now that all the fuss has died down, how great was it?

You tell me. I haven't seen it yet.

It's much harder to be a true hero today, because there's no more room for the fan to use his own imagination or even pick his own star. Everything's done for you. There used to be real mystique surrounding our stars. Today, with TV and modern communications and rapid travel there's little we don't know about the personal lives of our manufactured stars. My advice to you out there who want to be *real* stars is leave something for the imagination; forget about doing every TV talk show. Not only does becoming too familiar breed contempt; we all know that the more you leave to the imagination the more desirable you are.

Living in beach towns such as Honolulu and Los Angeles, I tend to meet quite a few bikini-clad ladies out on the sand. At night, when I see some of them in restaurants and discos, I am always surprised at how much better they look—some are almost unrecognizable. It's obvious to me that the more they cover up the better they look.

No one can bear (or is it "bare"?) the scrutiny of being

completely naked, literally or figuratively. That's why it's always better to leave something to the imagination. Stars and heroes are *always* more imagination than reality.

We've all thought about being rich or famous. I used to say: Give me the money, you can have the fame. But as I've gone through this world of ours I have seen fame open doors, take me places, and introduce me to people that no amount of money would have accomplished. Lines that others stand in disappear. Places that are completely full miraculously have room in the rear. If you say hello to a strange lady in New York she'll speak to you.

But the question is: Do you change as a person if you become rich and famous? From what I see with my rich and famous friends, the answer is no. Roots are planted deep, and more often than not, more money does not change one's life-style. Our cars may cost a little more and our houses may be a little larger, but this is only because we have to find something to do with that extra cash.

Let me give you an example—but don't laugh. My favorite thing to eat isn't caviar—which I have acquired a taste for and like very much—but a peanut butter and mayonnaise sandwich on soft, fresh white bread. That was my favorite as a boy growing up and it's still my absolute gastronomic choice. Give me a peanut butter and mayonnaise sandwich and a glass of milk and I am in hog heaven. On holidays, when others are feasting on great meals, I enjoy a bologna and cheese sandwich—unless I can get one of those Philadelphia hoagies.

I know people who can afford whatever they want, but they don't have butlers and chauffeurs and people doing things for them. Can you see me saying to a butler, "Draw my bath, fetch my high-tops, and put my gold jock strap on the bed"? Come on. That would never be me.

I've been friends with Bill Cosby since he was a relatively "po' boy" with just a lot of talent and a fascination for sports and jazz. It makes me feel good, thirty years later, to see how little all his wealth and success has changed him or his basic desires.

Instant wealth never changed Muhammad Ali or Joe Louis, but I can't say the same for a few other more recent heavyweights.

I once asked an owner of two pro sports franchises why he worked so hard—twelve and thirteen hours a day—all the time. Why not travel, I wanted to know, buy a yacht, go fishing? He said, in his very elegant and loquacious manner, "Wilton, my lad, the people I care for could not find time nor do they have the money to do what I might want to do. So I do what they do—I work during the week and enjoy the weekends with them." I believe many wealthy people drown themselves in work because they feel work is the only place they can be around their true friends. That's certainly the case with Jack Kent Cooke.

People are not aware that most new stars, stars of this generation, are not really comfortable with all the money they make. Most big stars strive to be the best at their given profession. With that success comes tons of money, which sets them apart from their friends, foes, and cohorts, the people they work with who don't make nearly the money they do. And this causes problems. You have all this money and want to go places, but your friends can't afford to go with you and they don't feel comfortable taking your handouts. You're forced to either go alone or go with people who are not your real friends. Invariably you become isolated and find that money has actually limited you in many areas that were often taken for granted when you didn't have the big bucks.

It's not much fun buying a big yacht if all the staterooms are empty and there's no one there to enjoy it with you. Your true friends have to work five days a week; they don't have the time to enjoy a yacht, anyway. So you fill your yacht with people who have money and leisure time, although they're not your friends. You're also surrounded by parasites who will appear day or night and be at your beck and call, no matter what. You get confused as to who's a friend and who's a parasite, because a lot of parasites are pros at what they do—they can fool you, believe me.

Is a friend in deed a friend in need? Not always. There are plenty of parasites who are there for you when you're in need—because they know they'll get paid back in spades. I've had guys do little favors for me that I needed at the time. Then they ask for a large loan, knowing that you're in their debt. I've obliged—and, of course, never seen them or that money again.

I know that having fame and money is a problem most of you wouldn't mind having, but don't be so sure. It's not as easy as it looks.

Here's a celebrity endorsement story with a different twist.

I was in Taiwan a few years ago with my female track team. As guests of the Taiwanese government, we were touring the city when we came upon what is commonly called "snake alley." I had been telling my track athletes that while in Taiwan they shouldn't be afraid to try the different foods. In snake alley, some "hawker" asked us to try some fresh snake blood, which he swore was good for whatever ailed us. I, who care very little for snakes anyway, was only interested in moving on, but my nice little group of young ladies razzed me for not practicing what I preached. So I was forced to undertake this most unpleasant adventure. Two men held this six- to eight-foot snake and with a sharp paring knife they split the snake's belly open. Blood squirted into a glass (about 10 ounces). When full, I was given the blood to drink immediately—which I did. To this day I'm still tasting that drink.

That's not the end of the story.

Just recently, eight years after my vampire act in Taiwan, a lady from the mainland of China, whom I had not seen in a decade, sent me a card while vacationing in Taiwan. She related how surprised she was to see this enormous eight-foot-high picture of me outside of this snake store. There was writing on the photo—in Chinese, of course—all about how I prescribed the drinking of snake blood for everything from A to Z, even as an aid to growing tall!

I think I need a good Chinese agent or a good Chinese lawyer. If I'm not going to get the kind of money Michael Jordan gets for selling Wheaties, they should at least give me a couple of snakeskin wallets.

In many ways, I found China dumbfounding. When I took walks in the city, crowds of people would gather, bowing and clapping until I disappeared out of sight. I didn't know what to do—bow back, wave back, or just stand there and continue to feel like a fool. I wasn't sure what provoked this admiration. Were they just stunned by my physical appearance? Was seeing someone of my size and color *that* amazing to them? There were some articles written about me, but since they were in Chinese I'm not sure what it was they said. Maybe they said that I was the black messiah or Confucius's cousin. Strange, those Chinese, but whatever it was, they seemed sincere.

I think I could be big in China, if only I liked Chinese food.

I *have always* been amused by people who make a point of letting me know they are not impressed with who I am. First, let me say that I *know* I'm no better than any other person. I definitely put my pants on one leg at a time like all men. But what are these people really trying to say? That they regard me no differently than anyone else? Well, guess what? I may not be better, but I *am* different. I'm taller, I'm more famous, I'm stronger, richer. You mean to tell me that it makes no difference to you who or what I am, because you're going to treat me like anybody else? If I were a bum it would be the same as if I were the president of the United States? Come on! The bum is a person and the president is a person. Right? So you're going to invite the bum into your house for dinner just like you would the president? Of course. I can see the president coming to your door and asking to use the phone because his car phone is inoperative and you responding the same way you would if a bum came with the same request.

All of us are moved or, if impressed is too strong a word, at least affected to some degree, by beauty, fame, courage, money, size, or the lack thereof. To say and act otherwise makes no sense.

.   .   .

Your everyday, garden-variety "celeb" is asked to give more to charity than anyone else. I'm asked to give everything from money, clothes, and talent to time. I used to give money to charitable organizations without a thought, but after reading so many articles about the number of organizations that are ripping off their donors, and the fact that only 10 percent of the original dollar reaches the charitable cause, I began to look for more meaningful ways to help the needy.

If you want to give to the needy, let me give you some advice. If you want to help without having to worry about whether you're being taken advantage of, donate your time. Get involved with organizations like Special Olympics, Best Buddies, or Operation Smile, organizations that need bodies to work with the aging and impaired. You might not know if the money you are giving is benefiting someone in need, but you'll surely know if it's a hands-on experience for you. You can see and feel the good you're doing.

I do a lot of work with an organization whose main purpose is to send doctors into Third World countries to restore people who have been deformed and crippled. Let me tell you, we are changing people's lives—and I can't begin to tell you what a glowing and growing experience it is.

While attending a tennis tournament in Florida I was asked by a TV crew to comment on the administration's position that athletes should not play in tournaments sponsored by unhealthy products like cigarettes. The feeling is that because athletes play in these tournaments they're endorsing the products, and that's sending the wrong message to kids.

Even though I'm obviously opposed to all unhealthy products, I feel that as long as athletes are not saying they are using the product, they shouldn't be asked to give up their chance to earn a living, any more than people who work in factories that produce junk food should be asked to quit because their product has no nutritional value.

When people see a famous personality they usually want to say something but are often at a loss as to how to start a conversation. They often remember something about you that connects you to them—even if it's really only a figment of their imagination. I was in Boca Raton recently attending a tennis tournament, and a seventy-year-old man came up to me and claimed that he went to high school with me. He had the right school, Overbrook High School in Philadelphia, so I said to him, "What year did you graduate?" He replied, "Thirty-seven . . . 1937."

I knew I was beginning to get a little peaked, but come on. I said, "Hey, my man. That's B.C."

The old man said, "What do you mean?"

"That's before Chamberlain."

But he held fast to his story, so I told him I would check my yearbook—and I really meant my "year" book, because I was only one year old in 1937.

I often get, "Oh, I remember you. We grew up in Philly together." Of course we never met or saw each other. What they mean is, "We grew up in Philly, separately at the same time." When I'm out on the road I must get that ten times a day, lines like, "Do you remember me? You signed an autograph for me when I was six years old." When you're famous, the bus driver may have had you on his bus one time, but to hear him tell it you took his bus every day to school for three years. And now, how can you not remember him?

Because I'm a volleyball player at the beach it's not unusual for someone to approach me and say, "We used to play on the beach together." After further questioning I'll discover they were on the same beach I played on—but I was on one end and they were on the other, with half a million other people in between us.

It's not really hard to talk to people of note. They're just like everyone else. You might be surprised to learn than an honest, cordial, "How are you doing?" is as good a way to start a conversation as any lie you can think of. When many people approach you with their little bullshit lies they think you're not going to question, call their bluff.

I used to go to the zoo, where there was a male rhinoceros. The rhino would stare at me, and I would hop over the fence and fake a charge at him and the rhino would high-tail it back to the safety of his quarters. Of course I was only bluffing, and if the rhino had called my bluff he would have found out I was as full of the same BS that most of the people who approach me are.

By the same token, I'm always amused when complete strangers speak to me as if I'm their long-lost friend. I may be going through an airport or walking on the beach or just going about my business on a trip, but people will come after me. The worst thing is that if I don't respond exactly the way they think I should, if I don't stop and say, "Hello, how are you?" but rather just nod pleasantly and move on, they think I'm an asshole.

An example: When I go into an airport and have to walk through the security gate machine, there may be thirty people in front of me and sixty behind me. The security guards, who normally don't speak to anyone, are all smiles when I pass and always say hi to me. Of course, they're only speaking to me because I'm a celebrity. Then they get miffed if I don't respond with the same enthusiasm. Well, who wants to speak with someone who just wants to speak to celebrities? They should be saying hello to all the little old ladies who walked by before me. The ladies would really appreciate the gesture. I don't. I don't go for that BS. If you're not going to speak to all people, don't speak to me.

I *sometimes forget* that whether I like it or not, there are people out there who respect me, who look up to me. There are tons of people out there who feel this way about athletes, actors, other celebrities. It's time we athletes and celebs give more of ourselves, do more to deserve this respect. I like the way Magic Johnson uses his off-season time. And I like Dave Winfield's involvement in the community, the work he does. We athletes always feel that we're being used—and we are—but for the good we can do our sacrifice is a small price to pay.

FOUR FAMOUS PEOPLE I ADMIRE

One of my favorite people is Magic Johnson, and not because he plays his position on the basketball court better than anyone. He looks as if he enjoys his work. The key here is enjoyment. His off-the-court involvements are something to be proud of, too. His All-Star Game, which raises money for the United Negro College Fund, is to be commended. He puts his money where his mouth is.

Another man I admire is Harry Belafonte, whom I've known for over thirty-five years. Belafonte has been credited with the statement: "The role of the artist is not only to show life as it is but to show life as it should be." He lives out that credo on a daily basis. His work with the starving people in Africa is evidence. Harry was a spearhead for the civil rights movement in the '60s. Without his support, both financial (which was significant) and physical, the civil rights movement would have had a lot harder time of it than it did. I know of no other entertainer who has been more important to the civil rights movement than Harry Belafonte. My hat's off to you, Harry. And I hope you get the credit you're due for your humanitarian work.

I like Margaret Thatcher. To me she's a pillar of strength and I'm sorry she stepped down from office. She's from this very conventional nation, yet she doesn't stand by convention. She does what she believes and feels is right. Sometimes she was pro-American, but if she didn't agree with us she said so and chose another side. A gutsy broad.

The man I most admire in the world is the pope, John Paul II, and I'm not even Catholic. He is probably the most influential person in the world, and this pope has taken himself away from most of the pomp and ceremony and made himself real. He's traveled the world like no other pope before and touched people both physically and emotionally. He doesn't extend his hand to have his ring kissed, he hugs people and holds them, making them feel that they're just as important as he is. I remember in Harlem when he stopped to talk to the young children, even though they weren't Catholic. He had nothing to gain from it really, but that's the kind of man he seems to be. He seems to make the people he hugs and touches become better people. The pope seems to possess that rare ability to transmit goodness from himself to others.

Celebrities should endorse products they know something about. Unfortunately, that is rarely the case.

Years back, Andy Granatelli and STP went hand in hand, for obvious reasons. He was a racer and automobile engineer; he knew a great deal about cars, so we listened to what he had to say. His credibility here was beyond reproach. Yet when you watch Lindsay Wagner or Tina Turner do a car commercial you tend to dismiss it as entertainment. I do, at least. (As I write this, I know both those ladies did car commercials, but for what cars I have no idea.)

Tina Turner and Lindsay Wagner are nice ladies, I'm sure, but they didn't get their reputations from being "grease monkeys" or test drivers for *Road & Track*. I dismissed their commercials because I questioned their credibility. When I'm in the market for a new car I'd like to know how the Andrettis, the father or the son, liked the car in question. Or if Shirley Muldowney, the drag-racing champion, did a car commercial, then I might be impressed.

I've done commercials for airlines and cars, and one might ask, "Where is *your* credibility here?" Well, my commercials were to show how much leg room and head room there is in, say, a Volkswagen. I don't think anyone can question my credibility when it comes to knowing about that!

In *the same* vein, I am definitely not impressed if there's a picture of a movie star gracing the wall of a restaurant where I'm going to eat. The implication is that this big movie star ate here, so "this must be the place." Few celebrities are gourmets. When I go to a restaurant, I don't want to know if Gregory Peck, Dustin Hoffman, or Tom Cruise have eaten there. On the other hand, if Julia Child or Wolfgang Puck had eaten there, I'd be impressed—but only if they said they'd come back.

Most *celebrities can't* and don't go to public places like beaches because of the continual harassment. In general the harassment is fairly innocent—a simple "Hello, how you doing?" doesn't seem like much—but if you're at one end of the beach and are trying to walk to the other, and a thousand people want to stop and say hello, that can ruin your day at the beach.

If you have to stop and say hello back, when do you get a chance to enjoy what you'd planned to do? If you don't stop and acknowledge them, then once again you're considered an asshole.

Some people get easily offended, and I get remarks like, "Hey, you think you're too good to speak to me?"

The key here is that most people don't care whether I'm having a good time. They feel I owe them. Their logic is, "Well, don't come to these beautiful places with other people if you don't want to be bothered."

Here's another one that gets to me—and it happens more often than you'd think: People who thrust their hand out for me to shake. I've been in men's rooms and seen guys come right at me, hands out, without washing their hands after taking a leak.

If I don't give them my hand, they don't understand. They get angry. Well, I don't think it's so hard to understand. I don't know where all these hands have been, or if they've been washed. I think it's pretty simple.

Yes, there are some redeeming sides to being famous. If you're in a bar, someone always wants to buy you a drink. It doesn't matter that you don't drink or that you can afford your own. Of course, if you don't accept their drink, then once again you're an asshole who thinks he's too good to let a peon do him a favor.

Along the lines of the previous item: If an average Joe asked you to buy him a drink, you'd tell him, "Get lost, chump." If I ask, you'd probably do it.

If Bob Crump asked you for a nickel you'd blow him off immediately. If Donald Trump asked you for five dollars, you'd give it to him without hesitation.

Why is this so? Most of us want to be close to people who are famous—or infamous—no matter how it's achieved.

People will wait hours to touch the pope, even when they're not Catholic. Courtrooms are overflowing when a famous trial is going on.

And this phenomenon is worldwide. The first time I went to Europe with the Globetrotters I stopped in the middle of the Piazza del Duomo in Milan, Italy. In the piazza were three American girls who had just come from Dayton, Ohio. When they saw me they rushed to me. "Oh, Wilt," they shouted. "We just read about you being with the Globetrotters. Can we have your autograph?"

Before I could sign, there was a group of four or five hundred people, mostly Italian, around me. They had no idea who I was, but they knew I was someone famous, so they were all clamoring for my autograph. They weren't going to miss out, even though I might have been the author of a book saying I hated Italy.

N I N E

On Hollywood:
A View from Tinsel Town

Since my basketball days I have been extensively involved in advertising, television, and the motion picture industry, and I've learned that the same truths that apply to the athlete apply to movie industry people.

Most actors and directors really believe that life in their cubicle—and their cubicle is strictly whatever new film they're working on—is important to the masses. They are always baffled when their film loses money at the box office or their TV series is canceled in midseason. They think everything they do is brilliant—while they're doing it—and they're always shocked when they're left in the unemployment office instead of making the acceptance speech they dreamed of at the Academy Awards ceremony.

When you are a celebrity, be it in sports or in Hollywood, you have a tendency to think that everything revolves around you. It's an easy trap to fall into. Only when you get a little older and a little wiser do you realize that, hey, man, everyone doesn't fall on everything you do. Just because you go out there and knock out "Iron Mike" Tyson you are not God. Kayoing Tyson may be a big event in the boxing world, and certainly a few other people in the world will read about it and be interested. But in the grand scale of life it's nothing to live or die by. The same is true in making a hit movie. It's fun, it can be creative, it can even be art—but, hey, it's still a fucking movie.

 WILTISM

Wisdom is a strange commodity. The more you have the more you realize how dumb you are.

I have lived for thirty years in what many people call Tinsel Town. The last twenty years I've lived in Bel Air, a plush, secluded area next to Beverly Hills and Holmby Hills. I've run across many movie stars of the rich-and-famous type at every turn. But I've come to realize they're no different than the average neighbor I had when I was growing up. You chat about the weather or other mundane things when you meet them at the mailbox or on the road as you drive by.

Still, I can't help but get a kick when I get a phone call from Farrah Fawcett, who lives next door, or from her housekeeper, asking me if she and Ryan can have some lemons off one of my many lemon trees on my property. What red-blooded American would find that a bitter lemon to swallow?

I've found that the bigger the name and the longer someone's been a star, the more real—as a person—he or she
seems to be. The ones who give movie stars and Tinsel
Town a bad name and image are the ones with newly
acquired fame, the people trying very hard to be "movie
stars," which they'll never really be. The bigger stars are
never surrounded by entourages and hordes of personal
guards. It's only the stars who crave attention who travel
with an excessive number of people. The real stars appreciate it when you admire their work, but they don't want all
that notice and attention. They do very little to try to draw
it. After all, you know that when you step out of a forty-foot
limo, people are going to look—if only to see what kind of
idiot needs a car that large just to go to the movies.

One of the most disgusting things to me is the selling of
Movie Star Maps, guides to the stars' homes. I don't know
what the legal ramifications are, but how dare they sell
away the rights of people to have privacy?

How would the people who buy these maps feel if total
strangers, some demented, were staring in their own win-
dows, watching every move they make? The folks who buy
these maps are usually intelligent people, but when they
come to Hollywood, go up to Sunset Boulevard, and buy
a map, they feel it gives them the license to become a real
pest.

It comes back to the "you owe them" philosophy. This
may be a subconscious feeling, but it's there: "You want to
be a star, then you deserve to have a little bit of grief. This
is the price you have to pay."

. . .

Is *television our* "Big Brother"? TV is telling you: This is the way it is supposed to be. Every girl in a love scene is pretty. You see very few interracial couples on television. How many good newscasters never even try for a job because they're balding? (As I've said elsewhere in this book, we all know you must have hair to work in front of the camera.)

If TV is Big Brother, he isn't the kind of brother I had, that's for sure. Or the kind I want.

I *wonder how* some of the products on television sell. The TV salesman tells you the product is worth seventy dollars, but he's going to let you have it for ten dollars—and if you act fast he'll throw in as a gift a set of steak knives, salad forks, a tablecloth, and on and on. Each item they're going to give you is worth more than the ten dollars you're paying for the original product, or so they say. What does that tell you?

It tells *me* that none of that junk is worth a dime.

I *don't know* why more people—especially older females— don't boycott some of the products that are advertised using only young, hard-bodied girls. If you believe TV, only good-looking young girls drink beer. I know that young girls age twelve to fifteen buy over 80 percent of all records sold and make stars out of whomever they like, but this is different. Pop music is a teenage product. Beer sure isn't. And it isn't only teenagers who buy cars, pizza, and jeans. Enough is enough with the young girls!

What set me off on this is the commercial I just watched.

It has a nine-year-old boy looking into a mirror and being told—by himself as he grows through different stages— how milk will turn him into a great-looking eighteen-year-old boy. The kicker here is, when he gets to be eighteen, the mirror image says, if you don't believe me, ask this beautiful young lady. Then this gorgeous girl pops out and says, "Come on, John, drink your milk. I'm waiting for you." It's not bad enough that they use sex appeal to attract us dirty old men, now they're down to nine-year-old boys!

Commercials are also saying that if you're a woman you can't be a little overweight or older than twenty-five and feel good about yourself. I would be highly insulted if I were a lady and were being told all this. As a man, I find it insulting when young girls are all we ever see and when we're told, overtly or subliminally, that this is what we want and are supposed to have.

It is time for more reality in commercials. You don't have to look perfect to be accepted. Let's start being real and stop all this false imagery.

How many awards shows are there, anyway? And how many do we really need? I mean, there is an award show for *everything*. I could fill this book with just the names of these shows. And why do they all have to be on television? I'm waiting for the day when they have an awards show to give an award for the best awards show.

During my postbasketball career I've done a number of TV and print ads. A few of the more noteworthy ones are the commercials for Volkswagen and TWA that I did over a period of five years. I also did BVD commercials for TV and print, and presently running on television is one I did for Sharp Electronics pitching their big-screen TV.

I've been fortunate enough to win several Clios. In advertising, a Clio is the equivalent of winning an Academy Award. I feel quite honored by this.

The last Clio I won was for a print ad for American Express. It was a striking picture of me and Willie Shoemaker. Many people have truly enjoyed this one, and of all the print ads I've done this happens to be my favorite— mainly because I didn't have to wear shoes.

I *have made* over sixty commercials endorsing nationally known products, and I am always aware of the "truth in advertising" law. I would never do a commercial for a product I didn't believe in. I do wear BVDs, I have driven a VW, and I like Sharp's 100-inch-screen television.

The most blatant disregard for this law is perpetrated by the tobacco industry. They glamorize the use of cigarettes in all their commercials. They use majestic settings filled with wholesome, healthy, glamorous people. The powers that be should force the cigarette industry to abide by the laws. They should force them to show cigarette smokers as they really are: in unglamorous settings, cloudy environments, and choking with all the other people who smoke.

T*here is one* commercial airing now that really irks me. It's the one from Oldsmobile.

You know the one I'm talking about. It says, "This is not your father's Oldsmobile." What they are saying is: We sold your father a piece of crap. This new Oldsmobile is the real deal. We screwed your dad but we won't screw you.

General Motors would have more credibility by saying that Oldsmobiles have always been great cars. Way back in the old days, when your father purchased his Rocket 88, he had the state-of-the-art car, and you have the state-of-the-art car now. Just because it's today, does that *always* make it better than yesterday?

Because people of color comprise more than 38 percent of the moviegoing public you would think that the movie industry would be in the vanguard of the equal opportunity issue. But you would be wrong. The movie industry is still back in the 1930s and '40s. The Eddie "Rochester" Andersons and Stepin Fetchits of today are the Eddie Murphys and the Richard Pryors. Producers give starring roles to comedians and let them make a lot of money, but they never cast people of color in the roles of real heroes.

Where are the Indiana Jones, Batman, and James Bond–type heroes of color? Heroes that girls "ooh and ahh" over and that guys want to be like? The movie industry doesn't give guys of color a chance to play these roles. They always go to a guy like Mel Gibson. Take *Lethal Weapon,* for example. He's the hero, the single guy women want to be with and men dream about being. The Danny Glover character is the family man, the conservative role. He's not the hero. And don't think that isn't a calculated decision by the powers in Hollywood, because it most surely is. Only comedians are given leading roles; it's okay to laugh at people of color, but not to idolize them.

So when you hear people say that minorities have made

great strides and graduated to new heights in the movie industry, don't believe it. I'm not sure it will ever happen.

I *learned on* my first film experience that typecasting has its rewards, because I was obviously cast perfectly. As a villain, I frightened everyone . . . even the animals.

When I was filming *Conan the Destroyer* with Arnold Schwarzenegger I had to do a lot of horseback riding. I was dressed like a great warrior, and all my garb weighed ninety pounds. I looked so ferocious that when my horse saw me coming he bolted and ran away. Everybody laughed and shouted, "Talk about feeling that you're not wanted." To mount my horse I had to sneak up on him from behind so he wouldn't see me and run.

When you're filming you don't always take off your costume when you break for lunch. Once when we were having a meal on location, the trainer tied a lion cub to a pole near the eating area. As the actors walked by they would stop and pet the lion. When I went over to pet the lion, the cub saw me and panicked. He almost broke his chain trying to get away from me.

For *Conan,* the producers and director wanted a bodybuilder as the villain, but none were statuesque enough to truly rival Arnold. I was chosen at the very last moment. The script was already written—without me in mind—so even though I was visible throughout the entire picture, my lines were short and few. This was fine for the filmmakers, who didn't want me in any way to overshadow Schwarzenegger. I want you to understand that *no* actor works any harder at his craft than Arnold. He is extremely smart, sensitive, and directable—but my size was intimidating, even to him. The director made sure, in most shots, that we were not matched too closely together. During the making of the film we staged many great fight scenes—unfortunately, most of them found their way to the cutting-room floor, because I simply overmatched him in that particular area. There was a great picture of the two of us in *Time* magazine that I later heard they weren't supposed to print because my biceps looked bigger than Arnold's. Image is everything in Tinsel Town.

Conan was shot in Mexico and most of the crew was Mexican. The crew liked me a lot and thought I would go on to become a movie star. But the hours and the regimentation are not to my liking. I *would* like to do at least one more action film, though. Being a movie buff all my life, it was like a dream come true. What you do on film seems to be indelible and permanent, which appeals to me.

One thing I must warn you of. Never go to dinner with Arnold and his buddies—unless you want to be embarrassed by the tricks they pull. While waiters race to the kitchen to place their orders, Arnold and his friends bend their knives, forks, and spoons into knots and bows. When the waiter returns, he's confronted with, "What's wrong with the silverware?" They did this two or three times one night in Mexico City. The waiters at first were excited and happy to have us in their establishment, but as the evening wore on, I'd say it was questionable at best whether they wanted us to ever come back.

What *do you* think about all those TV and movie stars who grace the front rows and prestigious seats at pro sports events? They claim they're there because they love the sport. Maybe . . . but maybe not. They sure enough love the attention. I never see them at summer league basketball games, even though many young NBA players play there. Why? Because there are no cameras. When the Olympics come to town they are right up there, but if it's just a regular track or swimming meet, the stars don't even know it exists. Most of these stars aren't true fans. Come on! If you really love something, you don't have to wait until it's nationally televised before you go.

In fact, since most stars hate to be bugged by the masses, this is the time when they should stay at home and watch the event on TV. It would seem to make more sense to go to the less publicized events, not the ones that create the most attention. But no, they pay these incredible prices because they can afford it for those show-off seats, or they get them for free from the owners, and the real fan is aced out once again. The true fan supported the program from the grass roots, and when the player matures and is playing in the big leagues he, the true fan, can no longer go watch. Either he can't afford to go, or the good seats are taken.

Now I know there are a few exceptions, a few famous stars who are true fans and will go anywhere for a good game. The likes of Billy Crystal, Jack Nicholson, and Louis Gossett, Jr., are not to be mistaken for the others. And don't get me wrong, stars have a right to go to the big games like anyone else. They work hard for their money, too. I just don't like phonies, and many stars are at the game for the wrong reason.

I also know it's a business, and these stars help attract fans and make money for the owners, but I can't go along with owners who only make good seats available for the big stars or big corporations, and forget about the little guys.

Another thing I get tired of is seeing the camera focus more on the stars that are around the floor than on the floor itself, where the action is. If I want to watch Arsenio Hall I'll watch him on his show, which I do. When I turn on the Lakers game I want to watch Magic Johnson do his best, not see how Dyan Cannon is dressed.

Being linked romantically with movie stars has not altogether eluded me. Yes, I have dated and had encounters with a host of them, but to me their names should remain private, as should our actions. I'm not the kiss-and-tell type. At least, I don't tell names. Numbers, yes; names, no. That's taboo for me. I dated more famous women when I was younger. Now, I'm less impressed with fame.

Also, I've found that most famous people find it more to their liking if their partner is not a rival, sharing the spotlight, especially in restaurants like Spago where people go to be seen. These places bore me. I prefer small, private places, like Dan Tanpas on Santa Monica Boulevard, or new places *before* they become trendy and "in."

Let me tell you a couple of funny stories that illustrate how phony some stars are at sports events.

During the 1976 Olympics, Mick Jagger was sitting in the stands next to me. He had one of his flunkies take a note down to a beautiful pentathlete who was getting set to perform in her high-jumping event. The message on the note stated that he would like to take her out to dinner after the meet. I couldn't help but think: What poor taste. This young lady was getting ready to perform in the biggest event of her life and all Mick could think of was getting lucky with her.

He had no idea that I knew the lady well, and her fiancé too, who was a shot-putter. I am sure that if the shot-putter had gotten the note it would have been a great date for one rock-and-roll superstar. He still wouldn't get no satisfaction, but his already big lips might have gotten even fatter!

Some stars shun attention while others feed on it. At this same Olympics I had a seat a few feet away from another star, this one a TV star. Because of my height, when I walked in I was noticed right away and was swamped with autograph seekers and well wishers. The TV star a few seats away was not getting any attention at all and it was driving him crazy. So he stood up and took off his hat, displaying his shaven dome, and stuck a lollipop in his mouth. And guess what—then people began to notice Telly Savalas, the great TV hero. He was immediately besieged by fans, which seemed to make him quite happy. Different strokes for different folks, I guess. Or, as he might say, "Who loves ya, baby?"

On Common Sense:
Maybe You Can Help Me Here

Just as there are things that piss me off about life down there, there are also things I just don't understand. Maybe someone can explain these things to me.

When I drive on the freeways, three out of four cars I see have only the driver in them. So why don't they make one-person cars? It would save on natural resources and it would be cheaper to build. Because of its small size there could be room for a lot more things. Cars and areas built for cars, like garages, freeways, and streets, occupy two-thirds of our metropolitan area ground space. Did you realize that?

. . .

I *have a* question for the person or people who invented the venetian blind: Why didn't you color one of the cords so that we would know which one to pull to open and which one to pull to close? I never know which is which, and I always get it wrong.

☞ **WILTISM** ☜

Compassion, goodwill, common sense, understanding, and love are just a few of the things in life that are free. Use them.

This is one I'm not quite sure about, so don't crucify me till you've given it some thought. (Besides, maybe next year I'll change my mind anyway.)

I'm not sure that if we got rid of all the so-called bad things in our society we wouldn't create an even bigger monster. I'm talking about cigarettes, booze, and things like that. If certain people were not allowed to drink or smoke, would they be uptight all the time? And how would they let off steam—by getting a gun and blowing off someone's head?

In the old days all our time that wasn't spent sleeping was spent hunting, farming, trying to survive. With all the free time we have now, what's a person to do? Some of us don't like to fish, hunt, or bowl, so without the vices I think we would be worse off as a people. We'd be a neurotic society and the pressures would be more than we could stand.

I remember hearing one doctor telling a patient, "I know I told you to stop smoking, but now I want you to start again. Because the effort it's taking you to keep from smoking and the effect it's having on your body is killing you faster than the smoking ever could."

I think that might be true of other so-called vices, too. But like I said, I'm not sure. One thing I *am* sure about is that smoking stunts your growth. I smoked a stogie when I was about fourteen—and I haven't grown an inch since.

When someone is rich we ask his advice on everything. We will take advice from any guy worth millions, yet we won't go to a professor with a Ph.D. on the subject in question. Why? Is this because the only answers we're looking for are the ones that will help us make money?

 **W I L T I S M**

Greed, envy, and fear are the cause of much human behavior. Too much.

Here are four things about food that totally throw me:

(1) If you are thirsty, why do you order very dry white wine?
(2) Unless you like being hungry all the time, why do you eat Chinese food?
(3) Why do people cook with alcoholic beverages? The heat evaporates all the alcohol out of it. If you like the flavor of blackberry brandy, why not just buy some blackberry flavoring?
(4) Why, after we have just had a grand meal and are completely full, does someone always come around and say, "Have some coffee"? Do we have an extra coffee pouch somewhere?

. . .

When I was young I gambled a lot. I played the horses and went to Las Vegas to play baccarat, poker, and games like that. I would occasionally win a lot. And when I'd win five thousand or ten thousand dollars I would come back happy and buy all my friends gifts. But if I lost one hundred dollars I would feel so bad, so low, so negative that I realized losing the hundred had more effect on me than the winning of ten thousand.

It seems the negative things in life have more effect on you than the positive. You hear the boos up there in the stands a lot more than you hear the applause: Fifteen thousand people in the stands can cheer you but when ten people are booing, you will only hear them.

Why? Is it because we're willing to accept the applause, but never the criticism?

Who would you believe the most, a preacher or a car salesman? I would choose the car salesman. Because both are trying to sell you something, but at least you *know* the car salesman shouldn't be trusted.

Why is fifty degrees warm in the middle of the winter and cold in the middle of the summer?

In America, people are thought of as intelligent if they can speak several languages. Yet in other areas of the world in which I've traveled, the ladies of the evening often speak four or five or sometimes more languages in the various nightclubs and social gatherings they are found at. No one considers them intelligent beings, just hookers doing their job.

Accumulating a lot of knowledge might not make you smart, but the proper use of a little knowledge does.

It's always amazing to me how your worth goes up after you die. I realize you can't do any more of what you did, but dying sure makes what you did better than what it was.

Marilyn Monroe is probably the prime example. I hear now from so-called experts that she was a great actress, yet when she was living she was just a sex symbol who, like all the other sex symbols, could not act a bit. There is more Marilyn Monroe memorabilia around today than ever. She gets more ink now than the president she was romantically linked with.

Come on!

If it takes dying to make you a hot item, or a more desirable commodity, what does that tell us about our values?

To me it says:

WILTISM

*You are only at your best
When you're laid to rest.*

I have owned Ferraris, Masaratis, Lamborghinis, Bentleys, Rolls-Royces, and Mercedeses. I have been driven many times in all of the rest of the world's most expensive cars. I won't even bore you by naming all the expensive American cars I've owned. But just recently, while driving a rented American car from the airport to my hotel, I was reminded of the beauty, craftsmanship, and other outstanding features that we take for granted in the average American automobile.

Not one of the fancy-dancy cars I've owned or still own has an air-conditioning unit that works half as well as the one in a Ford Taurus I rented. (And the Taurus is just an average-priced car.) It is also amazing how the radio systems in these moderate- to low-priced American cars are far superior to the systems that come in the high-priced foreign jobs. As I drove from the airport to the hotel I also noticed all the features that were illuminated on the dash, features that cars five to ten times the cost don't have.

I must admit I like hearing the sound of those powerful European engines. But if quiet is what you prefer, these average-priced American cars I've been renting can make the sounds of the gears shifting in your Mercedes or Rolls sound awfully loud.

But you say, "The resale value is so much better in these foreign cars." Well, when you're paying five to ten times the price, $170,000 for a Rolls as compared to $17,000 for a Ford, who cares about the resale value? If it's dollars you're worried about, the money you save initially buying a Ford can be invested; the interest on the difference alone far outweighs the resale value for a Rolls.

And forget about what an average tune-up costs on the foreign jobs; in some cases it's about one-fifth of the total price of your average American car.

So why do we buy these expensive cars? They don't get us to our destination any faster, if you obey the law. Even the lowest-priced car can do sixty-five miles per hour. No matter what you pay for your car it gets dirty like all the others. The batteries, headlights, and other features on an expensive automobile don't last any longer—definitely not three to ten times longer. No matter how much you pay for a car, the electrical system is eventually going to fail because all wires are pretty much the same.

Whether it's a Rolls or an Olds, after a time it goes.

To my way of thinking people buy expensive cars for the same reason they buy a first-class airplane ticket, or why guys who know diddly about boats buy huge, gorgeous yachts. It's because they can afford to, and more important, they want to show people that they can afford to. What better way to show the masses out there that you have attained a certain financial level? You can't invite them all over to your house, you can't take them all out to dinner, so what you do is buy one of these very expensive cars, ride around, and let everybody see you in it.

May I offer a suggestion to some smart American car company? Have a blind driving test. That's not testing a blind man's driving ability. It would be an opportunity for us to drive an American automobile and compare it with two or three of the more expensive foreign jobs, without knowing the make of the car. I'd bet you that people would have a very hard time distinguishing one car from another. The bottom line: The American car would be, if not superior, then pretty much equal. These tests will at least prove that the foreign cars are definitely not worth three to ten times as much money. The car test will prove, like the Coke and Pepsi taste test, that it is almost impossible to tell the difference. But at least Coke and Pepsi are going for the same price.

Are you listening, Mr. Iacocca?

. . .

By the same token, if my fake Rolex watch gives the same results and appears to be real for all who see it, and you can get a fake one for $75 to $100, why would anyone pay $30,000 for a real Rolex?

My fake Rolex keeps perfect time and when I wear it everyone is impressed. The watch cost me $75—which means it's probably worth about $30. Either the guy who sold me my watch is selling his watches too cheap or the Rolex company is selling their watches much too expensively.

As it was conceived, dancing was supposed to be an art form, but as I watch it on the dance floors of the various nightclubs I frequent, the art form has slipped a little. No, make that a lot.

Whether we want to admit it or not, most of us are exhibitionists. When we dance, we're out to be seen, and we really think we're good at what we're doing. But what we are doing is jumping, spinning, contorting, and acting like we are afflicted by some muscle disorder.

I can't imagine what we'll look like to the people of the future when they look back on videos—or whatever they'll be looking back on—and see us dancing. It's going to freak them out when they're told that this was one way of social relaxation and expression and a way to make us feel good.

Think about it! People who get all dolled up in their Sunday tights to go hopping around on a floor that has fluttering lights.

. . .

Why *do we* treat all horses like horses, no matter what color they are—pinto, black, white, palomino—yet some of us find it hard to treat all humans like humans because of their different colors?

W I L T I S M

Is there such a thing as a perfect age? I think not. But a good state of mind can make all ages seem perfect.

When we go on vacation, why is it we delight in traveling thousands of miles to foreign countries where we don't speak the language, we don't like the food, we don't like the accommodations, we don't know what we're going to see, and where the people don't like us, treat us rudely, and overcharge us for everything? Are we just taking a trip, or are we ego-tripping? I think it's ego. The farther away we go the bigger the lie we can tell when we get back: "Oh, I went way over there and had such a great time and saw this and that." All to impress our friends. Then, when our friends and associates take *their* vacations, they have to outdo us by finding an even more exotic place to travel.

Maybe next door is your better vacation. Canada is beautiful, vast, and diverse. We speak the same language—mostly—and the people are nice. Or even better, there is the good old U. S. of A. How many of us have visited all fifty states and savored what they have to offer?

Whenever *people are* asked, "Where are you from?" generally they will tell you what city. But I've noticed that if they name the state instead of the city, it means they're from some small town. They will say, "I'm from Iowa" or

"I'm from Kansas." For some reason they seem embarrassed to name the small town. I don't understand that.

Quaint little towns are where most people want to be, where people are friendlier, things move at an easier pace, and traffic is not a problem. Small towns are the beauty spots of the world. In Europe people will boast of being from one of the small ski towns or resorts. They know the villages are beautiful and are proud of them. Why is it that a small town in Europe is thought of as a quaint and refreshing village, and the same kind of town in America is "Hicksville"?

I *believe dining* room tables should be taller. They shouldn't stop at your chest, they should come all the way up to your chin. This way, when you eat you could scrape the food right to your mouth. As they are built now, you have to pick the food up and carry it over, and you drop a good portion of it on the way to your mouth. Taller tables would mean no more stained ties, shirts, and blouses. (If you still miss your mouth eating at these new tables, you've got a real problem.)

The extra height of the table would be no problem for those of us who are unusually tall or short, since most of us are about the same height sitting down. Most of my dates are a foot to a foot and a half shorter than I am, but when we sit down we're about the same size. (And I thank God for that, because it's important for other things too.)

When *I was* a kid and I would go to the doctor's office, I remember seeing a picture on the wall that portrayed the perfect breakfast: two eggs, bacon, toast with butter, and some milk. I'm sure you saw it too in your doctor's office, or the school nurse's office, or in health class. What's interesting about this memory is that these days, all those things they told you were perfectly healthy are now bad for you—the fat, the cholesterol, the calories, the sodium, the nitrites. They'll all kill you.

I'm sure they have another picture on the wall now depicting a new perfect breakfast. But before the printer's ink is dry the so-called experts will already be taking shots at it. Oat bran, the hot health food a little while ago, is already on the skids.

Why do we listen to these "experts"? I say we can call that BS and eat what we want—in moderation—'cause the experts obviously don't know nothin'.

Recently a young lady who was singing the national anthem before a NBA basketball game in Madison Square Garden forgot the words to the song. A referee who was there to do the game came to her aid. He whispered the remaining words in her ear. How embarrassing it must have been for her! But the point of this story is not her embarrassment, it's that our national anthem is so hard to sing that you need a ref to tell you whether you're singing it correctly. Why is this difficult song our national anthem?

After having heard our national anthem before games about five million times, I opt for "God Bless America" instead. It's a hell of a lot easier to sing and it has a much better ring.

But why a song at all? If you're strong on nationalism, as I am, the pledge of allegiance to the flag is much more in order. We all could join in and feel like we're part of the event. It would put a stop to all those would-be singers and also put an end to all those embarrassing moments we've had to endure.

And it would give us all a sense of pride.

Why are most real estate dealers women, and most car dealers men?

Women have that built-in mother image—perfect for a salesperson since we all trust mothers.

On the other hand, everyone knows that the person with the worst professional reputation in the universe is a car salesman. Yet men comprise 95 percent of the car sales force.

If we trust women with our largest investment I'm sure we would trust them with our second largest. After all, would your mother sell you a lemon?

In addition, a man would probably rather test-drive a new car with a pretty lady next to him than another man. It would also be easier for a woman to sell all those extras that dealers like to unload on buyers. What man has the resolve to resist a charming saleswoman?

Women buyers would relate to a woman salesperson. The female prospect would feel that if the saleslady can handle the car, she can also. And most women don't trust car salesmen because they talk down to them.

Some might say, "Men know more about cars than women." We're not talking about repairing a car, we are talking about buying one. How many salesmen know anything about auto mechanics anyway? When selling, most salesmen simply read off a fact sheet: "This car seats five. It has rack and pinion steering . . ." and so on. If you were to ask him to explain rack and pinion steering, do you think he could? No way.

As we know, car salesmen have the dubious honor—
along with lawyers, politicians, and now some ministers—
of being the most untrustworthy people in the world. And
all these professions are dominated by men. Real estate
does not fall into the same category—because it's dominated by women. Is this a coincidence? No. I think women
are much more logical when it comes to choosing something of real value.

On Sex and Love: What Rules the World

Does sex run the world? I think it does. The advertising industry tries to tell us what to eat, drink, wear, drive, etc. And more often than not, advertising uses sexy people, usually pretty women, to sell their products. What the sexy people have to do with the integrity of the product I'll never know. If sex can sell cigarettes, it can rule everything else, too.

I *have always* believed there is more than one true love for a person. I also believe that lust is more a natural part of us than love, and that one can spend every waking moment falling in and out of lust. There are a few of us who are fortunate enough to be in a position to fulfill our lustful desires. I'm one of those lucky ones. So don't be shocked to hear that if I had to count my sexual encounters, I would be closing in on twenty thousand women. Yes, that's correct, *twenty thousand different ladies.* At my age, that equals out to having sex with 1.2 women a day, every day since I was fifteen years old.

I have a feeling a lot of you are saying, "Come on, Wilt, stop all that bullshit." I say to you that there are those who know me well enough to know that I speak the truth. I'm not boasting, I don't see all this lovemaking as any kind of conquest; all I'm saying is that I like women, people are curious about my sex life, and to most people the number of women who have come and gone through my bedrooms (and various hotel rooms around the country) would boggle the mind.

I give the numbers here not to impress. I give them because it's like when I played basketball—many of my numbers were so unbelievably high that most people dismissed them as fables or found them impossible to relate to. Hell, I've done a lot of things that are hard to believe. Does that mean I should stop talking about them? Or that I should worry whether people believe me or not? I think you know the answer to that.

While riding on the bus when I was with the Globies, I once told a story the players found hard to believe. I told them that I once scored sixty points in twelve minutes of basketball. (In high school the quarters are eight minutes long, and during a quarter and a half of the second half, before being taken out, I scored sixty points, which gave me ninety points for the game—the Pennsylvania state record, which still stands.) The doubt didn't come from the fact that I scored the sixty points—the doubt came when I told them that the other team was *freezing* the ball. In high school there is no twenty-four-second shot-clock, and a team can freeze the ball as long as they want or as long as they can. But when the Globies went to Philadelphia I took some clippings back to the bus to show them I was indeed telling the truth.

So as I relate this story, I can see how people may feel that twenty thousand sexual encounters is a fictitious number. But a roommate who lived with me in Hawaii for a while asked me one Monday morning, "Wilt, do you have *any* idea how many women you've had visit you in your bedroom over the past seven days?" Before I could reply he pulled a list out of his pocket and began to give me the numbers for each day of the week. Thursday was the high—a total of six—and Sunday, like Friday, was only three. Thirty was his total. Then he said, "I wasn't even *here* all the time, so maybe a few slipped by me. How do you do it?" I replied, "Well, Jeff, many young ladies come to the islands and being so far from home want to try something different. *I* am the most different thing they can find."

Even though that week in Hawaii sounds like a fantastic few days, I'm afraid it doesn't come *close* to rivaling a birthday party I was invited to in San Francisco. At the party, I was the only male in the company of fifteen ladies of, how shall I put it . . . of dubious taste. Yes, I got all but one before the rising of the sun. I wasn't able to enjoy the fifteenth birthday girl but I did muster enough strength to sing her "Happy Birthday." This may help to clear up why I've never been married or even engaged to be married— though I have engaged. It may also put to rest the rumors that even I hear about myself from time to time, rumors that anyone who's single and lives in L.A. hears—"He's gay." I'm not.

I've always believed that one should sow his wild oats before settling down. Apparently, by being a little larger than most, I've got more wild oats to sow.

The one thing that *is* important is that I believe in fidelity where marriage is concerned, and my sexual appetite has not come *close* to allowing me to think about settling down from twenty thousand to one woman. (I view a wife or a steady girlfriend as one and the same.) Let it be known also that of the twenty thousand, *none* were married at the time—at least as far as I know. And I made a conscious effort to find out. Even as a single man, infidelity has no place in my life.

I wonder how many men would be married if they had my opportunities. I'm sure plenty who read the numbers will no doubt think my taste is not particularly high or that I am "easy." Well, I'm not a guy, like many I know, who gets drunk and believes that's what booze was made for— to make all women look good. I am a man of distinctive taste and most of the women I have encountered, the average Joe would have proposed marriage to on the first date.

I believe the lack of this kind of thinking has been the secret of a great deal of my success with the opposite sex. Having so many great-looking ladies, they don't intimidate me. In fact, normally it's the exact opposite. Since most normal males are perpetually in heat and most normal women are not, as a male you must learn to be convincing in your approach. No matter who the lady is, I convince her that it is an experience we both should not miss. It's important that they get to realize there is no loss of respect—and there isn't—no matter how quickly we get involved. Many women are afraid that if they allow an encounter too soon the man loses all respect for them. You know the old saying: If you get the milk for free, there ain't no need to buy the cow. But I say that if we lust in earnest for each other, that's *real* and we should act on this, because how many real things *are* there in life? Out of the three billion females in the world, in my travels I've seen tens of thousands of very appealing ladies. My twenty thousand is just a drop in the bucket. I'm simply more fortunate than most and I'm of a mind-set that allows me to try to consummate true desire. My appeal to women, as I have mentioned before, is that they find me different. They are intrigued, and they wonder if they can handle a man of my physical size. Of course there are scores of women who are terrified of having any sort of encounter with me. I'm not sure of their true reason for this attitude, though I do know a few of these ladies' minds have been changed when they get to know me.

I must confess I lean toward a natural-looking and active type. Glamorous-looking ladies do less for my libido than wholesome-looking ones. I'm sure this has something to do with the fact that, to me, an innocent-looking lady is a bigger challenge. Must be my competitive instinct. Yet I am constantly surprised when these innocent types turn out to be hell-raisers in the boudoir.

Race *relations were* a major factor in the NBA when I came up. Quotas and a star structure were well defined. Players of color were supposed to stay in their place and play supporting roles. Because I was so dominating, I was humiliating all these white players on the floor. *Then* I had the audacity, off the floor, to date white girls when I felt like it. Believe me, I never intended it to be disrespectful, insensitive, or brazen. I was just doing what was natural— chasing good-looking ladies, whoever they were and wherever they were available. I did this the same way no matter *where* I was; in Rome, Paris, Australia, or America. Remember, I had just finished a year and a half with the Globies, traveling the world dating girls of *every* nationality and color. I saw no need to restrict my dating in my own country. This was one of the things that helped me to become a "villain." Whites didn't like it, and people of color wanted me to be more attentive to my own kind so they could be "proud" of me. I am not sure this kind of thinking has changed much even today, three decades later.

With all the sex I've had, I never let it interfere with my playing. Being from the old (and dumb) school of thinking, I saw sex as a joyful activity, one that should take a long time and be relaxed. As a result, I only partook when there were no immediate chores to perform, like a basketball game to win. So little tête-à-têtes were no-nos minutes before a game. On game days, sex had to be very early indeed. My sex life suffered a great deal during the season—so I thank God that seasons were much shorter back then. Then, a season was six months. Now it can go as long as nine months. Maybe *that's* why I retired early.

The modern school of thinking is that athletes should not change their routine—and that if sex is part of that routine, it may be all right. I am not sure of that one. Last year, James Worthy of the Los Angeles Lakers was busted for allegedly soliciting two prostitutes who turned out to be undercover agents. His arrest came three hours or so before game time. At the time, the Lakers were on a four-game losing streak, so maybe James was just trying to change his luck.

When *it comes* to picking men, women don't really consider age to be a major factor. I know it's not so the other way around. Men don't fantasize about forty- or fifty-year-old women. But women like men who are forty or fifty or sixty. As a male you can hold your sexual position a lot longer than a female.

I have found that as I have gotten older, the desire for me hasn't waned as much as I thought it would when I was twenty-five and contemplating life at fifty. I must say that I am happily surprised.

As *an adult* I have always felt that I was blessed and possessed what I consider a powerful attribute—uniqueness. But I never fancied myself as being handsome or irresistible to the opposite sex.

Yet in some peculiar way I have found myself being the fancy of numerous women. Whatever it is that women find attractive in men is a multifaceted thing, I feel, so I am not sure whether they see me as a physical challenge or they believe that I am endowed with as much sensitivity as size, or, as I have been told by some, "You make me feel like a little girl again."

Women have said to me, "You need to be understood and loved like any ordinary person, even though you're this famous larger-than-life figure. You crave the uncomplex love that comes naturally to others. Because of your size and position this seldom occurs." That's what *they* think.

They see me the way men see the beautiful woman who's home alone on weekends because every guy thinks she already has a date, so no one asks her out. They think the same thing happens to me. It doesn't. Women are also taken with me because I'm more visible than anyone they know. Coupled with the self-assurance that I project, I become like a majestic mountain many feel they'd like to scale and conquer. Wilt as Mount Everest.

I have never been surprised by the many different types of women I attract. I'm always gratified and reassured to know that I'm desired, for whatever reason, so I try never to misuse this power. Even though I enjoy flirting, I never enjoy hurting. I never play with anyone's emotions, and when affection isn't mutual I try not to keep anyone on a string.

I am happy to say that I have as many female friends as male, maybe more. For me there's no difference. I discuss anything with them, go anywhere, play games, and enjoy all facets of life with them. As I said earlier, I was raised in a family with six sisters (and only two brothers), so I learned early in life about sharing with and caring for the opposite sex. Since all my sisters are very attractive and have had many pursuers, I had a chance to learn firsthand the rights and wrongs of courting.

A couple years ago Sean Connery was called the sexiest man in the world. How did this happen? When he was playing James Bond—agent 007—he was a very handsome man. Girls were falling all over themselves to get to him and guys were desperate to *be* him. When he was 007 he didn't have to be labeled sexy, he just was. But when he gets bald, a little paunchy, and ages a little, *now* they give him that title. *Now* he's the ultimate sex symbol.

Where is this BS coming from? It comes from the fact that, like greatness in sports, people can be called sexy when they're no longer threats.

A *lot of* women I date say things like, "I want to be treated like a lady."

Ah, well, normally if you *are* a lady you never talk about being treated like one. You don't have to.

(By my mom)

Beauty is only skin deep and ugliness goes to the bone. When beauty wears away, ugliness holds its own.

When looking at couples in a car I have developed a rule of thumb: The closer the two lovers are the shorter they have been together.

When each has a shoulder touching the opposite door, you know they've been together too long.

Many, *many people* have asked why I'm not married and have never been married. First off, I must tell you that I really do believe in this great institution—for some. But not for all. (And not for many, or for very long, as it appears today.) Marriage to anything or anybody is a commitment of body, mind, and spirit, and for me it just hasn't come together yet. I have met the body, but at the time I didn't have the mind. When I've had the mind, the spirit wasn't willing.

The question I ask myself, and have asked for many years, is: Is there a marriage out there that I would trade places with? In my case, I have to ask myself if I want to give up the freedom of bachelorhood, which allows me the opportunity to entertain life as I see fit. Or do I want to be curtailed by the laws and restrictions that our present society imposes upon a married man?

People often try to make me feel that without marriage, I have not experienced all there is to experience in life. But I've seen very few marriages that I truly respect. Of course, not knowing how most couples really act behind closed doors, it's hard to say for sure if they're happy. But too many don't seem all that happy.

A lot of people get married because they fear growing old alone. Bad news: My feeling is that they are not necessarily guaranteed any more comfort from family in their last days than they were from their solitude. Often the family they think will be there to share and care for them are busy raising their own families, with little time for their parents, even though they might love them dearly.

In actuality, the only reason to marry is to give your children a legal name—legal by society's standards. I don't see marriage enhancing love or making it stronger. Often it seems to work in reverse.

There are a couple of other things that I believe make marriages a tall order, no pun intended. Mostly, I believe there are many loves out there for us all, and each may have its time or place; to love more than one at a time is no disgrace.

Love can come and then love can go.
How long it will last I'll be damned if I know.

I am always amazed at the strength of the so-called weaker sex. To me, that phrase, "weaker sex," is a misnomer. In nature the strong survive, and it is a proven fact that women outlive men. There are many reasons why this is so. We used to think crying was a sign of weakness. Now we know and we are willing to admit that crying is not all bad. Women cry much more readily than men, and I believe this is one of their strengths. By crying they vent a lot of their emotions: joy, pain, frustration, and anger. Men, fearing they'll be perceived as weak if they cry, keep these emotions pent-up. So these feelings build up inside, and they work internally—often causing physical and/or mental illnesses, which shorten the life span.

Women have the rap of being more emotional than men, yet I feel it's just the opposite.

We all know how calculating a woman can be when going after a husband or even a simple date. Very rarely does a woman go after a mate frivolously. When a woman looks for a mate she wants to know how stable he is. Does he have a job? Will he be a good provider? Does he have a future? She checks out his clothes, his car, his friends. If you drive through Beverly Hills you will see hundreds upon hundreds of great-looking women driving expensive Mercedes-Benzes with their cute little kids next to them. You can bet your last dollar that their husbands, the fathers of those children, are ordinary-looking guys who are very successful financially. It's not that women are gold diggers, it's that when looking for a mate they use more sense. They look at the entire picture.

On the other hand, what does a man check out when he is looking for a mate? Her physicality. Maybe not *only* that, but let's be honest here—*mainly* that. He is not using his big head to reason this out, he's using his little head. To me this is an emotional response, not a rational one.

We, the men, are full of it—emotion, I mean.

I *find that* women who appear to have everything going for them—looks, education, talent, accomplishments, financial security—also seem to be very accomplished in the sexual side of life. It makes sense. To be sexually gifted is in keeping with the rest of their demeanor. These ladies take pride in *everything* they do. They put their work ethic into discovering more exotic and erotic ways of sexual sophistication. Women who are not so accomplished don't seem to think of trying to please themselves and their lovers. They seem to think that what comes naturally is good enough.

As with sports, some people have an aptitude for sexual prowess and some don't. But also, as in sports, all who work diligently at it can become the best that they can be.

When *it comes* to romantic love, a man has a strong attraction to a woman—and vice versa—for a period of approximately eleven to thirteen months. That's the period when you can't stop thinking of each other, you're calling each other ten times a day, and you can't keep your mind on any of your other activities. This is that beautiful time, that giving time, that wanting time. The time when you are full of love.

Years ago, people would have started a family by the end of this time period. Then their obsession would have shifted from themselves to their child.

Nowadays we find that couples that don't or won't have families are left with the dilemma of what to do with each other after they have come down from that total love high. I think that this in itself causes problems and leads to the changing of the guard, better known as a divorce. If the couple has a child, the chances of their staying together are greater and their relationship has a chance to be more fulfilling. I believe this is what Mother Nature intended.

I *was at* a party and when a girl asked me what I did, I told her I was a sanitation engineer. "That's great," she said, "But what *is* that?" I said I remove garbage from here and move it to there. And she quickly removed herself—without my help.

I have never met a girl who said her boyfriend was a garbage man. Their boyfriends are always engineers, doctors, or lawyers. I wonder if they've seen figures that show the average garbage man makes more than the average lawyer.

Which is the way it should be, since garbage men get rid of all the garbage that most lawyers are full of.

I *am all* for women being involved in all the things men are, but when it comes to women bodybuilders I have my doubts. (I should admit I'm not crazy about most men bodybuilders either, but in this chapter we're talking about sex, so I'll leave the men alone here.) I know that these bodies, which are supposed to represent health and vigor, are constructed by a great deal of discipline and sacrifice. But how appealing these bodies are is another question. And I don't think they're all that natural.

First of all, to attain this sculptured look requires a lot of severe dieting, which in most cases is done without doctors' supervision. And I won't even mention steroids. I've told you how I feel about them. Why would *anyone* take a drug which you *know* will hurt you and weaken you in the long run, when what you're trying to do is make your body stronger?

These bodies are also, let's face it, unappealing. Some of them are all lumps and veins. What the hell is appealing about a mass of nonproductive, overly developed pectorals (not breasts but pecs)? And that's the men! To see women looking this way is ridiculous. I know of no man who finds these ladies attractive.

At bodybuilding contests you often see a girl five feet five inches tall and weighing 140 pounds with huge, bulging thighs, who has just won the heavyweight division. Believe me, she represents a totally different image of what most men visualize as their five-foot, five-inch dream girl.

I have talked to Arnold Schwarzenegger about this subject and even *he* does not appreciate women bodybuilders for their feminine beauty. The lady he chose for his wife, Maria Shriver, bears this out.

Symmetry is the key to great beauty, and a great deal of that you're either born with or you're not. With my long legs I could never be a symmetrically perfect bodybuilder, but I couldn't care less.

. . .

Because I travel so much, a lot of my male friends—and some of my female ones—are always wanting to know where the girls are the most beautiful. What they really want to know is where the girls are the sexiest and the most sexual.

The men are always disappointed when I don't reinforce their fantasies and dreams about Scandinavian women, particularly the Danes and Swedes. Unfortunately, they are, in my estimation, very low on the list of sexy ladies.

First of all, they have that sexy reputation, and even if they wanted to they would find it hard, if not impossible, to live up to that. This reputation is not their doing, of course; it's manufactured by the usual propaganda machines—TV, movies, and magazines. It began years ago, back when the rest of the world had negative views and restrictive laws on premarital sex, the selling of pornographic magazines, and the use of sexual aids. Denmark and Sweden believed in sexual freedom. This less conservative thinking obviously perpetuates their sexual reputation.

But I have found that because the rest of the world—and Americans in particular—believe these things about Scandinavia, it's made their people very self-conscious, very sensitive when the subject is broached—verbally or otherwise. Rather than having loose morals and sexual inclinations, these people, generally speaking, tend to try very hard to let you know how promiscuous they are *not*.

Taking this into consideration, along with the fact that they are from a part of the world where people are not quite so gregarious as, let's say, Italy, you have a combination, gentlemen, that does not favor you getting, let's say, lucky in love.

That's the lowdown—and often, a let-down to American

men. But I know you want the real info, the gossip—you want to know where they are and who they are. Well, I won't disappoint you. Just remember, this is only one man's opinion. But *what* a man! (That's a joke, folks.)

The ladies of Canada and Australia are very nice and friendly. For some of you men out there, Bangkok may be the place of your dreams. There, for not more than a couple of bucks, a man can be treated like a king—or a queen, for that matter, if that's your preference.

But my advice, if you're an American, is to stay at home. Nowhere in the world do you have such variations of beauty, style, and pizzazz as here in America. Yes, American women have come a long way, baby!

Like you all, I've been caught up in the idea that the grass is always greener on the other side of the fence (or in this case, on the other side of the ocean), but once you get past those quaint, cute accents (if they speak English at all), there's not much else they have over the girls from the good old U.S.A.

Give me the intelligence and class of East Coast women, the charm and hospitality of the Southern belle, the daring and vitality of the women of the West. Yeah, they have it all in the U.S. They are the best.

Now, as far as you women are concerned, when it comes to men you should stay at home, too. Hey, if I'm any example of the American man, you can't go wrong!

☞ **WILTISM** ☜

Can you imagine how much better life would be
by allowing our minds and our thinking to be free?
But for us it seems we will always be
pawns and slaves of our society.

It always amazes me how the bathing suit issues of periodicals like *Sports Illustrated* and other so-called sports magazines sell so many more copies than their other issues. Men, there are a number of quality magazines out there full of gorgeous ladies in and out of clothes. I'm talking about magazines like *Vogue, Harper's Bazaar,* and *Elle.* You can pay a decent price and once a month you see all these same beautiful girls that you're seeing once a year in *SI* and *Inside Sports.*

T*his is another* "Maybe You Can Help Me Here" item, but I think it fits in this chapter better.

Why is it that the best time to go shopping is when you're the least hungry? Does this mean that the more you want something the more you'll accept anything, because everything looks good? A specific example: The hornier you are the more any girl will appeal to you, even if she's not the "right" girl.

Is that why they say love is blind? Meaning: The only way you really ever know if you truly like someone is to get to know them before you fall in love (by that I mean lust) with them, because if you are in love you can't see if you really like them? Crazy! But it really is true. Does it then follow that the best time to pick a mate is when you are least in love? Since love is blind, it can only get in the way of picking the right one.

Maybe the choosing of mates by parents years ago was not such a bad idea. They had a clear presence of mind, without all the emotional BS. We should go back into the records to see how those marriages fared, compared to the accepted way of choosing today. There's a subject for Oprah to explore.

Maybe what we need today is not so many marriage counselors who get paid for trying to save screwed-up marriages, but marriage brokers who get paid a fee to bring people together. Marriages fail at such a high rate now, could a marriage arranged by a broker be any worse? I doubt it. We now have call-dating, call for sex, call for laughter, call for everything else, why not a call to a marriage broker?

Here's how it works. You call up a marriage broker and say, "I'm looking for a wife. I'd like for her to be five foot ten, to read a lot, to be an excellent cook and to know how to swim." The broker replies, "Okay. I've got five of them. Let's look through our files. Here's Jane Doe, she's five nine and a half, she likes to swim, and she's a very good cook. She'd be a perfect wife for you. This is what *she's* looking for in a husband . . ."

Sounds great, huh? I'm going to open up an office; if nothing else, think of all the women I'll meet.

Even a wise man seems like a fool among fools.

We have all heard the phrase "Act your age." It's been used by all moms trying to get their kids to act more adult or grown-up. But now it's used to express how we feel about older people acting in ways that appear to be too young for their age. We're always making an issue out of marriages or relationships between people who have a big age differential. Why do we look at these couples with disdain? Should people of a certain age only have feelings for people their own age?

What does "your own age" mean anyway? We all know

there are adults who act and think like juveniles, and vice versa. Does anyone know at what age the desire for sex and romance leaves an individual? No! That's why no one deserves to be limited to a specific group.

Don't people ever look at what's really important, what two people have in common and if they're good for each other? If they are happy (which is undoubtedly the bottom line)? Maybe she's a good cook, and he likes good food. Maybe he's good in bed, and she likes what he does to her—old and young has nothing to do with it.

This goes for all the other surface things people see as negatives in relationships, things like racial and cultural differences. Too often, people aren't looking at the things that really count.

☞ **WILTISM** ☜

The making of a child can come from a moment of pleasure, but the making of a man can give a lifetime of pleasure.

Most men would think it a great achievement if they could make love to a thousand different women. But I've come to believe the greater achievement would be to make love to the same woman a thousand times.

TWELVE

On the Issues of the Day: Wilt's World

I have opinions on just about everything, as I'm sure you've noticed, including some important topics we haven't fully discussed yet: politics, crime, drugs, health, and other issues of the day. Dick Young, the late sportswriter in New York, used to write a column to discuss his views, which he called "My America." Well, I am a hell of a lot bigger than Dick Young—at least physically—so America isn't big enough. Call this baby Wilt's World.

As I noted earlier, I am a Republican. I supported Richard Nixon and Gerald Ford. But I am not a fan of Ronald Reagan or George Bush.

We have a lot of mentally ill and homeless people on our streets, which is a direct result of Reagan policies and actions. He had eight years to correct this injustice but chose to do nothing about what is a growing and tragic epidemic. Reagan did some things well, but to turn his back on the disenfranchised was unforgiveable.

Bush appears to be going through his term in office sitting on a fence—not committing to anything important. When you don't take a positive stand on something as basic as the Chinese attempt for freedom in Tiananmen Square, you won't take a stand on anything. That was a great civil rights issue, and the world knew the students in China were right. What was Bush's stand? I have no idea—and I don't think anyone else does, either.

George Bush learned the technique of noncommittal fence-sitting—ruffle no feathers and it will all blow away— as head of the CIA, and then refined it to an art form as vice president. It was easy, since he served at the feet of the master of procrastination, Ronald Reagan.

I wonder who really runs the Bush household? Is it George or Barbara? I have a feeling when it comes down to really running things, it's Mrs. Bush. I know if I had to pick a Bush to run our country it would be the Missus, not Georgie baby.

The *vote is* the most powerful tool we have as Americans. Yet it should be improved upon. There should be a box at the bottom of all ballots that reads "None of the Above." If you like *none* of the candidates in an election, you just check that last option. If the "None of the Above" box gets the most votes, we know we need to have another election with different candidates. If we had had such a choice in the Bush-Dukakis election, do you think George Bush would be president today? No way.

It's evident these days that even if you win you still may not be the people's choice. When Reagan beat Carter in the presidential election, was he really a winner? Almost anyone could have beaten Carter at that time. As we've seen, often only the lesser of two evils gets the most votes. Our government is based on the majority vote and I say that no politician should be in office if the true majority doesn't want him.

At present, when people don't like the choices they just don't vote. I've got bad news for all these people—that doesn't let the candidates know how they really feel. If they came out and voted for "None of the Above," wouldn't that be more revealing?

If one chooses to compare things, maybe a case can be made for legalizing drugs. Heroin kills about 4,000 people every year; cigarettes kill well over 250,000. Based on these facts alone, it seems logical to legalize heroin and ban cigarettes.

WILTISM

The higher you think you're getting, the quicker you're getting to the bottom. Drug users shouldn't say, "Let's get high." They should say, "Let's get low."

Let me consider a phenomenon I find distressing: organizations that are exclusive by race. There are many all-white organizations, and there have been for a long time. Today, every civil rights group—NAACP, CORE, EPA, and others—accuses these groups of being no different than the KKK, the John Birch Society, and all the other white supremacy groups. And we minorities are up in arms about them.

But we also have all-black organizations. There is an all-black ski club I know of, for example. You'll notice there is never any flak given to exclusive black clubs by the white majority. I believe that a great many whites are actually quite happy with these clubs, because they feel this is really the best way to deal with integration: If the people of color have their own things, the whites don't have to worry about them getting involved in theirs.

I realize the need and desire for all-black groups. They give people of color who would not normally do things like skiing a chance to participate and feel comfortable. In this context, when we use the term all-black it seems quite innocent. But we are really fostering the very thing we're trying to get away from.

I say the more groups we have, the more problems we have. You've heard the phrase "divide and conquer"? Well, it works. When you divide, you weaken.

When we divide into groups we weaken ourselves as a human race.

It *has been* more than thirty years since the movie *The Mouse That Roared* graced the silver screen, but that movie's philosophy is as true today as it was then. One of the best ways for a country to get ahead is to pick a war with the United States and lose. We support them, bring in troops to protect them, and give them all the money they need to rebuild their economy. Then they become world powers. Japan and Germany are prime examples. While our troops are protecting Japan, they're using all the money they would normally spend on defense to buy up America and the rest of the world.

So keep an eye on Grenada, Panama, and Iraq.

You might argue with this view, but from up here it appears that countries that work hard also play hard, and are better than average at games. It's like those accomplished women who are better at sex than the norm. The Germans, Russians, Chinese, and Japanese bear this out.

Take the Cubans. Under Castro they must work very hard to survive. And they are among the best in the games they participate in—boxing, weight lifting, volleyball, track and field. Before Castro, when Cuba was known for its nightlife, music, and gambling, they weren't that great in any sports other than baseball. When forced to work hard in life, they started to excel in games.

The Germans are another example. Look what they've done since World War II. They are one of the great economic powers—*and* a great athletic power. The Chinese are a hard-working people, so it's no surprise that when they choose a sport to learn they excel. They have been involved in international gymnastics and diving competition for only a short period of time, yet they are one of the world's powers in both sports.

Conversely, France, Spain, Belgium, Mexico, and many South American countries don't excel in sports. They don't seem to excel in anything else either.

Games and hard work go hand in hand. People who are willing to work hard can be good at whatever they do, whether it's running a country or running a race.

. . .

I *recently went* to Seoul, South Korea. I've been there a number of times before, but this time I was enjoying some nightlife. While listening to some very contemporary American rock music it made me flash on how much alike these places in various parts of the world were. I could drop you in a nightclub in London, Hong Kong, New York, or Nairobi, and from the music, the dancing, the drinks you're being served, even the types of people you encounter there, you wouldn't be able to tell where in the world you were. If you ask a girl for a dance in Tokyo or Timbuktu she'll dance pretty much like the girl you asked in Paris or Chicago. (Sex seems to be one of those universal things also—and I thank God for that.)

My point is that cultures and peoples seem to have all blended and become one, transcending all the differences we're supposed to have. And for better or worse, these nightspots have become the world's common ground.

Maybe we should have all those high-powered summit meetings in discos around the world. At least we'd know that everyone there would understand each other. We could use dancing as our means of communication—we could dance all our troubles away.

Why not? We haven't talked them away or disposed of them with wars.

B*esides music, the* most common denominator in the world today is sports. Every major country in the world today enjoys some form of sports. Sports, if given a chance, could be the one thing, the vehicle that bridges the gaps of communication between most countries. Nothing but war itself seems to command so much national attention. I think sports could be used to divert our attention from war forever.

International competitions seem to be nothing more than a healthy alternative to that other game that man has been destined to play from the beginning of time: the game of war. To call war a game may seem like I'm understating what war really is, but I feel the real reason we're willing to obediently march off to war stems from that cardinal urge man has to compete. The issues that seem to be the cause of all wars really are not the determining factors that lead us to them; it is simply our competitive nature.

From childhood, we are given toy soldiers and guns. We've played at being generals, fighter pilots, and all the "glamorous" things that go with war. These things are made so attractive that by the time we grow into manhood we look for a chance to play that game in the real world. It becomes nothing more than competition: My army is bigger and badder than your army. My battleships are bigger and badder than your battleships. It is just like determining who has the biggest and baddest football team in the Super Bowl.

We should have more sporting events like the Olympics. We should use these games to resolve arguments and issues that would otherwise lead to violence. Just like in the days of King Arthur, a champion could take up the gauntlet and do sporting battles in the names of king (or president) and country.

Think of all the lives that could be saved.

Humane killings are considered good when it comes to animals, yet we let people suffer endless pain. We force families to go deep into debt trying to keep people alive who are already, in a very real sense, dead. Do animals deserve more compassion than people?

I am not for us playing God, but if the only way to keep someone alive is by manmade machines—which is in itself playing God—it's wrong to withhold the final decision from the living loved ones involved. In these cases, the death wish should be granted.

I unfortunately lost both my mother and father to the disease of cancer. It's a terrible experience, not only for the sick but for the survivors. The emotional strain is indescribable, and so is the financial strain. When our family was trying to do all we could for them, I often wondered how families less financially fortunate dealt with such an expensive ordeal. The cost of dying—and of trying to comfort the dying—is a disgrace.

T*here are many* things that we can't do in a foreign country that foreigners can do in ours. Not only does this put us at a social and financial disadvantage, it helps to foster the wrongs some societies are involved in.

For example, South African golfer Gary Player came to America and made millions playing in our golf tournaments, while we of color are not allowed to play in his country. Now, Gary Player may be one of the nicest guys around, but I say if we disallowed people like him from playing here, he'd be a lot more apt to try to clean up that mess over there in his home country. As long as he can make his money here and return to South Africa to live the good life—or stay here and live the good life at the expense of others—why should he bother to try to change his country?

. . .

Trouble in large metropolitan areas often starts with gangs. These gangs are groups of young people, mostly in their teens or twenties, who seem to have nothing else to do but get involved in criminal and destructive acts. Can't we find other outlets for them?

I propose that the government give these groups jobs. Not just any jobs, but ones that let them blow off steam while they make money and are useful to society. Jobs like the cleaning and painting of neighborhood trash cans and public facilities; or the maintenance of green areas, the trimming of trees and shrubs, mowing of lawns, planting of flowers. There are many jobs these youths could perform, and such jobs can promote pride and dignity, which these gang members desperately need.

Another deterrent to the problem of juvenile crime would be the formation of groups—composed of adults—that are highly visible in neighborhoods. These groups would watch over things and ensure safe travel in their areas. The high visibility of policemen in some areas has been successful in preventing crime, but we don't have enough police to be everywhere.

We constantly hear about some older man or woman being robbed on the street as they're going to the store. Seldom does it happen if they are with a group. There are just too many variables that a wrongdoer has to deal with when encountering more than one or two people at a time.

Graffiti is one of the crimes that would come to an end if the government paid these kids to clean up, and if we had neighborhood groups on patrol. Just by showing that we adults care, we would show these young people that what they're doing is wrong. It's much like the relationship you have with your child. The more interest you show in his or her grades, the harder the child works to make you proud.

In this case it pays to be nosy, because when we're not, it costs us all.

☞ WILTISM ☜

We spend too much time feeding our bodies and not our souls. We spend too much time with what we wear, and too little time with how much we care.

A topic that I feel needs a lot more attention paid to it is the idea of owning firearms. To sell weapons like Uzis, assault rifles, and AK-47s—weapons used in gang warfare and major criminal offences—is ridiculous. I think—at least I hope—most people will agree with me there. But I also feel strongly that there are way too many crazies out there who like the feeling of power that a concealed weapon gives them. That's why I'm also very much against handguns.

True, you do need some way to protect your family and property. I personally feel that bigger is better here; it's probably safer to own a tank with a 55mm cannon mounted on it than any concealed handgun. If you can't get a tank, a shotgun is the best choice. It will stop your villain—or at least deter him, whether you can shoot it or not. Wouldn't you feel safer if your wife or loved one had a shotgun as protection, where all she had to do was point it? To me, that seems to be more protection than trying to use a puny pistol.

Most handguns are only used in little bullshit ways, like "settling" petty arguments in bars. Out of nowhere someone pulls a gun. (If he was carrying a shotgun you never would have argued with him. Or he wouldn't have been granted entrance into the bar in the first place.)

The point is that concealed weapons cause the most damage and the most trouble. They should be outlawed, and they should no longer be made. Ban them all. Even cops don't need them; shotguns are more persuasive.

I'm against all group labeling: Baptist, black, Republican, Armenian, Irish, female, male. I'm against every label. Every time we form a group we form a prejudice. Every group label you can think of has opposition from another group.

The Republicans don't like the Democrats just because they're Democrats, even if the platforms they're running on are almost the same. Irish Protestants don't like Catholics, even if both are hard-working coal miners from exactly the same background.

I believe it's these labels we put on ourselves, and the groups we belong to, that cause most of the prejudice we have today. Groups breed prejudice and hate. The more we can do away with group labeling the better we're going to be as a human race.

There's one in every neighborhood. You know, the one with the unkempt lawn or the one who never takes his trash cans out on the right day. I believe people owe their neighbors more respect. Roaches and rats often come around because of the personal neglect of one individual, but because pests don't pay attention to boundaries like property lines, we all suffer from one person's lack of caring.

There's a bigger point I am trying to make with this. This same kind of irresponsibility is being carried on as we pollute our rivers, lakes, and oceans. This affects not only our next-door neighbors but our worldwide neighbors. It's the same with air pollution, and even the residual effect of being around smokers.

Whether it's a lack of care for your lawn that mars the beauty of the neighborhood or the dumping of pollutants into the rivers that threatens life itself, it's the same damn thing. We all need to realize that a world with five and a half billion people cannot survive unless each and every one of us stops thinking on just a personal level and remembers that we all depend on one another.

Conclusion

One thing I have learned from writing this book is this—we all have views. And I would like to say to you: Do yourself a favor and write down *your* views. I am sure you'll find it as therapeutic as I did. You don't have to write them in book form or in a diary, just jot them down any old time. You'll be surprised how it will help you in life, how it will help you see things and think things through.

Because I wrote this book, I've already become more tolerant of people who seek my time, request autographs, and want to take my picture. When I sat next to Nadia Comaneci at the Goodwill Games the one thing I wanted was to take a picture of her, but I didn't dare. I just kept thinking about the times all these strangers drove me crazy. But after writing this book, and trying to understand different points of view, I realize how those requests can be honest, healthy ones.

Though fame can sometimes be an imposition, writing this book made me remember that it is also a blessing. It makes me feel incredibly good when people light up when they pass by in a car or walk by on the street and see me. Many never say a word—but their expressions say it all: "Wow! There's Wilt Chamberlain! I can't believe it!" I sometimes nod or smile in acknowledgment, but more often than not I try to project the feeling that I am *not* moved by their response. I'm not sure how other people of note feel or act when this happens to them, but for me, deep down, I feel like saying "Wow!" myself. I realize now I shouldn't try to hide the fact that I'm so flattered. Maybe now I won't.

I can remember driving to the beach one day and pulling up next to a truck at a red light. As I often do, I said hello to the driver: "What's happening, my man?" He said hi back, then did a double take before blurting out, "Wilt Chamberlain! I can't believe it! And you said hello to me! What a great day this is! I'm going to have a smile on my face the rest of the day. Thank you!"

Well, when I'm able to do that for a person just by saying hello, it makes me realize that all the inconveniences of being famous, of being a foot or two taller than the average Joe, are small in comparison to the smiles I can bring to people just by being me.

All of us can't publish books expressing our views, but so what? Write one just for yourself, your family, and your friends to read. It might be more rewarding to you than you think. Even if I had not gotten this published, I would have felt it a very worthwhile endeavor.

The one thing I am fearful of is that too often, people of note are given an opportunity to express their views *only* because they're famous. I mean, let's get real. What does Ivana Trump really have to say? Or guys like Lenny Dykstra and Dwight Gooden? A great year in sports at the age of twenty-one doesn't mean you should be able to write—or, in most cases, get someone else to write—your life story. I am cognizant of the fact that not everyone of note has something special to say. The one thing I have tried to stay away from is the notion that, hey, it's fifteen years later and I'm famous, so it's time to write another book. Too many people who become famous, in basketball or whatever, feel they *have* to write a book whether they have something to say or not. Not me. I truly hope you got something out of my *View from Above.*

I also hope you understood some of my views, even if you don't agree with them, and that you had a little fun while reading them. The one thing I want you to know is that everything I have said in this book is the truth—as I see it.

As my favorite movie star would say, "Here's looking at you." Even though my view is from above, never think that I feel I'm above you.

I will leave you now with my final and most important WILTISM: Peace.

Index